My Many Selves

My Many Selves
The Quest for a Plausible Harmony

Wayne C. Booth

Utah State University Press
Logan, Utah

Copyright © 2006 Utah State University Press
All rights reserved

Utah State University Press
Logan, Utah 84322–7800
www.usu.edu/usupreses

Manufactured in the United States of America
Printed on acid-free paper

Library of Congress Cataloging-in-Publication Data

Booth, Wayne C.
  My many selves : the quest for a plausible harmony / Wayne C. Booth.
     p. cm.
  Includes bibliographical references and index.
  ISBN 0-87421-633-8 (hardcover : alk. paper)--
  ISBN 0-87421-631-1 (pbk. : alk. paper)
  1. Booth, Wayne C. 2. Critics--United States--Biography. 3. Mormons--United States--
Biography. I. Title.
  PN75.B62A3 2006
  809--dc22

                              2005031116

It has amazed me that the most incongruous traits should exist in the same person and for all that yield **a plausible harmony.**[1] I have often asked myself how characteristics, seemingly irreconcilable, can exist in the same person. I have known crooks who were capable of self-sacrifice, sneak-thieves who were sweet-natured and harlots for whom it was a point of honour to give good value for money.

—Somerset Maugham, *The Summing Up*

[I would] portray myself entire and wholly naked.

—Montaigne, *Essays*

[Dorian Gray] used to wonder at the shallow psychology of those who conceive the Ego in man as a thing simple, permanent, reliable, and of one essence. To him, man was a being with myriad lives and myriad sensations, a complex multiform creature that bore within itself strange legacies of thought and passion, and whose very flesh was tainted with the monstrous maladies of the dead.

—Oscar Wilde, *The Picture of Dorian Gray*

There are two minds with two distinct natures, one good, the other bad. They really are evil themselves when they entertain these evil doctrines. . . . If there are as many contrary natures as there are wills in someone beset by indecision, there will be not two wills but many.

—St. Augustine, *Confessions*

I wonder if I will ever overcome my faults (lazyness, conceit, vague dishonesty, crudeness, etc.) to become a truly integrated individual. . . . I find myself very complex, psychologically, strange to say.

—Wayne C., College Sophomore, April 1940

---

1. Emphasis added.

Contents

Preface

Why, then, should I be concerned for human readers to hear my confessions? . . . What edification do they hope to gain by this . . . ? They will take heart from my good traits, and sigh with sadness at my bad ones.

—Bill Clinton, *My Life*

Every autobiographer faces problems that no novelist faces: as I write, my actual story still runs on. How can any first-person memoir present anything like a completed plot? It simply can't, and I thus have chosen what might even be labeled an anthology format: a sequence of quarrels among my conflicting Selves.

One major problem is that so much of what *I* find interesting, even exciting, about my diverse, often warring Selves would leave many readers snoring. Even the "laundry-list" stuff that burdens my files reveals something interesting *to me* about my life. Why did I ever buy *that* expensive paperweight (violating Skinflint-Booth), or why did I save *this* lousy eleven-page draft of an essay (surrendering to my Vain Self)? Why on earth did I take X to dinner, when I've always been annoyed by him? (Well, Vain-Booth was hoping the nonfriend might do a review of my new book.)

But why would anyone else ever want to read about that?

Some critics do claim that even the driest records of "meaningless" facts—the sections I find myself skipping when reading almost every other *LIFE*[1]—are meaningful. They even feel, as I *sometimes* do after reading Wittgenstein and other "ordinary-ists," that the ordinary stuff is more important than the extraordinary.

Here, however, I promise you that I will not record the list of the items my wife Phyllis handed me yesterday as I left for the grocery store. Nor the two items I forgot to purchase. Nor a list of my stack of unpublished, mostly uncompleted essays and books.

But even as I reject the laundry lists, you and I will face throughout this book the fact that the actual life I'm reporting, if viewed as a mere chronology, is quite ordinary, uncolorful, undramatic—not quite the grabber that Hillary

---

1. By using the terms *LIFE* and *LIVES* rather than autobiography or autobiographies, I have shortened this book by about twenty pages.

and Bill Clinton's stories have turned out to be. The boring fact is that I've never been physically abused, or awarded an Oscar, or had a spouse who cheated and was almost impeached. I've never been charged with rape or murder, or even with theft or cheating—fairly or unfairly. I lost no relatives in the Holocaust.[2] Though I was in WWII as a "clerk-rifleman," I endured no combat and have only one cheap medal, for being an accurate rifleman *in training*. I've never been president of *anything*, except the Modern Language Association for one year.

Should I feel regret, as I absolutely do not, that (unlike what Gore Vidal boasts about in his *Palimpsest*) I've never screwed or been screwed by celebrities? Should I spend time lamenting that my only connection with prominent politicians was bumping into Jimmy Carter in an airport lounge, long after his presidency was over? Is there any way to turn fifty-nine years of a happy marriage into a page-turner? Not on your life.

Even the death of our son at age eighteen—for us the most shattering of all events—is of the "everyday" kind shared this minute by millions around the world: *ordinary*, though devastating. Besides, that was thirty-six years ago and provides no narrative climax.

A recent ad for a new biography, *The Scarlet Professor*, tries to seduce readers with "Extraordinary *LIVES* make great reading." Right. But what's extraordinary about mine? A straightforward chronological account would read like too many of my boyhood journal entries:

August 25, 1935 (age 14½)
Got up at 5:00 and delivered papers. Had breakfast, then went to Sunday School. Passed the Sacrament.[3] Came home and had dinner. Great Grandmother Hawkins ate with us. After dinner played with Kip [Young], Junior [Halliday,] and Curtis [Chipman—a cousin]. Had supper, then went to church.

Just think of the difference between what I face here and what world-famous philosopher Bertrand Russell faced as he began his own three-volume *LIFE*. He and his publishers knew from word one that thousands, perhaps millions, of readers would welcome the books, even if, like me, they found themselves doing a lot of skipping. The work is full of his encounters with

---

2. I do have a son-in-law, David Izakowitz, whose parents experienced the horrors inflicted by Hitler and Stalin. His children, my grandchildren, would probably find a *LIFE* about those lost ones more dramatic than mine.

3. I've abandoned using "*sic*" for the boy's errors, though my computer keeps trying to correct them without my approval. All bracketed entries are insertions; parentheses within the quotes are always the diarist's.

celebrities we want to know more about. What reader would not want to hear about his conversations with D. H. Lawrence, revealing how much contempt Russell felt for him, or with T. S. Eliot, revealing how miserable the poet was feeling that day?

So it is clear that this *LIFE* presents interesting problems both for you readers and for me. My *non*plot—the quest for a plausible harmony among a crazy mixture of competitive selves—cannot rival such *LIVES* as Ved Mehta's wonderful story, *The Stolen Light*, about how he coped with being blind or Stephen Kuusisto's *Planet of the Blind*, a deeply moving account of having been half-blind from childhood on while pretending to have normal vision. What do I have that's as shocking—and thus gripping—as Martin Amis's account, in *Experience: A Memoir*, of how it felt to inform his two sons, ages ten and eleven, about meeting for the first time a daughter he had "absent-mindedly" fathered eighteen years earlier?

Though Amis's life is full of wonderful encounters with scores of celebrities and is loaded with dramatic moments, he still has to face the major problem I began with here: the nonplot threat endured by all *LIFERS*. As he writes his account of how his life relates to the life of his even more famous father, Kingsley, he puts that problem well:

> My life, it seems to me, is ridiculously shapeless. I know what makes a good narrative, and [actual] lives don't have much of that—pattern and balance, form, completion, commensurateness. It is often the case that a Life, at least to start with, will resemble a success story; but . . .[4]

And he then probes the "buts."

My hope for this *LIFE* is that, by revealing how my quite ordinary Selves have confronted—sometimes even battled with—one another, I can show how *all* lives, even the least colorful, not to mention *yours*, can be seen as dramatic in a sense quite different from the usual plot expectations. That hope tempted me at one point to include several chapters of speculation about the writing of *LIVES*—stuff actually more appropriate to an academic book theorizing *about* autobiography. I've cut a good deal of those intrusions by the Self I'll call Thinker-Booth, fearing that they sounded too much like a feeble echo of Henry Adams's wonderful *The Education of Henry Adams*.

In short, instead of tracing my life chronologically from an undramatic birth in 1921 to my scores of undramatic experiences yesterday (two of them blissful, the rest dull), I hope to engage you into thinking hard about how my conflicts of "Selves," of "Personae," of "Voices"—my "Splits" both deep

---

4.   Martin Amis, *Experience: A Memoir* (New York: Random House, 2001), 361.

and shallow—create another kind of drama: the quest for a harmony, or cho-rus, among those splits. (I don't know of any other *LIFE*, VainB whispers, echoing one enthusiastic manuscript reader, that has as vigorously reported such everyday splits and then pursued such an elusive but finally plausible harmony.)

Suddenly Moral-Booth, whom you'll meet throughout, snarls, "Cut that boastful sentence! It's silly, and it exhibits the egocentrism that you so often claim to have escaped." But then, after a moment's thought, MoralB adds, "I do have to admit that it's honest."

As you can see, then, you and I will face the tricky problem not just of who "I" am, behind the many Selves, but of who you are, as reader here:

- Are you a devout Mormon or a non-Mormon or an anti-Mormon or, like me, a fringer, still often feeling guilty about not being more active in the Church? Or does the very notion of reading about Mormonism turn you away?
- Are you a lover of teaching and scholarship, like me, or one of the thousands who these days spend their time attacking the acad-emy as corrupt—or at least attacking this or that corner, especially English departments?
- Do you know, as a few do, so much about my bibliography already that you'll find any reference to my work redundant and annoy-ing? (VainB again intrudes, "Put that as 'my fantastically impres-sive and sadly neglected bibliography,'" and then quarrels with Ambition-Booth, who argues, "No, it's a disappointingly short list of finally disappointing works! You could have and should have written much better works.")
- Are you in your twenties, never having heard the expression "If he fell in the shit, he'd come up smelling of violets," or in your eight-ies, remembering vividly how it felt to see your first airplane flying overhead at age ten?
- Will you condemn as banal, as many postmodernists will, my claim that our Selves are often divided and that it's fun and profit-able to play with their rivalries? Or do you find offensive any hint that your Soul may be disunited? Or are you among those extrem-ists who, combating the destructive excesses of in-dividualism, are certain that we are by nature inherently divided, not to say torn apart, and the quest for a harmony is absurd?[5]

---

5. My own transformation from "individualism" in the Mormon sense, with a soul unified from *the beginning* on, to a warm embrace of what might be called "we-ism" underlies

And so on. No matter who you are, or *think* you are, you'll find yourself differing with some of those possible "audiences." So as you read along, don't be surprised when you find yourself saying, "Enough of that—that chapter is for somebody else, not me."

In short, I cannot offer a page-turner, a mystery *LIFE*. Whenever you feel cast out, I suggest that you do what we all do when reading anthologies: skip forward to a title that suggests one of your own Self-splits.

Obviously, if you are still here, you haven't yet flung the book aside. So I ask you to please keep thinking about whether there is some true center of *your* multiple Selves and how *that* center resembles or contrasts with the "plausible" one I meander towards here.

None of us can ever expect any achieved harmonious revelation to be permanent: the next blow from circumstance tears us apart again. We don't need psychological theorists to tell us that those who have rejoiced in finding a full truce within—a harmonious core—often lose it quickly. Far too often the collapse ends in tragic civil war: irresolvable, sometimes even suicidal or murderous conflicts among the diverse voices. Facing bipolar disorder, schizophrenia, or whatnot, thousands of our brothers and sisters struggle daily to transcend the warfare, choosing among the flood of rival therapies: scores of medicines like Prozac and alternatives, along with a wildly chancy selection from the flood of new self-help books.[6]

Only those who happen to die in a moment of sheer bliss—like the murdered hero in the movie *American Beauty* or devout Christians blessed on their deathbeds—escape the miseries that circumstances impose, as "life" tricks us with a tornado, a car crash, a terrorist attack, or strong evidence of approaching senility.

Yet some of us, old or young, some of the time—part of each day, part of each season, part of each year—discover, by conducting our internal disputes

---

much of what I report in chapter 1. Years ago, after embracing the work of Mikhail Bakhtin, I put it like this: "We come into consciousness speaking a language already permeated with many voices—a social, not a private language. From the beginning, we are 'polyglot,' already in process of mastering a variety of social dialects derived from parents, clan, class, religion, country. . . . Finally we achieve, if we are lucky, a kind of individuality, but it is never a private or autonomous individuality in the western sense. . . . Anyone [who has not become a dogmatic individualist] respects the fact that each of us is a 'we,' not an 'I.' Polyphony, the miracle of our 'dialogical' lives together, is thus both a fact of life and, in its higher reaches, a value to be pursued endlessly." That Introduction to Bakhtin's *Problems of Dostoevsky's Poetics*, ed. Caryl Emerson (Minneapolis: Univ. of Minn. Press, 1984) reads to me now as almost a summary of what has continued to go on in my life and in this book.

6. A quick survey revealed that in the years 2000–2002 several hundred new self-help books were added to the forty-eight feet of bookstore shelving that I reported in *For the Love of It*. Last time I was in Borders, I measured *eighty* feet of self-helpers!

openly, the sheer fun of signing a treaty among the rival Selves or even set-tling on a genuine federal union of the rival states. Actually, by the end, as I've already hinted several times, I go even further toward harmony. My discovery, as a Mormon missionary, of what I now call rhetorology has granted me—or so VainB boasts—a splendid tool for conducting dialogue among the split Selves.

My hope is that as you read along, or even skip along, you will discover how, by confronting the rivalry in your Voices, the quest can finally prove to be worth it.

ACKNOWLEDGMENTS

How many thousands of names should be listed in the acknowledgments to any *LIFE*? Every friend, every enemy, every teacher, every student, every fam-ily member contributed to this *LIFE*. Even to the *writing* there are too many contributors to be listed.

So I'll now cut to an unfairly short list.

Thanks to Elaine Pfefferblitt for inviting me to write an autobiography and then enduring its rejection by her commercial "superiors"; to Adam Kissel, Will Stevens, Adam Jernigan, Robert (Steve) Nelsen, Robert Cuthbert, and Brandon Hopkins for careful editing; to my wife Phyllis, for having produc-tively criticized my life ever since 1944 and then for editing this *LIFE*; to my two daughters, Katherine and Alison, for more editing; and to Gerald Graff, who has supported the whole idea from the beginning. Adam Kissel has guided the book toward its goal with expertise and dedication. Thanks also to Robert Denham for help with the copyedited manuscript and other matters; and to John Alley, executive editor, and copyeditor Rebecca Marsh at Utah State University Press.

Part One

My Toughest "Self-Splits" and What Produced Them

It's a bit hard to distinguish those Self-Splits that have been potentially destructive, those that have contributed to my growth, and those that in retrospect merely amuse me. But for now, here are ten of the most intense conflicts that life has inflicted on the diverse Wayne Booths.

Or perhaps it should be put like this: Here are ten of the most interesting conflicts inflicted upon Wayne Booth by God—"God" in Booth's weird definition.

Chapter One

A Devout Mormon Is
Challenged by Rival Selves

So many of us begin strong and then flatten out. So many players in the game of life get to first base. Some reach second. A handful make third. But how few there are who reach home base safely. It requires continual striving to gain that mastery over self.

> —Gordon B. Hinckley, President, Prophet, Seer, and Revelator
> of the Church of Jesus Christ of Latter-day Saints

Long may the blood which was shed by the prophet
Stain Illinois . . .

> —Mormon hymn of my childhood,
> a curse long since expunged from the hymnal

I asked the personages who stood above me in the light [God and his Son Jesus], which of all the sects was right—and which I should join. I was answered [by Jesus] that I must join none of them, for they were all wrong . . . and all their creeds were an abomination in His sight.

> —Joseph Smith's later account,
> in his thirties, of his first vision, at age 14

Yond Cassius has a lean and hungry look;
He thinks too much; such men are dangerous.

> —Shakespeare, *Julius Caesar*

The trouble with you, Grampa, is you're always thinking, thinking, thinking.

> —Granddaughter Emily Izakowitz

Recently at a University reception, as I sipped my glass of wine, I spotted across the room the bishop of my LDS ward, who knows me quite well even though I hardly ever attend services.[1] The immediate impulse of the hypocrite in me, based on almost a lifetime of faked "observance," was to hide the glass. "That's absurdly dishonest," the Moralist in me shouted (silently), "and besides, he's probably already seen it." So I walked toward the bishop, glass in hand. He smiled warmly, we shook hands, and he seemed simply to ignore my violation of the "Word of Wisdom." We had a good brief conversation about "how's it goin'?"—as he sipped his coke and I sipped my wine. (Cokes were for a while banned by the Church because of the caffeine, but then they decided that the Lord meant to include only "hot drinks" when he gave Joseph Smith his health commands.)

I'm pretty sure that many a bishop would have called me in for an excommunication interrogation after witnessing such open violation of the ban on alcohol. Not this one. He doesn't want to kick me out, because he knows that I am still, in many important senses, a Mormon—one who goes on shocking some Mormons by listing himself in *Who's Who* as "LDS."

It is important now to have a look at the contrast between that eighty-four-year-old wine-sipper and the totally Devout Mormon Booth I was trained to be. To understand fully my diverse Split-Selves, the Mormon-Split is crucial. It may strike some readers here as irrelevant, but I still think of myself as a Mormon. (Of course, if you somehow detest Mormonism, you can just skip this whole chapter, in which I celebrate many of the true virtues of Mormonism.)

---

1. At this point non-Mormon readers may need a bit of dictionary work. LDS is the abbreviation of "The Church of Jesus Christ of Latter-day Saints." "Ward" is the name for the local congregation. The lay leader, unpaid for his demanding labors, is the "bishop." "Stake" is the name for a group of local congregations, and the unpaid lay leader is the "stake president." (I don't know how far up the hierarchy one must go to find a leader who is actually paid a full salary.) "The Word of Wisdom" was God's health code, given to Joseph Smith, the founding prophet, as a Revelation: it bans alcohol, tobacco, tea and coffee, etc.

In one sense my story is not different from that of scores of friends raised in other denominations who have told me, "Getting an education destroyed my religion; I was raised in faith, but pursuing reason got me into trouble."

But few of them were raised as I was: in a culture totally isolated from others. As their congregations met, they were surrounded by other denominations and probably by many secularists opposing all religion. In contrast, I was born and raised not just in a devout family belonging to a faithful congregation but in an isolated culture, with no non-Mormons surrounding us.

As I think about having lived for those twenty-one years encountering almost no one but Mormons (except for a wonderful chemistry teacher in high school, a Lutheran), I feel an especially strong kinship with all those in any isolated faith who met few or no rivals throughout childhood: any Muslim raised in a totally isolated Arab village and then sent to college in America, and any Jew raised in a settlement consisting entirely of Orthodox families just outside Jerusalem and then sent to the University of Chicago to get a doctor's degree.

I still feel kinship, of course, with everyone who was raised in *the one true faith*, but it is especially strong toward those who encountered no doubters or rivals until moving up the education ladder. All religious "lapsers" or "fringers" or "peripherals" encounter a quarrel between a loyal loving Self and a Self whom loved ones will consider to be a sad loss or even a traitor.[2]

There are many ways to label those conflicting Selves and the rival cultures that produce them: faith vs. reason; *mythos* vs. *logos*; closed vs. open; pure vs. corrupted; obedient vs. rebellious; loyal vs. evil. Sometimes the arrogant side of the thinker in me has labeled it, a bit stupidly, as "naïve vs. sophisticated." Back then the split was often thought of as "Zion" vs. "back East." For Erasmus, facing similar conflicts between full belief and unrestrained "reason," it was sometimes Jerusalem vs. Athens.

For all of us Mormons, Utah was indeed the unique Zion, combining both absolute faith and total commitment to pursuit of truth: divine knowledge. Many of our hymns celebrated the unquestionable truth that God had brought our ancestors to our "mountain home," leading Brigham Young to look down on the valley, back in 1847, and proclaim, "This is *the* place!" God

2. Whether you're Mormon or not, if you would like to encounter some deeper speculation by other Mormons dealing with these conflicts, see *Dialogue* (vol. 34, 2002), especially the introductory essay by Neal Chandler on the battle between *mythos* and *logos*, and "What the Church Means to People Like Me" by Richard D. Poll. For a splendid probing of the conflict within the Church between those who want to engage in "Apologetics"—serious argument about issues—and those who reject it, see John-Charles Duffy's "Defending the Kingdom, Rethinking the Faith: How Apologetics Is Reshaping Mormon Orthodoxy," *Sunstone* (May 2004): 22–55.

had established the true center where all of the virtuous would ultimately settle—and soon be resurrected into heaven.

My subconscious mind still floods daily with the hymns that identify ultimate reward with the beauty of those mountains surrounding our town. At this moment, one suddenly intrudes:

> O Zion! Dear Zion!
> Land of the free.
> Now my own mountain home,
> Unto thee I have come;
> All my fond hopes are centered—
> In thee.

We were all taught that when the apocalypse arrived—maybe next week, maybe next year—we faithful ones would all gather in Zion and then be taken to heaven, while the unfaithful would be destroyed or consigned to some eternal, lower status. (There was no need for a Hell: the lowest of the three eternal kingdoms, Celestial, Telestial, and Terrestrial, took care of that.)

The world outside Zion was where the unfaithful and sinful lived.[3] For some the path to damnation was California, but for most of us it was "back East" (often thought of as Chicago). I only later encountered liberal professors at the "Y" (Brigham Young University), most of whom had earned their higher degrees in Midwest universities. They saw "back East" as a place where one could find much of what is good about Western civilization. Yet for the orthodox as for me (until far into my teens, studying under those professors), the world outside Zion was just plain dangerous, crying out to be saved by our missionary efforts. Stories about how our missionaries were mistreated by "outsiders," even lynched, filled our Sunday services.

About the only "Eastern" idea I can remember being openly approved was the U.S. Constitution. As part of God's careful preparation for the restoration of our one true version of Christianity, the Constitution was holy. (Oh, yes, the Puritan escape from England was also part of the necessary preparation; I didn't learn until recently that some of my ancestors—on the side much neglected by me in my upbringing, the Chipmans, were on the *Mayflower!*)

Later, when studying and teaching "back East," with all my relatives rightly fearing that I was becoming a fringer or worse, I often did feel that I had escaped to an almost divine Athens: the thinker in me had cast off

---

3. Actually there were far more non-Mormons in Utah than I realized at the time. They were just talked down or ignored—as is still too often the case.

dogmatic ignorance and could now pursue truth, obtain learning, even become genuinely wise. That drive, at least, could be defended by a couple of Mormon slogans still deeply embedded in my mind: "The glory of God is intelligence" and "Man cannot be saved in ignorance."

Yet I was aware—during two years in Haverford, Pennsylvania, nine in Richmond, Indiana, and more than four decades in Chicago—that what I saw as the enviable side of "back East" was but a small and even threatened part of it. In many ways the culture I was entering, viewed according to my moralizing self's convictions, was radically inferior to the Utah scene. Those who lived back home had standards, including genuine service to others. Many of the outsiders I was meeting were—as I had been taught to expect— corrupt. And the Mormons who had become not just fringers out there but "Jack Mormons"—open rejecters—were often even worse: they smoked cigarettes and cigars.

Even now the contrast between the lives lived by insiders and those of many lapsers shocks me and sometimes drives me back toward being fully active. A fully lapsed friend who has had nine children reports to me that the four who are active LDS members have had far more productive, happy lives than the ones who broke away. While I would never argue that Mormons are on average happier than Catholics or Protestants or Jews or Muslims or Hindus or Buddhists (and so on), I feel sure that to be "affiliated" with *some* "congregation" is a genuine blessing.

The experience of my daughter Alison's conversion to Judaism is a prime example. When we attended our grandchildren's bat mitzvah and bar mitzvah, the ceremonies moved me to ecstasy.

I feel utterly confident that for a family to belong to any one of the *good* churches, with a supporting congregation, is the best inoculation against the destructive forces of our culture. As I sometimes put it to friends, I am currently inactive in at least five true churches.[4]

Still, it's not surprising that I sometimes came close to breaking away and becoming a "Jack Mormon." The thinker in me would sometimes *think*— but almost never say out loud to anyone—"All of those dogmatic 'faithful' ones threaten the world with ignorance and intolerance." Looking back now, I see this as a gross distortion. Those "dogmatic faithful ones" are on average among the most generous-spirited, most admirable of human creatures. Everyone there, from day one, is trained to believe in devoted, unpaid, pro bono service to others. No bishop gets paid a cent for his demanding service. No lecturer or singer or missionary gets any financial reward. Members of

---

4. I have a friend who believes that all of the worst atrocities throughout the world are committed by religions. He and I quarrel about that claim regularly.

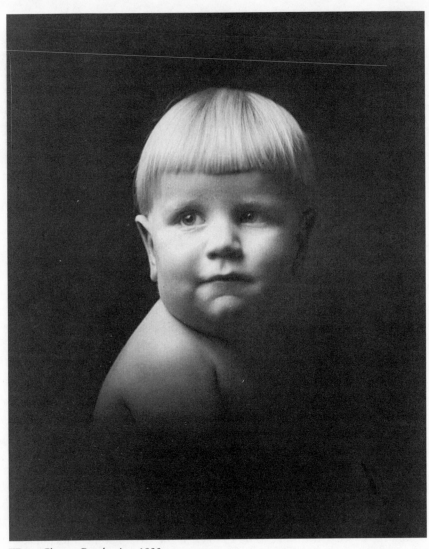

Wayne Clayson Booth, circa 1923

My parents with my father's parents, on the farm, around 1919–1920, *left to right,* Lillian Clayson Booth, Wayne Chipman Booth, Lovenia Jane Chipman Booth, Robert Ebenezer Booth

My father's family, *left to right, back row,* Ida, Irwin, Relva, Wayne (father); *front row,* Robert Ebenezer Booth, Irma, Lovenia Jane Chipman Booth, Manda

My mother's family, *left to right,* Zina, Lucy, Ann Elizabeth Hawkins Clayson, Lillian (mother), Ann, Merrill, Eli J. Clayson

the wonderful Salt Lake Tabernacle Choir are all "amateurs," in the sense of doing it only for the love of it, often driving from afar several times a week to rehearse. Can you see why I can never decide to obey other Voices and make a full break from a church that encourages such lives?

What Was It Like Living on the Inside?

If, as is highly probable, you were not raised in an enclosed culture like mine, it will not be easy to understand just how deeply it gets into your heart and soul—or as we sometimes would put it, into your bones. In American Fork, Utah,[5] back in the 1920s and '30s, almost all of the three thousand citizens were openly Mormon; a majority were descendants of immigrants. There were six Mormon congregations, each with its own "Ward Chapel." The few non-Mormons, a tiny minority I can't remember ever meeting,[6] had the only other church building, called something like "Community Church" or "Congregational Church." (Don't expect me to remember it, because it was something I totally avoided. Even as late as age fourteen, when I started delivering newspapers and had to ride my bike down the street passing that wicked church, I would carefully cross to the other side to avoid getting too close to the sinful.)

The family surrounding me even more tightly was huge by today's standards: four loving, authoritative grandparents; two loving (and slightly less bossy) great-grandparents; eleven living aunts and uncles; innumerable cousins and second cousins. Almost all were devout—or pretending to be. Surrounded by the pious, most of them exhorting me to do everything the *one right way*, for at least fifteen years I never met or talked with anyone I knew to be a non-Mormon. (A dim memory argues that there was a family of Jews who were tailors, but I can't remember encountering them.)

We did know a few families that seemed to be lapsing, like two aunts who had fled to California; they were always treated with explicit contempt behind their backs and with implicit anxiety and sometimes even open exhortation when they visited. When those two "lost souls" (my father's sisters) visited, we would face some paradoxes. My mother, more tolerant than most

---

5. Actually it was spoken as American Fark; most of our "or" words were pronounced "ar": carn, harse, fariner. Many Mormons have claimed that my cleverest essay was one that sprang from my struggling to learn how to say corn, horse, foreigner: "Farkism and Hyperyorkism" (reprinted in *Now Don't Try to Reason with Me* [Chicago: University of Chicago Press, 1970]). I still get overtaken occasionally by my young self and say something like "Cornegie Carporation" or "carnstorch."

6. There must have been non-Mormon kids in my school classes, but I'm pretty sure they never "confessed" to it openly.

of the family, would forgivingly serve them coffee, bringing out our one can of coffee preserved year after year on the most remote shelf possible. I remember their complaining—jokingly? behind Mama's back?—about how awful the coffee was.

The impact of dogmatic, monolithic truth was reinforced by the power of the stories my grandparents and two great-grandparents told. Five of the six (the Clayson, Booth, and Hawkins clans) filled my life with stories about how their parents, weavers and farmers in England, had been "saved" by being converted in the 1850s and then miraculously managed to cross the ocean and plains and become assigned by Brigham Young to found this or that tiny village. One grandfather was actually born on the thousand-mile trek across the plains; he and his mother were then carried the rest of the way in a shaky wagon. One great-grandparent had actually pushed a handcart most of the way. And all of them knew that the reason the families had made it alive and well, unlike many who died en route, was that God had rewarded them for their conversion and continuing devotion.

That closed-culture experience—what felt increasingly like imprisonment to the thinker, as he moved through his teens and was rebuked for asking dangerous questions—was reinforced by hourly, daily, weekly strict routines, the kind that most religions try to provide but which only a closed culture can fully realize. When *all* of your friends and relatives, not just weekly but every day, practice precisely the same rituals, which are also being practiced in every neighboring town—when *everyone who is anyone is a devout Mormon*—you become indelibly ritualized:

- Sunday mornings, from birth to age twenty-one: Sunday School (from age seven to twelve, it was always with anxious, bossy Grampa Clayson teaching us—sometimes angrily—that promptitude is next to Godliness; and we never missed any meeting unless we were seriously ill).
- Sunday afternoons: reading of scripture, with no athletic games, no movies, no swimming allowed (as you'd expect, we did some minor cheating on this one).
- Sunday evenings: "Sacrament Meeting," with prolonged sermons.
- Once a month, "Fast Sunday": no breakfast, as we honorably donated what the fasting saved to a Church charity, then attended a meeting something like a Quaker "silent meeting," with anyone free to "bear testimony." I stood up spontaneously at age ten and spoke nervously about how grateful I felt for living in the valley of the "mountains high, where the clear blue sky arches over the

vales of the free"—the thrill provided by the mountains that were visible through the east window of the chapel.

I'm sure that "bearing my testimony" was prompted almost entirely by the hypocritical desire to appear pious: no one my age had, to my knowledge, ever before borne his testimony voluntarily! I remember doing more than simply mouthing the clichés about divine Joseph Smith or the Book of Mormon.

- Tuesday afternoons, from early toddling to age twelve: "Primary" lessons in the chapel; all children required to attend, singing songs about Mormonism and various virtues: "Little purple pansies in the garden old . . . / We are very tiny but must try, try, try, / Just one spot to gladden, you and I."

- Tuesday evenings, after becoming a "Deacon" and Boy Scout at age twelve: "MIA" (Mutual Improvement Association), a semi-social occasion but with lots of religious preaching; sometimes basketball, sometimes even dancing, but all absolutely centered on Mormon culture: mutual improvement for everyone from age twelve to death—and then onward! That stress on mutual improvement is still one of the main attractions to my being active in the Church.

- Daily, in high school: Required LDS "Seminary" class, in a building close to the city school. The dogmatic teacher vigorously stomped on the thinker in me—the young man who, under the influence of a wonderful chemistry teacher, Luther Giddings, was moving toward Darwinism.

Meanwhile, we kids were taught at home to kneel every day for prayer before breakfast, kneel for prayer together before supper, and say a blessing on the food at "dinner" (always at noon). At bedtime each of us said an individual prayer, kneeling at the bedside.

Ironically, we were taught that one of the blessings of Mormonism is that it got rid of "ritual," especially Catholic ritual. I didn't discover until I was finally admitted into the Temple, just before leaving for my mission at age twenty-one, that the ritual inside that secret sacred spot was even more ritualistic than most of what the "wicked" Catholics practiced.

The major ritualized test of the difference between the virtuous and the sinful—because it was to some degree *empirically* testable—was the Word of Wisdom, Joseph Smith's message from God about the daily code: no smoking, no drinking of alcohol or stimulating hot drinks like tea or coffee, moderate consumption of meat. As I write about it, I suddenly am "hearing" the hymn we sang regularly about ourselves, the wonderfully pious Mormon children:

> That the children may live long
> And be beautiful and strong,
> Tea and coffee and tobacco they despise.
> Drink no liquor and they eat
> But a very little meat.
> They are seeking to be
> Great and good and wise.

That piety test was dramatized regularly by my family's attitude toward those who didn't quite pass it, even in minor matters like coffee or tea. When I was eight or nine, it was my daily job to lead our cow uphill about a mile to a (sometimes) lovely pasture. Often I was with a buddy who was walking another cow. He was the son of neighbors who attended services a bit irregularly, so I already suspected him of lapsing, but I enjoyed joking with him both in Sunday School and on our hikes.

One summer I learned that though their cow was almost ready to calve, they were still milking her. I reproached Tom about it: "Your family shouldn't be milking a cow that's gonna calve soon." "Oh, it's OK," he answered. "At least she's still givin' enough milk for papa's coffee."

My family told that story contemptuously again and again. Any man who drank coffee was clearly on his way "out"—not to hell, exactly, but to a different kind of damnation. He would be placed after death in the lowest of the three "heavenly" realms, the Terrestrial—still with a remote chance of redemption and ascent to the Telestial but almost certainly never reaching the Celestial, which was where my family expected to be. We would progress on through eternity, as God Himself had done—and was still doing. (Nobody ever mentioned that to broadcast dismissive anecdotes about neighbors was an unchristian act that might get you into eternal trouble.)[7]

The non-Mormons were even further down the line. Catholicism was the "great whore and abomination" described (somewhere) in the New Testament. Catholics, even more decisively than other non-Mormons, would never make it all the way "up there"—unless, of course, we managed to convert them.

---

7. The notion that God is a creature of "body, parts, and passions," a still-progressing, not-omniscient creature with whom we existed from the beginning and whose progress we could emulate eternally—that notion has naturally offended most non-Mormon theologians, Christian or not.

We saw Native Americans only once a year when they came through town selling pine nuts and begging for gifts. (We didn't have the designation "Native American" then and called them Indians or Redskins or, following the Book of Mormon, Lamanites. They had been turned "red" because of their having sinfully killed off, back in about 300 A.D., the other American descendants of the Twelve Tribes (white, of course), who were—but to explain that, I would have to give you a full account of the stories told in the Book of Mormon.) We were taught that they might possibly, if they converted somewhere down the line, be blessed by a color change, become "white and delightsome," and join us up there.[8]

No Mormons I knew had come from any culture except the British or European. Mexicans, working on our railroads—I can't remember what we called them, certainly not "Latin Americans" or "Latinos" or "Hispanics"— were lost souls because they were almost certainly Catholics and therefore sinners. African Americans were seldom mentioned, except in careless widespread metaphors like "there's a nigger in the woodpile"—that is to say, somebody's hiding something. We never even saw any blacks except for "shoeshine boys" (actually men) working fifty miles away in Salt Lake City hotels. We knew that though "Negroes" could become LDS members if they behaved right, the men—just like white women—could never be granted the blessing of holding the priesthood. We were certain, as even some Mormons today stupidly continue to believe, that blacks are black because God cursed Cain. Or was it maybe Ham?[9]

And what about the Chinese, who also worked on the railroads? The "Chinks" were simply good material for comedy: if you were doing a skit and needed a clown, what could be more useful than a "stupid Chink"? Otherwise, they weren't even mentioned.

Fortunately my family, unlike many, often faced openly the conflict between such bigotry and Christ's exhortations about universal brotherhood. Though God would ultimately punish the wicked, that was not *our* assignment. When "bums" came to the door during the Depression, for example, Mama didn't grill them about beliefs or faiths: she just fed them. Grampa always gave the Indians at least enough to bring them back next year. Though I can't remember anyone ever speaking out against the Church's racist

---

8. The word "white" in "white and delightsome" in the original Book of Mormon has now been dropped—so far as I can discover. The Church is working hard to become "international" and nonracist.

9. The Church about twenty years ago finally granted the priesthood and full equality to blacks, but it has not yet issued any kind of official apology for the century and more of racist interpretation of scripture. Fortunately some leaders, as Apostle Bruce McConkie did, have offered personal apologies for their own early racism.

doctrines, we all did celebrate our few living Civil War heroes on Memorial Day, since destroying slavery had been a noble cause.

So as I observed it, the bigotry was not primarily racist but doctrinal. And it sometimes was more domineering than I ever realized. Not so long ago (June 2000) the phone rang in Chicago.

"Hello."

"Are you Professor Wayne Booth?"

"Yes, I'm Wayne Booth."

"Well, this is Bland Giddings, hoping to have a chat with you."

"Giddings? The only Giddings I have known was Luther Giddings . . ."

"That's my point. I'm Luther's son, and I've read that you considered my dad one of the best and maybe *the best* of your high school teachers."

"Oh, he was, he was wonderful. He changed my life. How good of you to call."

We chatted for a bit, and then he said, "I'm a little uneasy about the next point. I'm publishing a kind of history of American Fork, concentrating of course on *my* family, but I've got one anecdote reflecting discredit on *your* Grandfather Clayson. I'm worried about how members of your family will react to it."

I told him to go ahead.

"Well, my father was hired to teach chemistry—as you know—at the high school. Your grandfather was on the school board, and he was running for election to be president of the board. And in his campaigning he promised that if elected, he would kick my dad out, because it was just plain wrong to have a non-Mormon, a Lutheran, teaching Mormon kids. When Dad learned about that, he just up and left, rather than hoping to fight it out, and went to teach in Idaho."

"Oh, man!" I interrupted. "That's just plain awful. But your dad never told me any of that. And how come he came back?"

"Well, your grandfather got defeated in the election, so Dad was invited back and came. That's how you got him."

I then raved for a few moments about just how wonderful Luther Giddings had been as my chemistry teacher, converting me to become a "chemical engineer," and about how generous it was of him never to have given me even a hint about Grampa Clayson's bigotry.

"Your father treated me almost like a son, and I felt him to be a kind of replacement for my lost father."

It took me several months after that conversation to realize that in one sense Grampa Clayson might be defended. Though Luther Giddings was not passionately anti-Mormon and in our frequent private talks after class he never openly attacked the Church, what he did do was stimulate the emerging ThinkerB. As one of the first non-Mormons I had ever talked with and as the deepest thinker I had known, he was, perhaps quite consciously, introducing me to at least some aspects of "the Enlightenment": faith in reason rather than superstition; belief in science as one absolute source of truth. I'm pretty sure he never labored deliberately to turn me into a Jack Mormon. I have journal evidence that he would sometimes lecture me a bit about not letting my problems with scriptural literalism lead to a break from what he considered a praiseworthy church. But I do remember his telling me one anecdote about the illegal real-estate dealings of my bishop; that was a real shocker. I wonder if he knew that such an anecdote might shake my faith.

It's hardly surprising that in spite of troubled thoughts, that hundred-percent culture kept me believing for a long time that Mormonism is the only true religion. I remember, even at age nineteen after ThinkerB had made me full of doubts, grilling a favorite liberal professor, A. C. Lambert, about whether I had or ever would have a full testimony. I strongly desired the moment of certainty that other people had reported as so thrilling. He looked uncomfortable and even sweated a bit as we chatted, leading me to suspect that he had never had a full testimony either. He finally said, "There are many different forms of 'testimony.' Many true believers never have the actual sensation of being visited by Christ or Joseph Smith. Don't worry about it." (I recently discovered a manuscript of his attempted book on the "2,000 Unfulfilled Prophecies of Joseph Smith." It's not hard to figure out why he never published it.)

STRUGGLES WITH DOCTRINE AND HISTORICAL CLAIMS

What, then, produced the wine-drinking chatterer who still hears daily commandments from his Mormon Self? The answer would require more than a full book, since year by year, decade by decade, I kept moving from closer in to further out and then back in again. Some problems I could simply resolve by saying, "So what? All churches present similar problems. Show me a better church." Others led me almost to the Jack Mormon request for excommunication: "I can never call myself a member of a church whose leaders can talk like THAT!"

The sharpest challenges to my faith were the conflicts between what I was taught in church and what I began to learn by reading non-Mormon books. They got me thinking more deeply about "free agency," a much-stressed Mormon doctrine crucial to the idea of eternal progress. How was I to relate my full free agency to the command to obey the authorities even when I disagreed with them?[10] Thus my embrace of the notion that God created us primarily to *pursue* free agency—free choice, free will—increasingly clashed with routine authoritarianism.

As early as April 1937, just after turning sixteen, the budding doubter rehearsed his troubles secretly:

Journal

I have been very friendly with Armis Ashby, who is a year younger than I, lately. He is about the most intelligent boy I know and we have long talks together. If anyone in our high school ever becomes great it will be he. We have both been raised in the Mormon Church and believe that there must be a God and that he must answer prayers but we are beginning to have doubts concerning many of the Latter-Day-Saint doctrines. We still believe that basically it is the best religion but when we see some of the things that are done, some of the rich church leaders it makes us wonder. I imagine that most intelligent Mormons go through the same period of doubt and I suppose that we will outgrow it or something. I think that some religion is necessary to an individual in modern life but my mind is full of doubts. I'm not just trying to act smart and show off but I really would like to have a talk with somebody who could satisfy all my questions on religion. The old testament is one of the things that is hardest for me to believe. It has some wonderful teachings but of all the fairy stories it seems in many of its books to be one of the most fairylike and yet some of our straight lased Mormons hold to every word as the word of God where anyone can see that millions of errors could creep in through faulty translations, the insertions of the translators own ideas etc. I am going to continue going to church in the hope that someday I will be able to have everything cleared up. I know that many of my ideas contradict themselves but I intend studying until everything is straight.

I quote that at length because VainB feels a bit proud about how that kid goes on facing a range of philosophical questions. Had he ever heard the word "philosophy"? Probably, but for him the questions are all "religious."

More than four years later, having gone back and forth again and again over many such issues and reading (superficially) a good deal of philosophy, the

---

10. These days free agency is mentioned even less often than it was then, while obedience has become even more prominent. The index to the hymnals now shows a great rise in "obedience" and a sad fall in "free agency."

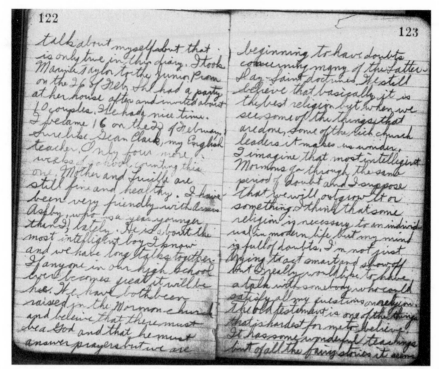

My handwritten journal, at age sixteen

troubled young man reported two interviews he was subjected to before being allowed to become a missionary. He wrote the following in his journal about both interviews:

> I felt the web of insidious phraseology [that they insisted on my employing] tightening about my once freely-thinking (not free-thinking) mind.[11] Such phrases as "Thy servant," "thy prophet," "thy great work," found a far too ready and unthinking way to my lips.—I hereby swear to not be fooled into religious blindness, into sentimental piety, into dogmatic belief. I will keep my perspective, if it is humanly possible.

And then the conflicting Self intrudes—the voice that would later produce many of my pro-religion arguments, especially in my book on the "rhetoric of assent":[12]

---

11. Again, in all journal quotations, the parenthetical marks are "his," not "mine." The few I intrude are always in brackets.

12. *Modern Dogma and the Rhetoric of Assent* (Chicago: University of Chicago Press, 1974).

I will also try to keep from doubting where belief is justified. There is a possibility that J. Smith did see God: although it is in a way unimportant. I should admit it if I can see enough reason; there is a possibility that the "authority" of the priesthood is important: if it is, I should not deny the importance when it is shown to me.

From then on, as different objections and problems arise, the journals are full of similar Self-Splits—most of them kept secret by Hypocrite-Booth.[13]

THE INFLUENCE OF OUTSIDERS' BEHAVIOR

Putting *belief* questions aside, how about *code* conflicts? As troublesome ideas kept poisoning the clear waters of faith, I had my first brief encounter with outside *behavior* as a Boy Scout traveling to Washington, D.C., in 1937, for the celebration of the organization's founding in—was it 1912? I was excited by almost everything I saw: the huge buildings, the museums, the stockyards. I saw almost nothing offensive—except the nauseating stockyard slaughtering in Chicago—because our pious leaders kept us pretty close together as a gang of Mormon scouts. Our tour was carefully organized to feature monuments and buildings celebrating the glory of our founding fathers. (I was, however, deeply shocked—and ravished—by the many nude paintings in the art galleries.)

My only memory of shocking immorality on that trip was not "out there"; it was the behavior of a man I had thought devout. When our train stopped in Denver for reloading, we went to a snack shop, where our stout, bossy, "bishop-looking" scout leader ordered a cup of coffee. That was shattering. How could a decent scout leader ever drink a cup of coffee?

Five years later, as a missionary in the Midwest (you'll meet him at length in chapter 6), I was for the first time surrounded daily by the Outside, good and bad, even as I defended, preached about, and often celebrated the Inside. Having decided that my "mission" was not to get people "under the baptismal water" but "to do good in the world," I found myself fascinated by the beliefs and practices of other religions. When I performed funeral services and baptisms (I never tried to do any actual converting, but as I "made friends for

---

13. A word about these journal entries I rely on. Some friendly readers of drafts have praised them, agreeing that they strengthen my portrait of the lifetime Self-Splits. But others have insisted on a lot of cutting—and I have often obeyed, painfully. VainB comforts me with Hemingway's claim that when you feel you're cutting out good stuff, you know you're writing really well.

the Church," some conversions did occur), I remember actually wishing that we Mormons had some ceremonies as "spiritual" as what I found in Catholic services. As I read voraciously the works of philosophers and theologians, hoping to find some compromise between inside and outside, faith and reason, my devoted Self kept fighting back, wrestling with the conflict almost daily in my journals.

Meanwhile, surrounded every day by people violating what I'd been taught were divine commands, what happened to my own obedient behavior? Well, missionaries are ordered never even to touch a girl, and I touched none for two long years—though I came close to "touching" Jeanne Wacker when she visited me on her way to college even farther "back East." Violating Church rules by meeting down in the Loop, we spent most of our time listening to music in record shops. But once in her hotel room, Luster-Booth thought a bit about the "possibilities" and then thought harder about what Jeanne would think about it—especially about his weird, official undergarments—while MoralB kept saying, "Absolutely not," and won.

Surrounded by code violators, MoralB felt a lot of genuine condemnation of those sinners. But nevertheless, honestly I must report (remembering Jeanne Wacker) that LusterB was simultaneously often longing for some sex. I remember his driving the mission car along a dark Chicago street one night. He looked up at the lights in apartment buildings and suddenly was beating time on the steering wheel: "Forty copulations and I've got none!"

So, even while MoralB felt deep contempt for those outsiders, who obviously were sinning from morn to night, I had to struggle with a rebel-Self who wanted "out"—or wanted at least some version of "free agency." Occasionally I felt driven to prove my independence.

Memory, 1943

After about fifteen months of fairly strict obedience, he (I can't quite say "I") decided it was time to have his first cup of coffee ever, to prove his independence—his Free Agency. He sneaked down from Logan Square Headquarters to the Loop, found an obscure coffee shop, looked carefully up and down the street to make sure no one saw him, slunk in, bought a cup, gulped it hurriedly, sneaked out, and hurried back to his job as pious Mission Secretary. Memory says that he felt himself a considerably freer spirit than he had been an hour before. He felt not a touch of guilt and a tiny bit of pride, because by then he thought that the anticoffee rule was silly.

I'm not so sure now that "silly" codes like that—"wear your yarmulke" or "kneel before entering your pew" or "pray every hour or so"—are mistakes. They can be important not only because they teach kids that there *are* genuine standards but also because they provide a chance to feel independent by breaking a rule that really doesn't matter much. If I were a kid trying to demonstrate my individuality now, living in any American city, where could I turn? To drugs? To a metal ring in my penis? Perhaps a good self-help book for parents these days might read, "Provide your kids with at least a few silly—or at least trivial—rules, so that they can enjoy breaking them without disaster."

The code conflicts inevitably heightened after I was drafted in 1944, soon after being released as a missionary.

Memory

I'm having a physical examination at the army Placement Depot (is that the right name?). The sergeant hands me a bottle and says, "Just piss in that." I smile at him and say—of course, intending it as playful—"Do you mind if I just urinate?" He scowls as if he'd like to hit me, then stalks away angrily.

The point? I had never heard anyone say "piss" except "behind the barn." And behind my smile I had been a bit shocked by his language in violation of what I'd been taught.

After two days in that Draft Center (what *was* it called?) the fringer began what turns out to be hundreds of journal entries about what he never called the "shocking immorality of the outside."

April 15, 1944, Camp Douglas

It has been interesting to note the progressive relaxation of behaviour standards during the last two days. Yesterday morning there were many who were silent, seemingly refined. Tonight I know of no one, including myself, who has not used profanity, & Bill Gay and I are the only two who have avoided obscenity. Some of them have gone out of their way to let me know (it has almost seemed) that humanity at its worst is worse than I had thought it. One particular "joe" has not entered one conversational piece without at least two "f___"s and a "bastard" or so. This is not so bad in itself—if it meant no more than "God-damn" means when said by the average soldier, I wouldn't care. But the spirit of obscenity is in the obscene words. When joe says "f___" he means "f___," & not just as a convenient expletive. (The tough-minded reader, if there ever is one beside myself, must excuse these bowdlerish "f___"s. They are justified, if not by the probability of so-called tender readers, but by my own need of leaning over backwards to prevent barbarization.)[14]

_____

14. As I copy that, I can't help thinking of the current policies that the *New York Times* and *Chicago Tribune* have on obscenities. When Gov. Bush, candidate for the presidency, got

The kind of *excessively* aggressive "lapsing" that HypocriteB has always avoided and condemned is dramatized by an episode in a little office in Shrivenham, England, in the summer of '45, where the army had established a mock university for GIs waiting for shipment home. I had been "hired," "promoted," to instructor of English composition. Some American professors had been brought over to fill slots. I was taken to the major in charge to have my job explained, and with him there was a distinguished-looking man in civilian clothes. The major said,

> "Oh, Private Booth, this is Professor Kimball Young, here to teach sociology. Professor Young, you may be interested to know that Private Booth is from Utah." (I already knew that Kimball Young was Brigham Young's grandson. I had actually read a good share of his book analyzing the sociology of polygamy.)
>
> *Young:* "You a Mormon?"
>
> *Booth:* "Yep."
>
> *Young* (pulling out a cigar from a pocket): "Jesus Christ! I just met another one two minutes ago. Let's have a fuckin' elders' meeting!"

I laughed, not offended, just amused at the excessive need to express his independence. But I can imagine how awful that would have felt to me a few years earlier or to any Mormon who had experienced no lapsing: How could a grandson of Brigham Young act like that?!

And how could MoralB go on with this testing the boundaries of code breaking? Toward the end of my time in Germany, I had a buddy protect me for an evening while I got drunk for the first time in my life, both to see what it was like and to express my free agency. And a bit later, in graduate school I tried a cigarette—again to prove my independence. After lighting up, I said to my friend, "Into whose face do I blow the smoke?" Got a good laugh and never touched a cigarette again, except the one marijuana cigarette I sucked a bit years later in southern France, *without inhaling.* Shocking, right?

"No more of that silly stuff," ThinkerB snarls. Let's get back to some *thinking.*

---

caught calling a newspaperman an asshole, the papers' policies did not allow reporters to use the word. Then in 2004, when Vice President Cheney used the f-word against a congressional opponent, the news coverage was amazing, with many deeply offended because Cheney said he felt better after his cursing. Having been in the army for two years, I no longer feel the slightest offense in such matters.

The Pursuit of Truth vs. Loyalty and Love

In the thousands of discussions I've read regarding the conflict between religious faith and the pursuit of truth through reasoning, I can remember no full encounter with the anguish this conflict imposes on someone who genuinely cares for the welfare or feelings of those who are unquestioningly faithful. It's one thing to suffer internally from doubts about whether to believe this or that doctrine or literal historical claim. My journals are full of "secret" evidence that I took as hard proof that this or that historical claim made no sense. But as everyone trained in orthodoxy knows, discovery of such clashing truths can produce immense pain, especially when the doubter has to choose between silence and a form of "whistle-blowing." To report openly on this or that historical fact or flat contradiction of principles or shocking incoherency in scriptures could shake the faith of loved ones, wound them, or even lead them to withdraw their love.

To suppress the discovery and pretend to have no doubts may circumvent such pains. But is it defensible to let this suppression create a hypocritical Self? Just as Darwin worried about how his scientific theories would disturb his wife's faith, all of us who love our faithful friends and relatives worry when we discover a fact that flatly challenges dogmas.

That conflict became acute for me as my thinking led to rejection of belief after belief. It's not just that MoralB thought it wrong to hurt the devout; he not only feared being hated or punished but did not want to harm the Church. Those conflicts deepened as the years passed. These days I often find myself defending this or that dogma I consider absurd if taken literally but support because of its metaphorical or allegorical wisdom. The conflicts don't go away.

It's clear now that the intellectual conflicts began, if unconsciously, very early. When the six-year-old boy's Daddy died suddenly, after he and his Mama had prayed passionately for God to do the healing, the effect must have been deeply troubling to the boy's faith, though memory yields nothing about that until years had passed. Mama confessed to me a couple of decades later that her faith had been shattered by God's ignoring her prayers. Taught to believe that to pray with a sincere and contrite heart would produce direct answers from God, and knowing that her prayers had been absolutely sincere and contrite, the "answer" she got was no answer at all. But for decades she never gave any sign to anyone of her loss of faith; she righteously and defensibly practiced what I will later call "hypocrisy-*upward*."

I'm sure that this experience made her much more tolerant of my later lapsing than Phyllis's parents were of hers. The Barneses had had no sharp moment of rejected prayers, no death of a child or spouse. They believed that every good in life depended on obeying God's commands. And when Mother Barnes saw signs of our lapsing—she could detect, for example, that we were no longer wearing the official undergarments—it felt to her like a total tragedy.[15] Phyllis's father reported to us, long after Luella died, that she wept through many a night as she thought about having "lost" her lapsed daughter: they would not be united in heaven after death.

THE ORIGIN OF HYPOCRISY

To avoid inflicting pain on relatives and shame on ourselves, Phyllis and I always tried to portray ourselves to the family as sincere "Mormons." We attended services fairly often. We showed no open signs of breaking the Word of Wisdom. We taught Church classes until the mid-Sixties. But perceptive observers—not only those who patted us on the shoulder to feel if the undergarments were there—could detect, in word and deed, that we were hypocrites.

Sometimes our posing was ludicrous. Once when her parents were coming to visit us in Indiana, due to arrive within a few hours, we were having lunch with the kids, with wine on the table. Suddenly the Barnes car drove into our driveway, an hour or two earlier than expected. Phyll and I scrambled frantically to get the wine out of sight.

Did we manage it? I think so. But I now wonder about the lesson in behavior that our action inevitably conveyed to Katherine and Richard (Alison was probably too young to do any interpreting). "Mom and Dad are hypocrites! Deceiving is the right way to go."

Long before that episode, something about me had made the family anxious. In Mother Barnes's letters to me in Paris more than a year before the marriage, she intimated a lot of anxiety about me, while disguising it as proud confidence that I would be a totally devout Mormon. (Although Father Barnes was equally devout, he had done a lot of thinking about many of the issues that troubled me—especially, with his Ph.D. in chemistry, the conflicts between science and miracles. But he never showed any signs of genuine lapsing, and he always joined Luella in blaming me—seldom to my face—for having corrupted Phyllis.)

---

15. Active Mormons—those who have qualified to go through the Temple ceremony—are expected, or rather, required, to wear specially designed underwear that has been specifically blessed for the wearing. Special "holy" symbols, derived originally from the Free Masons (Joseph Smith had been one), cover the nipples and navel. The garments have changed greatly over the years. For my grandparents, the arms and legs had to be fully covered, and some (legend says) wouldn't even take them off to bathe. Today you can't tell for sure whether a jogger in shorts has garments underneath.

One of the worst times occurred much later when Mother Barnes agreed to come to Pennsylvania in order to help care for two-year-old Kathie while Phyllis was giving birth to Richard. With Phyllis in the hospital, Luella and I confronted each other daily, and she saw it as the proper time to convert me back into total devotion. Here's my half-miserable journal entry of that time—ignoring the praise that loving Luella deserves for traveling cross-country to tend a grandchild. I can't remember any more painful example of how my Selves quarreled.

> *July 28, 1951*
> Presence of Mother B. makes a wonderfully unpleasant-pleasant situation. She is good with Kathie, and in everything but her passion for doctrinal conformance, a "good" woman. Yet all her qualities depend, or seem to depend, on her doctrinal conformance. With Phyllis away, I find it very trying to live with her. She delivers me ill-disguised sermons, in the form of anecdotes about acquaintances of hers who have been physically blessed or cursed according to their conformity or lack of conformity. She [recently] picked up Renan's *Life of Jesus*, read a bit, and confronted me about it, horrified.
>
> "What do you think of that book of yours I was just reading?"
>
> I spar, to avoid pain, both for her and myself. About the only thing I do well with her is look her in the eye. With all her feeling of virtue and superiority, and with all the guilt I would expect myself to feel (having put on my undergarments, after a fashion, for the duration of her stay), with all the wrongness of my position, I feel completely in the right, because of all my fears about this really frightful situation, the threat of hurting her is predominant. . . .
>
> How long an open discussion can be averted at this rate I don't know. My novel [the never-finished *Polygamy Smith*], if it is published, will break everything into the open, but probably before that some slip of Kathie's or some chance discovery will throw everything into the light of their horrible disappointment. They are so vulnerable—that is my chief feeling—so awfully vulnerable. . . . I shrink from the revelation that must sooner or later come to them of our defection.

It's obvious that the diarist is understating his pain and anxiety: his whole life—especially when facing the loving devotee, hour by hour—is in tension. VainB, who has always longed for total approval of everyone, is losing it.

HypocriteB had suffered intensely in a nasty event a year earlier, when we were still in Chicago. Our ward bishop and his counselor made an official visit to complain about our irregular attendance.

May 1, 1950

The Bishop's visit was painful. I hedged: "Each person must work out his own destiny, Bishop; right now my habits are to stay away from church, and you must respect my decision. Perhaps later I'll discover my error and return." But I said nothing about the impossibility of return, in his sense of the word. I could no more stand up to that man and tell him that, to me, everything he believes—everything—is a colossal lie than I could stand up and tell mother the same thing.

Why would I have put it like that? I certainly did not believe that every Mormon belief the bishop accepted was false! The antiliteralist sounds foolishly arrogant to me—but he's anxious.

> The high point of his plea came when he suggested that, although I said I enjoyed staying home on Sunday with my family more than going to church, I had no assurance that God would not see fit to take my family away from me, as punishment.
>
> "Now, you say that your daughter has been having several bad colds. You don't know but what they might turn to pneumonia, and then where'd you be!" That he is an MD made, I suppose in his eyes, his whole plea more effective. Then his companion capped the whole thing with: "Wayne, you must have spent from $1200 to $1500 dollars on your mission. Don't lose that investment!"
>
> I was tremendously guilt-ridden throughout the interview. To lose the esteem of those one esteems—and I do like, at least, some of the members—is always tough for me.

The bishop would no doubt have been convinced, two decades later, that my son Richard's death resulted strictly from our misbehavior.

Will my assertions here that I still believe in God—according to my definition—lead the stricken ones to forgive me? Will it help to confess my genuine embrace of many of the Church's values, especially the exhortation to serve others? Will it hurt to confess to more moments of HypocriteB's concealment of actual beliefs? Would it help if I offered his "mythic" embrace of many obviously impossible "historical" claims that most Mormons claim to embrace literally? Two Selves dispute about it:

> *ThinkerB:* You've been overly hypocritical throughout here; you've not offered a single example of the historical discoveries that led you to reject this

or that central Mormon claim. Are you just a coward and hypocrite, afraid of expressing the truth? Are you simply imitating the Mormon authorities who, over the years, have hidden what they knew about the atrocious, "God-driven" 1857 massacre of 120 "gentiles" in Mountain Meadows, Utah? Is serving *your* faith more important that what you know as the *truth?*

Family-and-Church-LoverB: You're absolutely wrong; the *LIFE* is going much too far with its silly report of objections. What's the point of revealing all these doubts and conflicts that will upset friend after friend, relative after relative? You've either got to cut all that or stipulate that the book cannot be published until the year 2050. Or, at the very least, you could explain why, for you, so much of the Bible and Book of Mormon present wonderful mythical truths. Just last week I heard you arguing with friends that the Adam and Eve story gives a truer account of our origins, allegorically, than the one offered by dogmatic Darwinists.

LIFER: Shut up, you two. Why can't you just let me get on with it?

How to Handle the Guilt

I won't list more of my "behavior lapses" and "belief lapses." But what about the question of obedience to those basic LDS commandments that still do seem admirable?

One that I admire most is the strict requirement to give the Church a full 10 percent of annual income. If I were God, I would have made it more progressive, with 90 percent from the billionaires and .05 percent from the impoverished, but it is still a daily, yearly reminder that something in "the world" is more important than merely adding to your possessions. Statistical studies show that Mormons give a lot more to their Church than do members of other denominations; they might also give more to other charities. Phyllis's father told us, and I believe him, that his annual giving was about 20 percent.

Yet it has been many years since I paid a full 10 percent tithe to the Church, and by now I give relatively little. The definition of what is "full" is a bit shaky, and some are inevitably tempted to lie a bit to get or stay in. That was the route I took at first. Here's how I put it in a letter to Phyllis from Paris four months before our marriage. The letter shows the soldier as a lot more hostile to this commandment than I feel now.

26 Feb. 1946
Dearest, . . .

Mother just wrote me this: "Wayne, I wrote a letter to you explaining that the Bishop said he could not give a recommend to the temple for anyone who had not paid tithing. Don't let this spoil your marriage." I had been a little angry at the tone of an earlier letter written by your parents, but I must confess that nothing they said was as obviously full of evil portent as that quote from Mother. I'll probably send some tithing, but we must be honest and admit to ourselves at least what it is I shall be doing. The Church says, in effect, you may buy your way into eternal marriage. Mother says, in effect, you mustn't spoil your chances for a happy marriage by refusing to pay the blackmail. And I say, in effect, I'll pay the blackmail, not for the eternal marriage, which, if possible under any circumstances, would not be aided by paying a purchase tax, not for the happiness of which Mother speaks, but simply to keep her and the Bishop and all our relatives and friends and pious well-wishers quiet. The way the whole system is cleverly contrived to keep anyone who has emotional ties within the system safely tied in every other way, angers me, my love, positively angers me. I'm nearly as angry as my B.Y.U. prof was when the church first enforced the "no tithing—no job [at BYU]" policy. As if anyone who pays tithing in order to keep his job would gain anything spiritually from having given. But I'll show them. For every dollar I send home to the nice, considerate Bishop (and the trouble is, he really is nice and considerate and thinks he's doing a fine favor), I'll give two dollars to the KPD [German Communist Party]. That'll show 'em!

So I sent some cash to a bishop, and Phyllis and I were married four months later *for eternity* (in a manner of speaking). That time my lies were utterly defensible—the kind that don't hurt *anybody:* what I label hypocrisy-*upward.*

But again I have to ask, does the "good" of maintaining family love outweigh the "good" of being truthful?[16]

Eleven years later, HypocriteB did lie, blatantly. When my mother decided to marry Ray Davis after thirty years of widowhood, I wanted very much to attend her wedding ceremony in the Salt Lake Temple. But of course I couldn't attend without our bishop's "recommend," and he knew that I had been moving closer and closer to a point *beyond* the fringe. On the one hand, I was still a successful teacher of an adult Sunday School class, but on the other hand . . . well, the bishop had so many doubts about me that he sent me from Richmond to the stake president in Indianapolis, about seventy

---

16. For a wonderful current revival of traditional accounts of how to deal with conflicting goods and evils, see Michael Ignatieff's *The Lesser Evil* (Princeton: Princeton University Press, 2004). He works hard to restore our ability to think hard—following Aristotle's *phronesis* (prudence), Machiavelli's *virtù*, and the Jesuits' "casuistry"—about when and how to balance one evil against another.

miles away, to be interrogated. HypocriteB managed to get his signature by employing promises, some faked and some genuine. I could state sincerely my devotion to Mormonism, and I felt fairly comfortable making an utterly fake promise to pay full 10 percent in the future.[17]

Since then I've never subjected myself to an interview, and I've never paid 10 percent. How, then, can I go on calling myself MoralB? Well, it's easy: every year at tax time I obey the commandment—according to *my* definition of what it *ought* to mean. I calculate my total charitable giving for the year to make sure that it comes to *at least* 10 percent of our total income.

That proves that I'm still in good standing "up there," right? It is my God's will that I devote one-tenth of my "increase" to His causes, right? Actually, in the view of all of my current Selves, divided or united, when we consider our present income, the gifts ought to be a hell of a lot higher than 10 percent. Sometimes they are.

But why, then, do I not give more to the Church itself? You'll find answers to that question, explicit and implicit, through many other parts of this book. And you'll detect, as at this moment, a lot of suppression of annoyance, even anger, about some Church purchases squandering money that tithepayers thought was going to God's causes. So I feel a lot of uneasiness about it—not quite guilt, perhaps, but . . .

Who Wins Within Me Now?

That my youthful version of "inside" is totally abandoned should be obvious by now. I'm afraid that some Mormon readers here will misinterpret what I've said so far as too much on the side of the skeptical ThinkerB, showing nothing but contempt for the sexist-patriarchal-puritanical-racist culture that clashed so sharply with what I later embraced "outside." "You've made it sound," they must feel, "as if you had been 'enclosed,' 'dominated,' practically 'enslaved,' and then you were 'freed'—even 'saved'—to become the VainB you are stupidly proud of being right now."

But I hope it's obvious that I see it all quite differently. Though in some ways I was freed by moving "out," in other ways I was endangered. I was often tempted to be sucked into a culture—as in that example of actually trying marijuana—that strikes me today as in many respects far more threatening to my diverse Selves than the culture I was raised in. Obvious in everything

---

17. In the Temple, by now a bit out of date on procedures, I was initially puzzled to see all of us in attendance pinned with a little card reading "Time Only." It took me a few minutes to remember that since Mama was already married for eternity to my father, she could not be married to Ray "for eternity": it was for "time only."

that follows, as in my "faked" annual tithing, is the sustained centrality of Mormon influence—conscious and unconscious.

> *MormonB (whispering):* You see, I am absolutely still a Mormon.
> *ThinkerB (from his intellectual pedestal, wineglass in hand):* That claim is just absurd! Don't you see that it's not hypocrisy-*upward* you're practicing as you go on using the Mormon label; you're just CheaterB practicing plain immoral cheating. Don't you feel annoyed right this minute by the new Church policy on X, Y, or Z? And what about your daily violations of the Word of Wisdom—tea, coffee, alcohol (though never cigarettes)?
> *LIFER:* Well, really—can't we agree that those violations are unimportant? If the complaints about the Church leaders' bossiness disappeared, you know that we would have no trouble abstaining from caffeine and wine. We could even have the thrill of attending Temple ceremonies!

Quarrel over, temporarily.

I won't allow my moralizing self to spend time adding another tirade to the innumerable public attacks on the grotesque, often cruel, sins in our present culture; he is especially tempted to deal with how the wealthy and their minions in Washington are behaving. Instead I just want to underline how much greater the clash was for someone raised in the fold than it ever can be for someone raised—even in the most devout religious family—in our mass-mediated consumerist culture, in which we meet from too many directions the claim that "anything goes." There is no longer—for too many—any remotely clear ethical code. My quarrel with the "loss of ethics" has been implicit in all of my teaching and writing, much more so than I often realized. As some critics have lamented, Booth is nothing *but* a moralizer.[18]

I still believe that being enculturated with moral norms can be harmful when the code is imposed thoughtlessly and with sheer dominating authority. But I can't give up my gratitude for having been indoctrinated with a code, at least some portions of which I still embrace—even claiming to do so "religiously." Like many on the political and religious "right" and "left," I fear our "true values" are disastrously eroding. I also fear that too many, on the right and left, pursue their codes destructively, as when an anti-abortionist kills someone for favoring free choice or our president takes us to war because he is sure God wants him to.

---

18. It's hard to resist here citing the "values" implicitly taught by most successful TV series or the "values" pursued by our business world, as revealed in business after business since the Enron revelations in 2002.

My main point is thus my daily gratitude for having been indoctrinated into the *fact* that there are serious moral limits to individualistic code breaking. There are genuine values in the world, and when you violate them you— even if you are a multimillionaire president of the country—*you* are guilty. I feel lucky (or blessed) to have been spared the miseries that I see others suffering or producing in their victims when they "go too far," thinking that "anything goes" and shouting "I'm OK, you're OK" or "Greed is good!" The Mormon teaching that "standards are real, not just invented," though formulated differently in different decades, continues with me now, and I see many moments when, if I had not been indoctrinated from day one, my so-called Thinking might have landed me in disaster.

Chapter Two

A Pious Moralist Confronts a Cheater

It is impossible for a man to be cheated by anyone but himself.

—Emerson

Nothing so much prevents our being natural as the desire to seem so.

—La Rochefoucauld

Know thyself? If I knew myself, I would run away.

—Goethe

One must not cheat anybody, not even the world of its triumph.

—Kafka

In early spring of 1946, the frustrated Staff Sergeant Booth is in the occupation army in Bremen, Germany, longing for shipment home. The morality-trained twenty-five-year-old—still the "devout" Mormon you have met—is now teaching a "lit-comp" course to other GIs waiting for shipment home. He has been put up with several buddies in a quite fancy house that the U.S. army has taken over.

Browsing through an impressive domestic library, he is tempted to steal a couple of books, but they're almost all in German. Then he comes to a shelf of miniature musical scores, mostly of string quartets: Haydn, Mozart, Beethoven, Brahms! Would it not be right to steal them from the abominable Germans? Besides, he thinks, "If I don't take 'em, somebody else will." He picks just a dozen of them out—of course feeling guilty, apprehensive—and hides them under his bed. Finally, a month later, he hauls them home.

They still sit on my—not his—shelves, reproachfully but usefully.

I would now return them to anyone from that family, if I could ever find the name. MoralB finally, in one sense, wins—but to little effect. He often sneers at me, "How on earth could you have committed an offense like that?"

I wonder how many of the professedly honest men and women I've known have committed as much cheating as I have.[1] If this were a self-help book, I would censor all that follows here, laboring to invent a man who practices only life-enhancing, morally and intellectually defensible values. But as I

---

1. Influenced by the many revelations in 2002–03 of business cheating through recent decades, I asked a friend, experienced for most of his life in resolving traffic controversies, "What percentage of Americans do you believe will lie or cheat for personal advantage?" Without pausing even a second he said, "About 95 percent." Only slightly shocked, I then asked, "What percentage will lie or cheat even if they know it will harm others?" "Oh, much smaller. Only about 50 percent." If you are skeptical about such estimates, you should have a look at Erving Goffman's many accounts, in book after book, of how universal are the arts of masking, posing, "performing."

work at creating a harmonious Self who enjoys probing the conflicts, I must at least pretend to offer a wholehearted exhibit of honesty. And reporting the cheater's quarrels with the moralist is an essential part of the quest.

The better side of my Mormon Self—or should I call it my Platonic or my Augustinian or my John Deweyan Self—is not at all happy about most of the offenses you'll read about here. Stealing those music scores from Germans who, for all I knew, were admirable anti-Nazis or even Holocaust victims, is simply unforgivable. I was harming others. (Phyllis, penetrating editor, asks, "Do you mean to imply that if they had actually been known to be Nazis, your theft would be forgivable?" Well, ah, er, I'll think about it.)

Though I'm sure I've never lied as persistently as our political leaders or CEOs do, it still shocks me to rediscover a Cheater-Booth who was not just willing to cheat to win this or that bit of cash or praise, but sometimes even seemed to enjoy cheating for the sheer fun of it. A friend who read an early draft was also shocked and then advised me to report more moments when morality triumphed: "You're far more trustworthy than your chapter suggests." I hope it's true that if I totaled up all of my choices, I'd find far more in which "doing the right thing, whatever it costs" triumphed over cheating. What does it say about me, then, that I find stories about CheaterB more fascinating than stories about MoralB, even when they embarrass me?

Not long ago Phyllis discovered that we had underpaid a repair company by about a hundred bucks, and they didn't know it. What was my immediate silent impulse? "Forget about it; they've overcharged anyway." Her response was automatic: she just sat down and wrote a check, with MoralB's full support. I now still wonder, "Why on earth did I want to cheat them?"

Would I have been able, without her help, to talk CheaterB into making out that check? I hope so, but the initial impulse to forget about it was really there. That vile deceiver is still surprisingly alive in me, though by now MoralB usually trounces him.

Interlude

I have just now told her about that repressed impulse to say, "Just ignore it."

"How could you marry a man," I joke, "who is inclined to cheat—and stay married to him for fifty-nine years?"

"Well, I *thought* you were a man with total integrity."

"Well, one of my Selves was just that! I hope you've noticed."

"Oh, yes. I live with *him* all the time."

Another recent example, considerably less defensible: As we are preparing a dinner for twenty or more relatives in our rather chilly Utah "mountain cabin," I must go down from the mountains into "town" to shop for a few groceries and perhaps some wood for the fireplace. We check to make sure that even on Sunday the Harmon's grocery store is open; phone book says, "Open twenty-four hours every day." Driving up to the store fifteen minutes later, I see that the car lot is entirely empty. I go to the door; it's locked. I feel a bit cross at the managers: why did they place deceptive information in the phonebook? Isn't that commercial cheating?

As I turn to leave, I notice a pile of firewood bundles lying outside the doorway. I scan the scene, see no one in any direction, and without a moment's hesitation I pick up a bundle of the firewood and carry it casually to my car, feeling something like "What fun!" I drive off, and suddenly a rival voice nags, "Why are you stealing that wood? Is it to get even with them for not being open?" I'm tempted to take it back, but CheaterB wins: What does it matter? After all, we've given them a lot more profit during our month here than that wood costs. And I've not actually hurt anyone!

After shopping at another store, I drive back into the mountains, feeling more and more self-reproach, not just for the stupidity of it—what if someone had caught me?—but for the sheer wrongness of stealing. I debate all the way about whether to tell Phyllis about it. Finally, entering our driveway, morality triumphs: I will tell her.

And I do. She is shocked—not fully surprised but rightly annoyed. "When you joke these days about fearing that you'll become a senile klepto-maniac, maybe you should take it seriously." It takes only a few seconds for me to agree with her: the theft is indefensible, and I will certainly pay them next time I'm in the shop—emphasizing, with a plausible smile tacked on my face, that we needed the wood and intended to pay all the while.[2]

Now there's a debate with the LIFER: Should I confess such behavior here? What will my grandkids think—in the unlikely event that any of them read this far? I hope they'll find it a bit instructive about whatever cheating they're tempted to do.[3] Maybe my telling about it will lead them to see the superiority of Phyllis's response. Will they see that what they actually "are" now can possibly be transformed by aspiring to *be* someone better?

THE (COMICAL? SHAMEFUL?) HISTORY OF IT

I'm still puzzled about where CheaterB came from, raised in a culture that preached so strongly *thou shalt not lie or cheat or steal*. One part of me aimed

---

2. Oh, yes, skeptical reader; I have made the payment, anonymously.
3. A recent study, purporting to be "scientific," claims that something like 90 percent of children interviewed admitted that they had done some cheating or lying to their parents.

to become the most morally admirable creature in history. How could anyone who was as moved as I was by Jesus's attacks on hypocrisy start out, so early, not just deceiving others to further his own interests but actually enjoying the acts of deception?

Before addressing that question, consider a further selection from so many embarrassing memories:[4]

Age Four and a Half

A policeman comes to the front door of our two-room, no-toilet apartment. He shocks Mama by saying that it's not her he wants to talk with but me. Someone has broken the windshield of a police car as it sat on the street in front of a neighbor's house.

He looks at me suspiciously. I'm scared.

"Do you know anything about it?"

I know absolutely nothing about it, but I immediately tell him, in some detail, how it all happened.

"It was my friend, Sammy, next door. He didn't do it on purpose. We was just playing with throwing rocks up over the roof from behind there [pointing to the rear of the neighbor's house], and he threw a rock way up over the roof [gesturing with my arm] and it come crashin' down on the car."

He knows at once that I'm lying. "Look, kid, nobody your age could throw a rock that far." He sounds angry. After he leaves, Mama makes me miserable with her punishment—no physical blows but her standard chant:

"Oh, Clayson, how disappointed I am in you!"

I can't remember feeling guilty about how much harm my lie might have done to Sammy if the cop had taken it as true. I'm glad to say that I have no other memories in which my conniving threatened serious harm to others.

Age Seven

My uncle Joseph is a "champion" marble shooter, winning marbles by the bagful. Five years younger, I have never won a single marble. I long for those wonderfully colored objects, so I steal his bag and hide it at the back of a remote closet. It doesn't take long for Joe to catch me. Punishment? I'm locked by Mama in a dark closet, weeping for what feels like hours. Mama is *deeply* disappointed in me.

---

4. I don't have to tell you that LIFERS' memories are unreliable. We'll have a look at that problem a bit later.

From that time on I was quite careful about stealing only when I could be pretty sure I would not be caught.[5] But:

Age Eight

Returning alone from a Church service, I see a looseleaf folder hanging on a fencepost. I look around, see no one, tear off the string attachment, and carry the folder home, excited about having some blank pages for my drawings.

Mama recognizes immediately that it's a voters' registration notebook; it is election time. She marches me back up to the violated house and orders me to take the notebook to the voting official and apologize.

A good lesson CheaterB took from that? Don't steal anything that your parents can identify.

He went on stealing paper and pens and pencils for decades, whether or not he had enough money to buy them. Even today when I see any desirable writing supplies lying unprotected, nobody watching, I sometimes have a hard time clamping down on the Cheater. I usually win these days, but will I always? In my pursuit of plausible harmony, "I" sincerely hope so.

Age Eight to Yesterday

I have always lied about how much I've read—though far less these days than as a kid. From about fourth grade on, having proudly skipped a year, I "had read everything." I would lie to teachers about classics I'd barely looked at. I would bore fellow students by trying to make them feel inferior for not having read the latest *Atlantic Monthly*, one that I'd only skimmed through. By late high school and through college, the way for VainB to prove his superior intellect was to show that he had read this or that impossibly difficult book. To see others embarrassed by their "ignorance" gave VainB some slight bit of pleasure: "I'm getting ahead—even if I have to lie to do it."[6]

---

5.   I'm sure that this memory explains why I also remember a family joke about a boy put by his mother in a closet as punishment. When she wonders why he's stayed there longer than required, she comes to take him out and says, "Why are you still in here?" "Well, I've spit on your dress, and I've spit on your shoes, and I've spit on your coat, and I'm just sitting in here waiting for more spit."

6.   Daughter Alison pleases me by scribbling here: "This does sound worse than you are. It's a necessary hypocrisy even to get by in academia, no?" "Of course, dear, but isn't mine a lot worse than yours?" We'll be meeting in chapter 6 some forms of hypocritical posing that I do think morally defensible. That will entail considerable labor at distinguishing defensible and indefensible deception: the subject of my currently back-burnered book on "hypocrisy-upward."

But now back to cheating that wasn't related to ambition or vanity.

Age Fourteen

As a "deacon" (Mormon boys are ordained into the priesthood at age twelve) I am assigned the task of going door to door and collecting from ward members their monthly "fast Sunday" contribution, the amount they have saved "for the poor and hungry" by skipping breakfast that morning. I collect what I can, then quickly pocket about a fourth of it before turning the rest over to the bishop.

Decades later when I confessed this sin to my aging Mama, she refused to believe it.

"Your memory must have made that up. The boy I knew could not have done such a thing."

"But, Mama, didn't I do a lot of lying to you? Didn't I often steal a bit of cash out of your purse?"

"Not that I can remember."

Age Fourteen–Fifteen

I am often assigned the paid job of distributing free newspapers or brochures house to house. I become quite skillful at burning a large fraction of the copies in our furnace; that saves a lot of time and labor. Then one summer I hide a bundle of them in a street irrigation culvert.

That one was stupid: as soon as irrigation water entered the pipe and flooded, the stack was discovered, easily traceable to me. Punishment? Can't remember, but the humiliation of it is still vivid. I had forgotten the lesson, "Make sure you're not easily caught. Whatever cheating you do must be done intelligently." Meanwhile I was constantly nagging myself to stop such awful stuff.

Perhaps the most shocking example occurred when I became a newspaper delivery boy and subscription seller. For quite a while I failed to sell any subscriptions at all, and I never became very good at it. Yet I claimed success from the beginning, reporting increasing sales totals—sales that I actually was faking.

Age Fifteen

The company gave every delivery boy a small cash gift for each subscription sold. Naturally the money-grubber Self wanted to earn a lot of money, while the honors seeker figured out that since the cash gift for each subscription was almost large enough to pay for a full month of deliveries, he could chalk up a fake subscription at very small cost. So his divided selves faced a dilemma: if he entered fake subscriptions, his chance of winning the contest went up fast, while his income went down only a small amount for each subscription. Which was more important, fame or cash income? The egoist won, hands down, and his subscription rate went up and up, finally leading to his winning a contest.

Suddenly the whole episode, with its fame-winning façade, crashes. He contracts Bright's disease and hears a doctor speculate about possible death. He has to turn over his routes and records to the boss, and they reveal a total jumble of dishonest subscriptions and careless juggling of data: a huge cash debt (actually quite small, as I consider it now) and incontrovertible evidence of nonexistent subscriptions.

His boss turns out to be a generous man; he waits until the boy is back on his feet and attending school again, after two months at home, before he shocks the mother by revealing his discoveries. He does not turn the boy in to any authorities; all he insists on is some more work, without pay, until the losses have been paid off. (Does the diary reveal the truth of any of this? Not at all. It reads as if the boy were now simply working for his old boss again in a new job. Does it confess to any guilt? Not at all. It never acknowledges that the crazy desire to be number one had produced an atrocious hypocrite reveling in being a winner.)[7]

It's puzzling, given the guilt I feel about that now, to remember *not* feeling guilt through most of this cheating. One would think that with all of the sermonizing and punishment most of it produced, I'd have felt more than just anxiety about being caught. My journal entries do *imply* a lot of guilt about not achieving an ideal character: entry after entry about how I must try to be more honorable, a "better boy." But I never recorded, nor can I remember, anything like the remorse I feel now about stealing the music scores in Germany—or about most of the offenses we're coming to.

Age Seventeen

Four or five of us high school senior boys are discussing sex. One of them says how much he longs for some *real* sex, not just petting or masturbation. I intervene, with something like this:

"Don't you realize that all the girls are longing for it too? And that if you just push harder, you can get almost any one of 'em within fifteen

---

7. This recollection is quoted, with some alterations to the third paragraph, from an article in *The Michigan Quarterly Review*, written for an issue containing diverse memories of "Secret Spaces" (vol. 39:3 [Summer 2000]: 442).

Wayne C. in high school

minutes. I've had full sex with many of 'em just this year—they just cave in if they know you're serious."[8]

They all look surprised, a bit shocked. Nobody seems to doubt me. Two years later, at BYU, my cousin Parker Chipman meets me in the hall.

"Are you still having as much sex as you told us about back then?"

"Oh my gosh. Did you believe my story?"

"Of course I did. And it *almost* changed my own behavior."

Age Nineteen

I have been hired to tend a hamburger stand, a quarter of the way up the mountain where BYU conducts its annual Timpanogas Hike. Collecting payments for hamburgers and soft drinks, I pocket some of it—and never get caught![9]

This one did produce immense guilt—so strong that I didn't mention it in my journal. Here I was cheating everybody, and it gave me no credit whatever for skill or manliness. Any six-year-old, even a girl, could have gotten away with that easy one.

Age Twenty

Another student and I are working as irrigators on the university farm at thirty cents an hour—a five-cent raise from last year. Since much of the work is just standing and waiting for the water to flow, we both get a lot of reading done; that's not cheating. But then my buddy gets an offer to work several hours a week on another job. He asks me if I'd be willing to cover him in a scam, continuing to report his sixteen to eighteen hours a day, with me actually doing some of his work. He'll pay me half of what he gains by the scam.

CheaterB agreed—though the journal reports only mild moral concern. After all, we were both being underpaid!

From Age Seven to Twenty-Five

I stole quite a few books. (This offense now really shocks me.) I can't remember how many—some from bookstores, a few from school libraries, a couple from a detested teacher's desk. Sometimes I would buy a book, read it quickly, and return it to the store as if unread. Books felt like my life-blood; could it really be a crime to add to the essential nourishment? I drew

---

8. I'm pretty sure my lie didn't include the word "fuck."
9. It must have been a very small percentage, right?

the line with friends' books; when I would "steal" one of them, I would secretly return it later. (Though I often cheated family, I somehow always held back from cheating friends.)

The most outlandish book theft—one that HypocriteB is strongly tempted to censor—took place in Blackwell's bookstore in Oxford, when I was a GI waiting for shipment home after the war.

July 1945, Age Twenty-Four
In the riskiest theft I ever committed, I stole three books—all of them, of course, of high intellectual value—and did not get caught. (I think, but can't prove, that two of them were books Phyllis had written a request for.)[10]

If I had been caught I would have been court-martialed, kicked out, perhaps ruined for life. Maybe not that bad, but it would have been awful. And what is especially shameful is that I had enough money in my pocket to pay for those books! Understandably, the journal does not mention the theft, nor do my letters home to Phyllis. Does it seem to you that I am even more embarrassed about the stupidity of that one than about the dishonesty of it?

Some years later, MoralB did triumph: I mailed Blackwell's some money to repay the theft (without giving my name).

The cheating memory I regret most—even more than my stealing of the music scores in Germany—was committed in Paris in late December of 1945. Everything about it is sheer, undocumented memory; quite understandably, there's not a word about it in my journals or letters.

Climax
The Germans had launched a surprise counterattack, producing what is now called the Battle of the Bulge. Our army was short of infantrymen to charge back, and they began interviewing us clerks in Paris for return to combat. As I went for my interview, I felt both terrified and torn apart: honor commanded my "surrender to combat," but by now, after all I had seen of what combat meant for those who managed to come back, I could not face it. What could I do?

Well, the clerk did the best job he could do faking bad vision—he could not read the vision chart. The doctor looked suspicious.

"Any other excuse?"

---

10. Reading that, she writes in the margin, "Don't blame me; the books you sent me were secondhand!"

Suddenly he thought of one. "I do have fallen arches. They got me turned down for the Navy." (That was an honest story. The Navy rejected me because of my arches; the infantry took me in spite of them—in itself a neat comic irony.)

The doctor looked at the mildly misshapen feet, decided that I was not fit for combat, and let me escape back to my clerkship.

If I had been a conscientious objector or complete pacifist, escaping combat at that point would not have been shameful. But I was a passionate anti-Nazi, a total supporter of our army effort. I was convinced that we were in a noble cause. (I still view it as inescapable, though hardly noble.) Yet I lied in order to avoid my own probable death at the front. The fact that it was my feet that really saved me doesn't mitigate my vision lie at all. CheaterB had joined all those other guys, from presidents on down, who—as we learned later—used this or that dodge to avoid the draft. Full shame.[11]

Isn't that more than enough about my cheating Self? Should I go on and report my two—*only* two, I insist—moments of cheating as a student? Should I diminish readers' contempt by boasting about never, from my late teens on, cheating a student or colleague and never (consciously) cheating my family or close friends? And how about never, never—in this book—lying about *anything*? VainB could fill this chapter with self-touting moments when morality won. Do I not deserve a lot of credit for clamping down on that VainB? Yet now I surrender to him.

Just One, 1975

I have been invited to speak at a conference on pluralism, along with Professor Boaster and others: fee, $300 each. We all accept. A few months later, as the plans for the conference move ahead, I receive an invitation from President Johnson's university in Texas: fee for the talk, $1,000 (I think; certainly it was the highest I'd ever been offered). Without even a moment of doubt, I say, "Sorry, I'm already committed."

A week or so after the conference, I learn that Professor Boaster had been invited to take my place in Texas and had accepted. He had written the director of the pluralism conference saying something like "Sorry, but

---

11. If what I've just said seems exaggerated to you, have a look at almost any biography of our presidents—for example, Robert A. Caro's account of President Lyndon Johnson's road to power (1981) and Michael Beschloss's (2001) accounts of Johnson's daily lying, or Mark Crispin Miller's story of how all our modern presidents, especially the Bush family, have lied (in *The Bush Dyslexicon*, 2001).

my doctor has ordered me to take things easy, so I just can't come." Then he went to Texas to collect his much higher "honorarium." My reaction when I accidentally learned of that? Total contempt—and a bit of pride about having defeated at least my money-grabber Self.[12]

SOURCE OF IT ALL

Where did my unusually strong willingness to deceive come from, given my Mormon heritage of contempt for it, and why should I bother to report it here? Am I not poisoning my image? (*Writing* about it doesn't poison *my* own image of my Selves; after all, I've been living with these facts since that first episode at age four and a half.)

Well, perhaps some of it sprang from partially defensible motives. If you have no money and you need a pencil and paper for writing, is it really wrong to steal a bit—if you're not stealing from a beggar?[13] My sister was equally short of cash, but I can't remember that she ever stole or cheated; her only compensation for grief was probably when, as a two-year-old who had lost her stable family with Daddy's death, she collected everything she could lay her hands on and constructed a little "secret" pile in this or that corner. Maybe we both were trying to get hold of something that was truly *ours* after the disastrous loss.

In any case something weird was going on in my picture of my Self; it was more than just hardwired selfishness. A strong part of me was taking real pleasure (or at least seeking some reward) from whatever my successful cheating demonstrated. Was it a search for cleverness—outsmarting the conventional victims? Was it rebellion? I did sometimes think of my actions as clever, and I did sometimes think of them as admirable rebellion against stupid codes.

I see a strong difference between my public posing as pious and the behavior of some other sinners who openly and courageously broadcast their sins as rebellion—or simply as hoaxes. My offenses were always "protected" by HypocriteB, the skillful performer of public piety.

So again: Where, oh, where did the impulses come from?

---

12. One beloved reader, whom I will not name for fear of hurting her feelings, writes in the margin: "I question using this anecdote. It only puts Professor Boaster down and reduces you to VainB." To which I answer: "Par for the course."

13. Nathalie Sarraute, in her memoir *Childhood*, reports getting caught stealing some candy in a store. When she is grilled by parents about just *why* she would do such a terrible thing, she simply shouts back, echoing Bill Clinton's explanation of why he misbehaved with Monica Lewinsky, "Because I wanted it."

One possibility is that I was thumbing my nose at the mysteriously cruel God who had betrayed Mama. If He could be a cheater, why shouldn't I become one? Had it not become clear to my unconscious soul that cheating was built into the very nature of things? What would a God who would kill my father care if I stole a few pennies or cheated my newspaper manager? I lived in a world run by a cheating God—or at least a God who was deliberately confusing.

It must have strengthened such convictions to be surrounded by relatives (including Mama) who played hypocritical roles in public. I can't remember examples of their doing it viciously or destructively. But they were clearly masking themselves as pious public personae, different from the people I met in private. That experience must be shared by almost every member of every church: "The mother and father I live with are not the ones whom members meet in church on Sunday morning." Just how much of my relatives' hypocrisy was I consciously aware of? I can't reconstruct it all, but it's not hard to think of many examples.

- One of my uncles faked, in dead winter, a total physical collapse, requiring him to be carried uphill to his high school where, after the doctor was called, he jumped to his feet, laughing at his victims. I can remember loving that story, as my uncles told it again and again. I wished that I had that kind of courage.
- I didn't learn until late in my teens that Gramma Booth was cheating daily by secretly drinking a cup or two of tea.
- When I was assisting my absolutely trustworthy aunt, Relva Booth Ross, in writing her autobiography, she told me the following:

  > As a teenager, the only argument I ever had with Father was over me wearing my corsets too tight. He and Manda [her sister] quarreled over high heels, but with me it was corsets. One night when I was going to a dance, he made me go and loosen them up. When I came out, he said, "Did you do it?" I said yes—but when I got to the dance I tightened them again.[14]

- I wonder how old I was when I learned that my Great-Gramma Hawkins fermented beer from fruit juice in her cellar.
- Uncle Joe would boast to me about how he got away with this or that infringement of the rules.

---

14. *The Autobiography of Relva Booth Ross: With Lives of My Parents and Grandparents*, ed. Wayne C. Booth (Provo, Utah: J. Grant Stevenson, 1971), 20.

- Grampa Clayson in his public sermons was visibly, passionately kinder, gentler, more tolerant than the man we lived with.[15]

The more I think about such examples, the more I'm convinced that most or all of these relatives were at least partially aware of their own hypocrisy. My Booth grandparents had, by the time of my father's death, lost all four sons, with four daughters remaining. What kind of God would allow that? God is up there, all right; He must be. And the only way we can hope for better treatment from Him is to claim both publicly and privately to be the most pious church members in town. But meanwhile, in our hearts we suffered a good deal of questioning.

MoralB Fights Back and Wrestles with HypocriteB

Whatever the reasons for my frequent cheating, moral judgments (often joining VainB, who aspired to win the virtue prize) were constantly intruding. MoralB wanted not just to appear pious but to *be* virtuous. The commandments about visible behavior I obeyed scrupulously: I never smoked; I never drank (until the army); I paid my tithing regularly; I never missed church voluntarily; I accepted every assignment from every authority without ever talking back. When my school buddies went watermelon-stealing, I refused to go—I would not allow myself to be seen in public as a thief, even while practicing theft in private. I did raise occasional problems for my Sunday School teachers by asking tough questions, but there was no explicit code against asking questions. Indeed, one of the most prominent doctrines then—more prominent than now—was that God had granted us free agency, and to exercise it we had to do honest thinking about our choices.

Inevitably, the conflict between the would-be saint and the actual sinner took a different form as my faith in many of the literal Church doctrines diminished and my own commitment to "virtue"—to be honorable and do good in the world—expanded. My awareness of a virtuous tension—just how much doing good in the world depends on our willingness to put on honorable and cheerful masks—rose as I observed more and more posing in people I genuinely admired.

This was especially true as I saw how my beloved BYU professors survived steady pressure from authorities to be more orthodox. They were sometimes sent up to Salt Lake City to be grilled by the Church authorities. One time Professor Poulson was called up because a student had reported his revealing in class that he didn't believe in a personal devil.

---

15. Phyllis remembers that when her father was stake president, she thought quite explicitly, "Oh, if only the members out there who think he's so great could see the man I live with at home—two entirely different people!"

After he returned from Salt Lake City, I privately asked him how the interview had gone. "Oh, it was OK," he said. "When they asked if I believed in a personal devil, I answered, 'Of course I do: all of my devils are personal.' They laughed, we shook hands, and that was it."

That's hypocrisy of the constructive kind, right? Though the word was never used among us, it was always implicitly there, as it was in my conversations with other professors. The silent voice was always saying, "We don't take the Church literally, but we think it does good in the world, and we hope that by supporting it—*and concealing our doubts*—we do too."

My full account of hypocrisy being saved for chapter 6, what about the rest of my life? Well, much of it has been plagued by a strong sense of my being a cheater—in danger of being caught. Long after I'd stopped actually stealing anything (except one package of firewood), my nighttime dreams still show me being caught. As late as July 1952, when my family was living for a few months back home in my mother's basement, my journal reports my sleeping miserably, dreaming every night about guilt.

> I wake each morning completely exhausted. It's partly the hard bed, partly being in mother's house, and partly a general uneasiness about being "found out": obviously I could not have as good a deal as this Ford Foundation Fellowship unless I had somehow cheated to get it. [I really had not!] I have, in fact, cheated so many times in my life to get things, particularly money (always petty amounts, and always in completely safe situations; always safe) that now that I have a large bonus honestly, my unconscious won't let me believe it.

"Did you yourself," I hear some of you readers asking, "at some time develop greater honesty, before achieving it *totally* here in this book?"

Well, I've already given you some evidence of that. But the triumph was never total. As you've seen throughout, I can never resolve the conflict between total sincerity and the desire not to hurt others. But I do claim that my many moments of hypocrisy these days are never performed in order to cheat others. It's always only to "do good in the world." If I were to express sincerity in every moment, a lot of store clerks, and even some colleagues, would be more miserable by the end of the day.

Whether or not my self-defense is sound, I am convinced that defensible hypocrisy is the kind practiced when we are trying to live by some moral command superior to "thou shalt be openly sincere at all costs."

Shall I cheat a bit now and delete the least defensible examples from this chapter? Too late.

Chapter Three

The Cheerful Poser Comforts a Griever
or, A Would-be Tough Guy Meets Grief and Conceals the Tears

Griefs, at the moment when they change into ideas, lose some of their power to injure our heart.

—Marcel Proust

Well, every one can master a grief but he that has it.
—Don Pedro, in *Much Ado about Nothing*

What, man! ne'er pull your hat upon your brows;
Give sorrow words: the grief that does not speak
Whispers the o'er-fraught heart and bids it break.

—Malcolm, in *Macbeth*

Grief is itself a med'cine.

—William Cowper, *Charity*

To put on a cheerful face, disguising one's grief, saves the world immense pain.

—Anonymous

Disaster #2[1]

In late July of 1969, Phyllis and I and our fifteen-year-old daughter Alison were on a three-day drive from Utah to Chicago. At the end of the second long day we checked in at a motel in Grinnell, Iowa. Alison's brother Richard, three years older, had flown back to our Chicago home some weeks before, and he had reported that things were going well both with his girl-friend and with Donico Croom (Nickie), the student who had been living in our house instead of with his mother in the projects. Richard's older sister, Katherine, was in Minnesota on a summer job.

After the three of us had dinner, eager the next day to be with buoyant, witty Richard, I phoned home to say, "we're almost there." The phone was answered by Nickie, who had been sharing the house with Richard. When I said "hi," he seemed to be choking, or even sobbing. After a moment I intruded. "What's up?" And finally he said,

"Richard's dead; he got killed by a car."

The fact that we felt our lives totally *shattered* by that should surprise no one. And you readers can predict that my attempts to write about it will land us all in muddy waters. If the organization of the next few pages confuses you, please forgive the Griever, now having to pose as a disciplined author (you will be reading the seventeenth draft). I've attempted a whole book about the death and the grieving, but diverse other Selves have always cancelled it. Why torture yourself day by day, dealing with all that? What good will it do the world? How can you reconcile the claim of total grief with the obvious evidence that the grief has not continued to be total?[2]

Only much later did it occur to ThinkerB that the tragedy curiously had unified my life for once, wiping out the conflicts among Selves. By destroying all ambition, all vanity, all hypocrisy, all thought about anything but the loss,

---

1. We've already met disaster #1, the death of my father when I was six years old; I say more about it later.
2. Grieving memories were revivified recently when Nickie died, in his fifties, after years of coping with diverse illnesses.

50

John Richard Booth, age 17, 1969

it had produced a total focus—by no means deserving the term harmony but a weird kind of total centering.

Grief took over everything. I felt, we felt, the inexpressible sense of having had our lives utterly destroyed by an infinite loss.

How long that miserable "unity" lasted I can't say now, but for quite a while there were no rival Voices intruding; there was only the sobbing, the despair, the hopeless effort to console Phyllis and the girls. As anyone who has experienced such a disaster knows, nothing anywhere about anything matters except *that*. You have been stricken, and only one "you" has survived: the Griever. And for the rest of your life such moments crop up again and again. As I write now, grief intrudes. What I'll finally call "temporary miserable unities" take over—but they are a far cry from achieving the "plausible harmony" that this book pursues.

Before describing how we coped with that moment, a few facts about the boy we had lost and how the loss occurred. Brilliant, generously loving, challenging—Richard was a boy who had given us hardly any of the "adolescent torturing" that was so common in his generation and that seems even more common today.[3] He'd been away in England for a year, taking a break before college, and he had decided on a career as an actor. Teaching English was his fallback position, if and when the choice of acting didn't pay off (as was likely: there were, he had heard, ten thousand unemployed would-be actors in London at that time).

Back in America for a few months, he was driving with his girlfriend, Tucker Lincoln, to visit her parents. Our aging second car heated up. He unscrewed the lid of the radiator; it exploded into his face. He staggered into the highway. A nurse happened to be speeding along, and . . .

Even now, as I write that, I am suddenly in tears again. I turn off the computer and only slowly pull myself together—which in this context means a slow acknowledgment of how I am actually again almost torn apart. There, a few moments ago, sat the Griever, and here now is the LIFER posing as a productive ThinkerB writing *about* grieving: utterly different Selves.

Loss of a child, says ThinkerB, has to be ranked at the top on the scale of relative grief. It's true that to rank griefs can be silly; losses of all kinds can feel infinite at the time. But I can't resist making the claim that to lose a long-loved child is even more shattering than to lose an aging father or mother. That's because you have invested more in that child than you have invested in your parents. The science-fiction writer Orson Scott Card gets it right as he deals with the death of his seventeen-year-old son: losing a child "is the worst thing in the world. Once you have children, you realize that you are held hostage by those children. They are more important to you than yourself." To lose one is an "infinite loss." (The only losses I can now think of as perhaps even worse are the recent reports of adolescent boys, hopeless druggies, bankrupting their families by misusing credit cards; those kids are *really* lost, while our Richard is still the Richard we loved.)

---

3. Katherine, who surely knew Richard more intimately than I did, writes on the manuscript: "That's not true. You worried about him and fought with him a lot." Well, yes, I'm sure you're right. But by *comparison* with . . .?"

A memory about ranking that still annoys me dramatizes the problem of the phrase "infinite loss." A friend came to console us, once we were back in Chicago. "Oh, I do feel so sorry for you," he said. "It must be awful. Of course it would be even worse for my wife and me because we have only the one child and you have the two remaining daughters."

I was tempted to slug him. And I never forgave him, though of course I hypocritically suppressed my fury. I even realized, thinking about it long afterward, that in one sense the friend was right: in sheer terms of *future* calculations, loss of one in three is easier to recover from than loss of the only one. But his stupid (was it cruel or a botched attempt to console?) offense was his not realizing that in the moment of such grief, no calculated ratings make sense; infinite losses cannot be ranked by some cost-benefit analysis.

How Did My Selves Cope with It?

The first intrusion of another Self sometimes distresses me even now: how quickly the Griever came in conflict with VainB, who insisted on presenting an image of a man *not* destroyed. Even in the first moments, I pretended that I felt totally competent to drive back to Chicago. It was as if I were saying to myself, "I am a *man*; I am too tough to be destroyed. Let me take charge."

Fortunately, my friend and boss, Provost Edward Levi, hearing the news back in Chicago, insisted on sending a driver to drive us home. VainB protested, "Thanks a lot, but we don't need it." Levi rightly overrode me, knowing that no one in danger of uncontrolled sobbing should try to drive a car for several hours.

It wasn't long before other Selves intruded too. Shouldn't the guilt-ridden father/husband blame himself for not having instructed his son more effectively about car radiator dangers? Shouldn't the money-hungry Self take the advice of the insurance lawyer and sue the innocent nurse whose car hit him as he staggered into the highway? (I'm still deeply grateful to MoralB for refusing that one.)

And how should the increasingly questioning Mormon deal with it all? My doctor-bishop had predicted that my lapsing might destroy my child (chapter 1). Was there any sign that we thought he had been justified in his prediction? Were we personally to blame? I think the subject was not even discussed, except when we were angered by hints from devout Mormons that at worst God was punishing us or at best he had need of Richard on the "other side."

By then I did not, and I do not now, think that a meddling God decided to kill my son, whether to punish us or for any other reason. And I am strongly convinced that belief in a literally meddling God is about the most spiritually destructive of all "religious" beliefs. At the same time, I still cringe at the pain or anger I may be producing right now with that statement for any devout Mormon reading here. For them nothing is more scandalous than rejecting the notion of providential intervention.

What surprises me even now is that I had a clear moment when the event produced a quarrel with God-the-Meddler in a dream shortly after the crash. I am in a huge card game—about twenty of us squatting on the floor in a large room. God is dealing the cards in total chaos: flipping them this way and that, upside down, off to one side. I suddenly jump to my feet and shout at Him, "I will have nothing to do with a dealer who deals nothing but chaos," and then stalk out of the room. Clearly, my unconscious was still wrestling with questions that my conscious self had thought were long settled after I had declared myself an atheist during WWII.

As we longtime "fringe Mormons" suffered, did we appeal to Mormon counselors for spiritual healing? Not at all. But we did debate about where Richard should be buried—in Chicago, our home at the time, or in Utah, the spiritual home still in my heart. It was clear to me that he should be buried in "my mountain home." We purchased a cemetery plot in Alpine, my ancestors' hometown, and took part in a fine, generous memorial service in the church there. Somehow Phyllis and I both felt that though Richard had been totally inactive in the Church and we were obviously fringers, we were still in the deepest sense Mormons.

As we tossed the soil into his grave, surrounded by those beautiful mountains and those loving people, I felt absolutely certain that I would now again become totally active in the Church. What did it matter that I had this or that disagreement with this or that official doctrine or practice?

Did I keep that "promise" to myself? Obviously not. When we visited Earlham College, we joined in an equally moving memorial that the Quaker Meeting held for Richard. I spoke, sobbingly, in that "silent" meeting and felt (dramatizing the problems of chapter 1) just as strongly tied, emotionally, to that congregation of Friends as I had felt in Utah with the Mormon brothers and sisters.

After that, other somewhat shallower conflicts among Selves emerged. Quite soon there intruded the Self-Reproacher, who would occasionally rebuke me for not being more helpful with Phyllis and the daughters. And soon the "world" intruded. I had a talk scheduled for a conference, and I pulled myself together and gave the talk, showing no signs of grief (I think), while still inwardly miserable.

I worked hard to relegate my expressions of grief to the private journal, while enacting a *somewhat* cheerful recovery everywhere else. I even attempted, as Phyllis remembers gratefully, many little "affirmative sermons" to my three fellow grievers about the meaning of life and how to place this major loss within the larger picture. Was I doing the same cost-benefit analysis that my dastardly colleague had done when he claimed that his loss would be greater than mine? Not really—or so I'd like to claim. I *hope* that I was groping for a version of "religious language" that could genuinely console.[4]

As every griever could predict, comfort for all of us was elusive—for a very long time. I had a dim hope that the beloved literary works we'd read in the past would help us cope; they did not. I reread various poetic elegies; they bored me, as I found myself thinking something like "That bastard Milton couldn't have been feeling as bad as I feel, or he wouldn't have been able to turn out anything as complex as this 'Elegy.'" I tried several times to write effectively about our sense of loss, but the effort was too painful. I tried reading various novels in which death or disaster is coped with: Dostoevsky, Kafka, Edith Wharton's *Ethan Frome*. No go. Even music failed to console for a surprisingly long time.

Then it happened that Saul Bellow's *Mr. Sammler's Planet* came out, and for some reason Phyllis and I both found that it really did help. With all its faults (as I see it now), the way Bellow reveals Sammler's grappling with loss and disaster pulled us, partially, back into life. And meanwhile, real solace was gradually emerging from music—from both listening and playing chamber music together. Why music consoled us more than literature I'll never be able to explain.

Even so, the comforting was at best only partial.

After a few months I tried to write a brief memoir of Richard's life, but that also proved far too painful. I finally did pull myself together and assemble and publish the letters he had written us during his year in England— wonderful letters that still arouse both grief and joy when we reread them or discuss them with friends.

On through the years, Phyllis and I both have often posed publicly as less shattered than we have felt. And that posing, I would argue, has been useful—in fact, one of our best tools in coping with the grief. Grappling together with the problem of how to deal with it, we have only rarely had disputes of the kind that produce a rise in divorce rate among couples who have lost a child. We went on grieving (in a sense, even until today). But we learned that if you can put on the mask of good cheer, the mask sometimes

---

4. I have to confess that the *public* displays of grief and comfort after national disasters—Oklahoma City, September 11, President Reagan's death, and on and on—almost always annoy me; they're too full of self-touting and obvious pretense. But one can't say that without confessing, as my next paragraph dramatizes, that no words, no ceremonies, are adequately consoling at such a time. What is really annoying is the way the media play up trivial "disasters" while playing down daily disasters like the fact that every fifteen minutes an American is killed in a car accident.

becomes—at least for the moment—the real face. Acting out cheerfulness cheers you up.

A recent study claims that 92 percent of couples who have lost a beloved child end up in divorce. I can't believe the rate is nearly that high, but I do understand how the new relation that emerges can prove shattering. The grieving father looks at the grieving mother and sees not the cheerful, vital, witty woman he had been living with but a ten-years-older, weeping, spiritless lost soul; the grieving mother looks at the grieving father and sees not the cheerful, vital, ironic man she has been living with but a ten-years-older, sobbing, spiritless lost soul.[5] In other words, death of a child is a *temporary* death of at least two others, not to count the changes it produces in the lost one's siblings.

Just how much hypocrisy, then, did we practice over the years? Quite a lot. Usually when chatting with new acquaintances who asked, "Do you have children?" we would both answer, smiling cheerfully, "Yes, two daughters," without mentioning the loss. Only after decades did we sometimes say, "Well, we had three, but one child was killed." Sometimes that would lead to embarrassing tears, so even now the honesty is rather rare: why impose our grief on strangers?[6]

For now I'll put on a cheerful mask and spare you most of the sobbing that went on from July 25, 1969, through the next few years, except for one key sample:

Nov. 28, 1970 [O'Hare Airport, sixteen months after the death]

Dream last night
I am singing, and someone says, "You don't sing much any more—and especially that song." I go on singing:

> Wa-atch the stately ships
> From their moor-orings slip;
> Spread their wings, and die
> In the after-glow.

I wake, that is, *half* wake—oh, yes, I realize that it is Richard who spread his wings and died. Only now as I write about it do I remember that the words of the actual song are really "Spread their wings, and *go*." My dream ruined the rhyme in order to do some healing.

---

5. Phyllis continues to claim that this portrait of me exaggerates—that I was steadily a comfort, helping her to survive. What I'm sure of is that we both helped each other.

6. As I am doing now?

Sometimes Phyllis and I still wonder how we managed to survive that potentially annihilating loss. Our answers are often an underlining of the claim that our willingness to pose was one of our rescues. And for a great deal of that affirmative posing in the face of disaster, we are in debt to the Mormon upbringing that dominates so much of this book. As Mormonism had taught us, even when disaster strikes, you should sing that wonderfully moving hymn, "Come, Come, Ye Saints":

> Come, come, ye saints, no toil nor labor fear;
> But with joy wend your way.
> Though hard to you this journey may appear,
> Grace shall be as your day.
> 'Tis better far for us to strive
> Our useless cares from us to drive;
> Do this and joy your hearts will swell—
> All is well! All is well!

Is that why I've always been so deeply moved by the ending of T. S. Eliot's *Four Quartets?*

> Quick now, here, now, always—
>> A condition of complete simplicity
>> (Costing not less than everything)
>> And all shall be well and
> All manner of thing shall be well
>> When the tongues of flames are in-folded
>> Into the crowned knot of fire
>> And the fire and the rose are one.

OTHER DISASTERS, STARTING AT AGE SIX

I suspect that most people who casually encounter me see me as among the most cheerful of men, at least among those my age. As this book often suggests, I actually feel cheerful a good deal of the time—probably much more often than the human average among us creatures from the time of the Fall (millions of years ago) until now. "Things" have mainly gone well for me. One British reviewer of my recent book, *For the Love of It,* gave as her reason for hating it: "I just can't stand an author who tries to sound so relentlessly cheerful and nice." Was she right in assuming that the "nice" author implied throughout the book actually had many unnice, uncheerful moments as he wrote it? Of course. The very act of writing affirmatively about our

My mother, Lillian Clayson Booth

My father, Wayne Chipman Booth

chamber-music playing, always treating the negatives lightheartedly, was a kind of masking-over of my actual musical life. There are, for example, few references to the deaths or illnesses of friends and relatives that occurred during the several writing years. That I relentlessly detest that reviewer for detesting my being "relentlessly nice" is in no way a claim that the relatively unified Booth encountered in the book is the one *real* Wayne Booth.

As ThinkerB reminds himself of the many similar examples of cheerful posing, he becomes—I become—increasingly aware of how often such maskings have actually merged into self-deception. I would think of myself as having recovered good spirits, and only when looking back on it would I discover that I had really been almost in total despair, deep down inside. Yet somehow the posing often helped—especially when it avoided producing despair in others.

Putting such spiritual comfort aside for now, let's have a look at some other major disasters, along with a few minor losses, and consider how the Griever has been treated by other Selves.

The first major disaster, perhaps even more influential on my life than the death of my son, was the loss of my father not long after I turned six. To sense fully what that loss meant to me, you must receive hints about the Daddy he was. Memory, no doubt selective and unfair to Mama here, portrays him as an absolute ideal, practicing none of the nagging and punishing that Mama flooded me with.

1925, Provo

We're living in a tiny apartment in Provo, Utah, where Daddy is working toward his A.B., financed by Mama's elementary school teaching.

Daddy says, "Clayson, would you like to help me milk Blackie?"

Thrilled, I run after him out to the cow shed. As he's done before, he squirts a stream of milk into my mouth, straight from the teat: warm frothy milk, much of it dripping down my chin. Wonderful! On other occasions he fills my cup to the brim, and I drink it while he goes on milking. Daddy smells like the cow, warm, a mixture of milk and manure.

Same Location

Daddy says, "There she goes," and Mama and I run to the front window.

"Who?" I shout.

An old woman is riding her bicycle down the street (Fifth West, in Provo) in a long black dress, looking like a witch. Daddy says, "She says the world will come to an end tomorrow."

I am not just puzzled; I'm terrified. But Daddy comforts me. "It's OK, Clayson. We don't believe she's right."

1926, American Fork

Daddy is playing the violin and I am singing along with him. Ecstasy.[7]

Daddy is working summertime as the "Smith-Hughes Representative," the government consultant to farmers to help them make their farming more scientific. One day he takes me with him on a visit to Alpine, six miles away. We drive up in his new Chevy, and as we drive home just before sunset, he allows me to sit on his lap and pretend to be driving. I notice that the setting sun travels fast, behind the trees to our right, keeping up with us as we drive south. I ask him how that could be. "How can the sun move as fast as we're moving?" He explains it in detail, making me feel almost like an equal. I feel very good, sitting on his lap, "driving" the car, in the light of the sun whose traveling my Daddy can explain.

I am pumping my little red wagon up the slight hill, on the sidewalk, to meet Daddy when he comes down from his teaching at the high school. I have learned that he teaches "agronomy": how to be a good farmer. He longs to be a farmer. (I later learn that Mama had talked him into leaving the farm in Highland, three years before, to go back to college, because she refused to live miserably on that comfortless farm any longer.) He comes down the hill, I meet him, he hugs me, and he pulls me home in the wagon as we sing together. Bliss!

Daddy is singing:

> Old zip coon he played all day.
> He played till he drove his friends away.
> He played and he played by the light of the moon,
> But he never played anything but . . .
> Old zip coon he played all day.
> He played, etc., etc. (an endless repetition, with me picking it up more and more as my solo).[8]

Daddy is singing:

> Good morning, Mr. Zip, Zip, Zip

---

7. Gramma Booth told me later, long after his death, that when he was in his late teens he played in a dance band! I can't believe it—that saint playing dance music! And she confessed, he actually came home a bit drunk one night. I never met that Daddy.

8. It never occurred to me until recently that the singer's being a "coon" might have been racist. I can't reconstruct whether Daddy was thinking of a black singer as he sang. I certainly wasn't; I'm pretty sure I didn't even know that African Americans existed.

With your hair cut jessas shortas mine.
Good morning, Mr. Zip, Zip, Zip,
Yore shorely lookin fine.
Ashes to ashes, an dust to dust
If Camels don't kill ya
Then Fatimas must . . .
Good morning, Mr. Zip, Zip, Zip,
With yore hair cut jessas shortas
Your hair cut jessas shortas,
Your hair cut jessas shortas mi-i-ine.

Daddy has driven us somewhere, through the winter snow. On the way back, I've gone to sleep in the bitterly cold car, wrapped in a blanket on Mama's lap. When we get home they wake me, and I am shivering and miserable; it feels like the end of everything. But as Daddy wraps me more warmly, hugs me, and carries me through the snow into the cold house and puts a hot water bottle into my cold bed, I feel his love warming my soul.

Fall 1926
We have moved from the rented "Croppers" to a purchased house and small lot, a few blocks further west—a house less well finished: only cold running water, no indoor toilet, no telephone. Daddy has big plans for remodeling. And he now has a large lot behind him on which he can do a little farming—just two or three acres, but for him the apple and peach trees and small potato lots are much better than nothing. We still have Blackie the cow, which I pretend to help him milk. But Daddy is working very hard in the second year of teaching. I can't remember seeing as much of him; fewer games together, fewer songs. . . .

February 22, 1927
Daddy gives me a fine pocketknife as my birthday present. He demonstrates carefully how to use it without cutting myself. Mama objects to the present: "You should have waited until he's older." I try to cut into a hard piece of wood, the knife slips, and I cut my left index finger badly. Daddy doesn't chew me out, but he teaches me again how to hold it. The scar is still prominent.

Early April 1927
Daddy comes home from the high school one day and goes to bed midday, obviously feeling very sick. He has been working too hard all morning in the spring sunshine, helping to put in the grass for the high school. A doctor comes; more doctors come. Someone takes Daddy to the hospital in

Lehi—a *long* way away, three whole miles—for tests. They conclude that he has Addison's disease.[9]

Now Daddy lies in the little living room that smells of medicine and lilies. Mama is obviously anxious, but she tells me that he'll get well because she and I have prayed about it hard and long with "sincere and contrite hearts."

April 27, 1927

I am out playing in the backyard with my new pocketknife, remembering Daddy's warning about being careful, and someone screams: "He's gone!" A lady (Mama?) comes to the door and shouts to me, "Run across the street to the Jacklins' and have them phone your gramma to tell her your daddy's dead." I carry the message, feeling unsure about what it means.

I can't remember any feelings for the next few days, only something awful about the room where we viewed Daddy in the coffin, looking utterly unnatural; the room now smelled not just of lilies but embalming fluid. The house was filled with Mama's sobbing.

A Few Days Later

Daddy's funeral is to be held not in the ward meeting house but in the huge Tabernacle downtown. That is because so many people admire and love him. I feel rejected because I am not taken to the funeral. Later people often say, "Your Daddy drew the largest crowd we've ever had for a funeral" (or did they say, "the largest for a young man, only thirty-five"?).

Everybody loved Wayne Chipman Booth; everyone thought he was the most virtuous, most promising man in town. My only surviving aunt, Ann, now says that he was her dream man and that his marrying my mother, her oldest sister, was her dream marriage. Everyone felt an immense loss—and I rather slowly discovered what a transforming loss it was for me.

Everyone now seemed to expect me to grow up quickly and be as admirable as he was. My name was quickly changed from my middle name, Clayson, to be his replacement: the second "Wayne C." Mama would say often, weeping, "You have to be my man now, *Wayne C.*, now that Daddy is dead. You are so much like him!"

---

9. Would I have learned that term then? I've looked it up in medical books again and again over the years, always shocked at how soon the description, which I just looked up again now, gets repressed: "progressive atrophy of the adrenal cortex." My memory does not want to record details about that death.

Thus the puzzled little boy was driven to emulate the imagined father, and I see myself still doing it, in both constructive and destructive ways. At age seventy-two, when VainB was for no good reason wondering how many people around the world were at that moment reading one of his fabulous books, he wrote a silly journal entry: "When I die, I can be sure at least that a lot of people all over the world will be sorry to lose me." I didn't note that I was thinking of Daddy, but now I feel some mystery in that entry. Is that what I've been working to "achieve"—the image of my father as the ideal man? Well, I have to answer, "Yes, partly. That *is* what some of my Selves—not just VainB but many others—have hoped to become."

From that catastrophe on, memories of griefs and responses resist being fitted into any clear pattern of Selves. The Lover in me is shocked, for example, to find almost no memories throughout this tragic period about my sister Lucille. She was then one and a half years old, to be two in June. (She died in 1997; I felt considerable grief then, in a sense infinite like all major losses, but not as intense as the event in 1927.) I do have many memories of her from the year before—my cute baby sister. But Daddy's death had apparently wiped her out from my scene—temporarily, of course, though I still often reproach myself for having never honored her as much as she honored me and for having teased her so much. She later told me that she didn't remember anything about the death—or about the next (minor?) disaster.

A Few Weeks after Daddy Died

One night my cute little dog Tricks, the gift of Uncles Eli and Joseph, does not return. Next morning he's still gone. I can't find him anywhere. A neighbor comes and tells me that he has seen Tricks lying beside the road, maybe hit by a car. I run up to the place he has described and find Tricks, dead. Killed by a bulldog, a neighbor says.

My instant grief was even stronger than what I had at first felt when I heard "He's gone!" It must have felt like just one more blow proving how awful life can be. Intense sobbing. From today's perspective, that loss seems relatively trivial. But that's not how it felt then.

A Few Weeks Later

I am playing in the sun, lonely, near the east entrance of our house. Mama comes out to order me to do one of my daily chores.

"I won't."

"Wayne C., why are you being so naughty these days?"

"Mama, you keep after me so much I'm gonna run away!"

"Do you know any more good jokes?"

And she stalks back inside.[10]

That does it. I'm furious. I quickly walk to the street and start out on the six-mile walk to Highland, where I know my cousin Jim is again visiting from Canada. I walk and walk, not having realized just how long this runaway would take. A farmer I happen to know comes along from behind in a wagon.

"Where you goin', Clayson?" (He hasn't learned the "Wayne C." label yet.)

"Up to Highland."

"Your Mama know where you goin'?"

"Yep," I lie.

"Like a ride?"

"Sure would."

I climb up on the seat, and he takes me most of the way there, at one point through a water-flooded gully that presents no problem for a horse and wagon. When I get to the farm, Aunt Relva, Jim's mother, is horrified, knowing that Mama in her grief will be doubly distraught at my disappearance. Neither she nor my mother has direct access to a telephone. (For all I know, the self-centered kid didn't think once about how miserable his Mama's life was or what anxieties he was adding to hers.)

Making it clear that I have been very naughty, Aunt Relva loads me into her Model A Ford that she manages to drive even though she has lost one leg. "We gotta get you back, right now; your Mama must be very upset." As we head for American Fork, we soon come to that rain-flooded gully, and Aunt Relva does not dare drive into it. There was nothing for her to do but take me back up to the farm, where Jim and I play throughout the afternoon.[11]

I have no memory of how I got home or how Mama reacted. She must have been deeply hurt, even furious, but perhaps too grief stricken to know what to do about a naughty boy who would treat her so cruelly as I had with my little runaway from tragedy.

---

10. The memory of the last two speeches here is firm and precise—unlike many memories. Those were our words, I am confident, partly because of her later confirmation.

11. Was Mama still totally ignorant and anxious about where I might be? I now believe—or I hope—that Relva managed to find someplace where she could phone one of our neighbors to find Mother and reassure her.

1928

With mother now teaching third grade, we cannot afford to keep Daddy's chosen house and lot, and we move to the cheapest apartment available— just one inside cold-water tap; no inside toilet.[12] With a stove in only one room, when winter comes, the house is bitterly cold. As I climb into the icy bed, I shiver and sob, crying, "I want my Daddy." Then I dream, night after night, that he is alive again—ecstasy! I wake to face the disaster and sob again.[13]

As these night miseries continued, Mama would sometimes come into the room to comfort me. But too often the comfort would turn into the basic exhortation, "You've got to be the man of the house now," with explicit instructions not to cry so much.

1928–1929

I am in second grade, enraptured by beautiful Virginia Shelley, with whom I sang duets at the county fair. I dream about close companionship with Virginia, both asleep and awake. I repeat the fantasy of taking her hand and, using my magical powers, floating both of us up over the crowds. Everyone looks up at us, enviously. It starts to rain, but I just silently wish, powerfully and successfully, that we remain dry, while the rain pours down on everyone around us. It is thrilling, flying over the crowds of people down there look- ing up at us as they get soaked in the rain. My Daddy may be dead and I may be a weeping sissy inside, but up here I am a beloved hero, possessing powers over the falling rain of life.

The misery of Daddy's death was reinforced a year later by the death of my most warmly loving grandparent, Gramma Clayson. Like Daddy, she had won my heart with everything she did.

Autumn 1928

Gramma is lying on a cot—is she ill?—out on the east side of the house up the street from us, at Third North. The lawn, the large tree, the hedge, and her face are vivid in memory. (I can recover little else about the scene—not what I was wearing, not what she was wearing, not how the house was

---

12. I remember longing for the inside toilet we'd had a year and a half before, for the first time, at the "Croppers," just a block north of Grampa Clayson's. Whenever I could, I would go up across the street to use Grampa Clayson's inside toilet.
13. That's the reverse of our usual awakening from nightmares, when we're relieved to find the everyday—if the reality isn't even worse than the dreams.

decorated. After reading many memoirs full of vivid physical details—clothing, furniture, scenery—I'm shocked by how few such "grabbers" my memory provides.)[14] Gramma says she may have to go to the hospital, but she offers to read to me. I accept. She reads from *A Girl of the Limberlost.*

December 1928

Gramma Clayson is much more visibly ill, lying in the bedroom. Someone has brought her a milkshake. As I sit beside her bed, she offers me a taste of it; it is the first milkshake I have ever tasted, and it's as good as the ice cream we make for ourselves on rare celebration days (like the 24th of July, "Pioneer Day"). She offers to read to me, but I can tell that she is too weak to do it. And then she says,

"Wayne C., I have something very important to say to you. Will you promise to do what I now ask?"

I promise.

She takes my hand.

"What I want you to promise, Wayne C., is that you'll always be good to your mother and take care of her. Won't you?"

Recording that event, at age fifteen, I wrote, "I promised her, in tears, that I would but I don't know how well I have succeeded although I have tried."

I have remembered that promise often for the rest of my life, sometimes feeling guilty.[15] I was seldom as good to Mama, or even as appreciative of her good qualities, as she deserved or as I might have been had I not been such a damned ambitious egotist, myself the absolute center of God's universe and maybe destined to become a God of another planet,[16] trapped as a would-be "intellectual" living with a mother who had read hardly anything of importance! In any case, Gramma's plea is fixed forever in my soul.

December 23, 1928

Someone comes to tell us that Gramma has been taken to the hospital in Lehi. Then someone calls to say that she is dying. No adult with a driver's

---

14. Of course, I could provide irrelevant details—for example, the precise color and shape of my shoes on the day, at age four, when I learned how to tie a shoelace, or the precise shape and location of our first telephone, or the color of my proudly worn first long pants at age five. But such memories don't help the people appear as vividly as they must have appeared at the time.

15. This account was first written back when I had just turned 72; I've doctored it only a bit in recent drafts. Now in 2005, my feelings are the same.

16. Oh, yes, we Mormon males were taught that, and still are—though a bit less aggressively.

license is around. So Uncle Joe, age twelve, insists on driving us in the old Model A Ford, scary-fast, but we get to Lehi too late. Gramma is dead, like Daddy. I do not remember the funeral (was I even there?), but I remember Joe boasting that he had driven that car at thirty-five miles an hour. And the memory of grief-stricken loss is *almost* as great as the loss of Daddy.

Meanwhile I had already heard of the deaths of two male cousins about my age, and my Booth grandparents had told me often about how Daddy's death was for them the climax after having long since lost three younger sons. How often they told me about Uncle Irwin's having been killed, at eighteen, trying to hop a freight train![17] The lessons of infinite loss and of how to grapple with grief were thus reinforced from age six on.

THE POSING NONGRIEVER, HYPOCRITEB, IS BORN

Throughout my early school years, teachers at the beginning of the year always asked us, "Who are your parents?" I would name my mother and then would have to say, "My Daddy's dead"—and burst into tears. To cry in front of the whole class became increasingly humiliating, more and more proof that I was a sissy.

> *Fall 1933, Beginning of Seventh Grade in a New Building*
> The teacher makes the standard request, and again I sob. I can hear some giggling in the room. After class, alone in the hall, I swear to myself—crossing my heart—that *I will never cry about anything ever again* in my whole life.

The result of that weird oath—which I literally obeyed for some years—now seems a bit pathetic, especially given the following sad moment:

> *1935*
> Junior Halliday lives across the street and has become my closest friend. He is slight, not really healthy; he has had bad sinusitis from childhood. But he's bright, lively, fun to talk with about ideas. When *Monopoly* first comes out, we play it at least once a week for months on end. We bicycle together. We ride down to Utah Lake and picnic in the water willows. We go on a "six-mile" hike for our Boy Scout merit badge, far above Highland on the foothills. We watch a lizard in the sun. We grab its tail, and it drops the tail and escapes.

---

17. The coincidence of my uncle and my son both being killed at eighteen has often been talked about by the family—sometimes implying that God had something in mind.

Soon after we've turned fourteen, I learn that Junior has to have an operation for his sinusitis, so he cannot go with me to Mutual Dell up in the mountains for the annual weeklong, wonderfully exciting holiday. Enjoying myself blissfully, I am one day told that Junior is terribly ill. Next day Junior comes up to Mutual Dell, and we have a quiet farewell beside the mountain stream; I hug him goodbye and never see him again.

I feel grief stricken, but—here is the horror—*I do not weep.*[18] I am a man! Men do not weep. I have learned to fake nongrief.

It took me many years to stop feeling proud about that hypocrisy and recognize the cruelty of it. What must it have meant to Junior's parents as we later stood in his bedroom, which they had kept exactly as he left it, when I failed to weep as they sobbed and hugged me?

But back now to the times when I openly grieved.

1928, Age Seven

My mother as widow and my grampa as widower decide to pool resources and join our two families. We move into Grampa's much nicer house, and I find myself not only with a good toilet but surrounded by relatives: Uncle Joe (twelve), Aunt Ann (fifteen), Uncle Eli (eighteen). Aunt Lourena, wonderful pianist, is in college. Uncle Merrill, clarinetist, is already teaching in a seminary somewhere. Aunt Zina has just been married. Aunt Lucy and Uncle Roy and cousin Lucy and the other "insignificant younger ones" live in Preston, Idaho, as later will Aunt Lourena and Uncle Orvil.

The point of that prolonged listing is that upon moving into that crowded setting, the boy who had been his Mama's center, especially after his Daddy's death, has now become not much more than a troublesome peripheral. Not only are Daddy and Gramma gone, but VainB's previous sense of being at the center, maybe even Number One, is now lost. So I inevitably experienced what looks to me now as an "identity crisis"; VainB must find new ways to restore his status in the world. I'm now sure that at least some of the cheating I reported in chapter 2 was a response to the world that was now demonstrating itself to me.

---

18. Dream, September 26, 2000: After writing that yesterday, I dreamed last night that I was saying farewell to my beloved friend Max Dalby, both of us now (in the dream as in real life) getting old. It is clear this will be my last time ever with him. And I break into uncontrollable sobs, going on for minutes; it feels like the end. And it is obviously related to having recorded yesterday the fact of *not* weeping over Junior.

1929

In spite of my uncle Joe's constant mean teasing, I want to play "manly" games with him, and he won't let me. I hate him and he hates me. We quarrel whenever we're together, yet I want to be with him all the time. His pa (Grampa, of course, no doubt miserable because newly widowed) often beats Joe with a razor strop because Joe does very bad things: he sometimes does not come home when he's supposed to; he talks back; he doesn't keep his promises. He makes alcohol by fermenting fruit juice. Worst of all, he is mean to me, and Mama then tells Grampa, and Grampa beats him.

1927–1932

Mama is very different from the attentive, playful mother she was before Daddy died. I can't remember her laughing very often, can't remember her playing the piano any more,[19] can't remember even seeing her much after she began teaching school and doing a lot of Church work. My life includes little fun with anybody.

Even my memories of summer, when Mama was free of teaching, are mainly about working hard: housework; working all day with Joe weeding potato patches; picking fruit; mowing lawns (he and I did the "Tithing Office" lawn, a huge one, and were rewarded with something like fifteen cents, enough to buy a root beer across the street at the A&W); peeling peaches and pears for bottling; turning the butter churn.

So, much of our fun together was lost. The Mama who had doted on me earlier—reading to me, teaching me to march around the piano, singing with me as she played—that mother had "died" with Daddy. The Gramma who had loved playing games with us kids was also gone.[20] Grampa was so distressed by our presence that he sometimes said to Mama (so I was later told), "Lillian, I sometimes just feel like flushing them down the toilet." My only hope for fun in the house was Uncle Joe, and most of the time that was not fun but torture. Joe was miserable himself, and he had good reason to find me annoying. I was tall for my age; Joe short for his, and people would tease him: "You'd better watch out, Joe. Wayne C. is catching up on you." Joe found ways to handle that:

---

19. Decades later she "took up" the organ and became a church organist. Memory probably has suppressed ways in which she kept up on the piano.

20. The portrait of her by her daughter Ann, published in 2001, makes it clear that her presence had made the family scene a lot more fun-loving than it had become after her death when we moved in (*The Life and Blessings of Ann Clayson Larsen: My Personal History, 1913–2000*, private publication).

Joe takes me behind the barn and beats me up, just after his miserable pa has razor-stropped him.

Joe loves to tickle me on and on, with me pleading for him to stop, through hysterical laughter and on to tears. He won't stop until I vomit or until someone rescues me—Mama or our miserable hired helper, Alice Welsch. I want my Daddy.

Joe has wrestled with me and has thrown me down; he is sitting on top of me and is pretending to spit down into my face. The spit comes out of his mouth and almost drops and he sucks it back in—again and again. How can I ever get even?

Even so, I want desperately to play games with him; he plays basketball with neighborhood kids and won't let me join in. One evening when we go up to the barn to do our chores, Joe to milk the cow and me to throw the hay down, Joe jumps over the fence and starts playing basketball with the neighbors behind Monita Abel's. I want to play too, though Mama has told me I must come right back after doing the hay because she needs me for some other chore. I go under the fence and keep trying to enter the game, pretending to take part, jumping in from the edges but never really getting hold of the ball. After dark we go back to the barn and do our chores and return to the house, very late. Mama is furious. I claim that it was Joe's fault, but Mama whips me for the first (and last) time using a large stick. I cry only a little. Then, VainB goes to Joe and proudly exhibits his welts by taking his shirt off: I'm as tough as you are! I am becoming a *man*, taller than Joe, as tall as my father was!

Joe takes me to the County Fair, and after wandering around a bit we come to a boxing ring. Eight or ten kids are being blindfolded as the gloves are put on. Joe volunteers me for the "blindfold slaughter" (I can't remember our name for what Ralph Ellison calls the "Battle Royal" that he was subjected to).[21] I put on the gloves as they blindfold me, stumble terrified into the ring, then blindly stagger about, swinging my gloved hands, hoping to ward off the blows but feeling really bitter, as I listen to Joe and the other spectators laughing hilariously at us getting struck and swinging back, almost always missing the striker.

Whatever that experience is, it is not being a man. Would my father ever do a thing like that to me? Of course not. Yet I didn't refuse to do it; that would make me even more of a sissy.

---

21. For Ellison's full account of how awful the blind slugging feels, especially when you're black and there are hostile white spectators, see *The Invisible Man*, chapter 1.

Did I ever get even? In a way, yes—as you'll see later.

It's clear to me now that from Daddy's death on I was both trying to be a man and passionately longing for a surrogate father. Miserable and in his early teens, Joe wasn't even close to filling the huge gap. Two of the more plausible candidates, Uncle Eli and Uncle Merrill, were soon off the scene. Grampa Clayson was the obvious choice, but in his unspoken grief he provided little solace. I'm sure that the other grampa, Ebenezer Booth, living half a mile away, would have served somewhat better had we lived with him and Gramma Booth. But unlike the daily, hourly Clayson intimacy, we visited them only about once a week.

That longing for a father went on for many decades, involving not only the teachers I've named and my mission president. I found no real mentors in the army. But in graduate school a father-hero did emerge: Ronald Crane, literary critic and historian. Without my ever thinking about it in this way, I now see my adulation—though he deserved it—strongly intensified by my sheer longing for Daddy.

All of those "replacements" are now dead, and the few tears I've shed over them have all been kept strictly private as I've maintained my cheerful pose, never breaking down while offering testimonials at their funerals.

Another and even deeper repression didn't reveal itself to me for decades. I'm tempted to give it a title referring to a standard joke among psychologists: *Oedipus Schmoedipus, As Long As He Loved His Father.*

It was sometime in 1968, and I was chatting with Saul Bellow. Somehow the subject of the oedipal complex came up—how kids deal with fathers and especially with fathers' deaths. Saul was defending Freud's theory, and I replied, a bit impatiently,

> That whole business about the oedipal complex is silly. Freud talks as if a child never gets over his feelings about his father—the whole business of wishing the father dead and then feeling stupidly guilty about having killed him. Saul, I have to tell you that my father died when I was six, and I can't remember a single moment when I felt personally guilty about it. I've never been haunted by any sense of being blamed. Oedipus Schmoedipus, as long as he loves his *mother*!

A night or so later I had—for perhaps the fifteenth or twentieth time of my life—the following dream:

> There is a man's corpse in our family garden. The police are investigating a murder, and they think I am guilty. They are about to find the corpse. I

know that I *am* guilty. I killed the man, and they're going to catch me. I wake up, both terrified and flooded with guilt.

And then I was flooded with the sudden realization that such guilt had been with me from the beginning. In my unconscious, I "knew" that I had killed my Daddy.

It now seems impossible to deny that such unconscious guilt, reinforcing the oedipal complex, had deepened my grief, earlier and later, and at the same time reinforced the need to be a *man* and not show grief.

My proud resistance to grieving—even contempt for it—continued for a long time. When my beloved Grampa Booth died in 1939, I wrote about his funeral like this:

> It was cruel the way Grandma Booth had to suffer over his death. Everyone coming in the house would loudly sympathize and emphasize her sorrow— till she was a nervous wreck. The funeral wasn't bad in this respect, but I don't like funerals in their present form—I don't know how to change them, unless we can change the traditional outlook on death as something sorrowful. All that . . . their crying amounted to was either self-sympathy at having lost a valued loved one, or sentimentality. There was [not], and never is, any sorrow for the dead ones, but people won't admit that they are weeping selfishly.

VainB, now eighteen, is still boasting that he is so manly that he can resist grieving. Shortly before, on the day his Grampa died, he had written, "I do not feel in the least bit badly about it, although I loved him more than most people do. He was a fine man." No grieving![22]

I somehow learned over the years, as beloved teachers and colleagues died, that my grief need not be suppressed. My mother died at age seventy-two, and though I wasn't as shattered by hers as by the earlier deaths, for some time it was devastating. I suddenly felt that there was no "ceiling" left over my head: I was now the top among the living in the closest part of the family. That feeling gave no pleasure. That there was no "ceiling" meant that I no longer had a Mama to tell me, "Wayne C., you are the man of the family."

By that time I had long since rejected the notion that grief should be suppressed. In the hospital in Salt Lake City, I had a wonderful final conversation with Mother, impressed by the way she was coping with certain death. Two years later I described it in a memoir as follows:

---

22. And too little attention to grammar.

Her death, which came from a sudden heart attack at the end of her world tour, was one of smiling courage and even good humor. She could not help knowing that she had lived a more steadfast, honorable, and unselfish life than most men or women achieve; she had nothing to regret and nothing to fear, and she faced death without complaint or self-pity. Those who saw her at the end felt, as all who had known her knew, that here was indeed a great woman.

We had been able to talk openly about many matters long suppressed (though I did not bring up the question of the afterlife, not knowing whether she still expected it). It was mainly about what we had meant to each other, with her teasing me a bit about always having blamed myself for failing to achieve. Her expressions of pride in Alison, Kathie, and Richie are still with me now. She showed not a hint of grief about her own forthcoming death.

Only a few hours later she did die, and I found myself there in the hospital sobbing almost as uncontrollably as I had over Daddy's death. A young doctor pulled me up from the shelf on which I was leaning and offered me a sedative "which will ease the pain." I was tempted to hit him, as I pushed the drug away and shouted, "No! I don't want to hide it!" The notion of suppressing the full grief seemed stupid, even wicked. Perhaps it was my memory of how I'd treated Junior's death that produced such an excessive response. But at least I had finally managed to defeat the hypocrite and express my feelings honestly.

So—three major losses by the age of fifteen, a fourth by the age of forty-four, and a fifth at age forty-eight: my father, my favorite grandparent, my best friend, my mother, and my son—not to mention the many later losses of favorite colleagues: Arthur Heiserman, Sheldon Sacks, Ronald Crane, Perrin Lowry. It won't surprise you, as I revise in 2005, that these increase day by day now: Robert Streeter, Charles Wegener, Chauncy Harris—and on and on.

How do I now feel about those diverse losses? Does ThinkerB still think of Daddy's death as a catastrophe? How could I? My whole life since Daddy died would have to be repudiated if I were to say that his death was a curse. I now would be an entirely different person if he had not died—maybe a better one but possibly a lot worse. I probably would have encountered a brother or two and some more sisters. I would certainly have been less weepy, less taken up by reading as a way to avoid social contact. I would have felt less pressure to "act like the man of the family." If that different man wrote his *Life*, it would also be entirely different—quite possibly that of a totally unquestioning Mormon. Mama would not have lost so much of her faith. Daddy would have engineered my Church loyalty.[23] And my soul would have felt no explicit injury to its belief in a God who responds to direct pleas.

To reject this life that I have had since Daddy's death, including the maskings that have helped us all to cope, would be like rejecting the gift of life itself. And that is just the opposite of how I feel about that gift. My gratitude to "God" (as I define Her/Him/Them/It) is so great, especially for my life with Phyllis, that I am deeply puzzled when I read arguments by authors like Samuel Johnson (whom I admire greatly) asserting that human life is nothing but misery, that its only compensation is the hope for an afterlife.

But this is not the place for further speculation about that—and besides, if I were writing this a few days or weeks after Richard's death, it would be far less affirmative; it might sound like an imitation of Johnson. (Unless, of course, I were writing hypocritically for some audience whom I would try to protect from grief.)

One more point about the deaths: they do not now, not even Richard's, lead me to fear or hate death. My own losses feel—at the moment, though I know I won't feel that way when the next death of a close friend comes—"accommodated" into the universal path: "dark, dark, dark, we all go into the dark." Almost all of the authors whose poems I collected in *The Art of Growing Older* are dead, and I will before long be dead. Although I cannot say, "that does not matter to me," I can say that I embrace it as absolutely "entailed" by the very fact of creation, whether we think of it as a divine miracle or as evolution. If you are going to have creatures as highly individuated and mentally aware as we are, you must accept the death of each individual and thus a sense of loss in those left behind.

Conclusion? There is no conclusion to grief, unless one dies early. How will I deal with the next loss? Who knows?

What I do see, throughout this account, is the continuing effect of that earliest loss, Daddy. Even at this moment I see signs that VainB is emulating that heroic father. So that motive must be added to the sources of my ambition—which I sometimes defend as the *defensible* kind of striving. Such emulation is reassuringly different from VainB's mere competitive ambition. It is a defensible mixture of envy and rivalry and productive modeling: the desire to *achieve* Daddy's every virtue, not just to *appear* to have done so. It

---

23. But what do I know about what he would have done or how I would have responded? Prof. Poulson, who had taught Daddy at BYU, suggested to me that my father, before his death, was already "maturing" and having deep doubts about the literal historical claims of Mormonism.

could even be called the desire to re-create, or clone, the lost beloved. I must resurrect the most loving, cheerful, productive man in the world. I must love everybody, cheer everybody up, and thus become superior to those Selves who fail in that mission, those I do not love. And that can sometimes prove almost intolerable, as my beloveds have tried to teach me, when my cheering-up feels like criticism of their tears.

Of the many paradoxes in my life, this is one of the most striking—and confusing. When I lose control of the cheerful self and snap back or snarl or shout an angry attack, I afterward curse my Selves for violating my ideals. And I dread the thought of how I may behave when—as could happen any moment—I am stricken with another major loss.

Chapter Four

My Many Selves Confront
the Man Who Believes in LOVE

*I am inordinately self-centered. . . . There is only one thing in the world worse
than being talked about, and that is not being talked about.*

—Oscar Wilde

*I must write as though I were a person of importance; and indeed, I am—to myself.
To myself I am the most important person in the world; though I do not forget
that, not even taking into consideration so grand a conception as the Absolute, but
from the standpoint of common sense, I am of no consequence whatever. It would
have made small difference to the universe if I had never existed.*

—Somerset Maugham, *The Summing Up*

*Man, whose joy consists in comparing himself with other men, can relish
nothing but what is eminent.*

—Thomas Hobbes

*This [Brutus] was the noblest Roman of them all;
All the conspirators save only he
Did that they did in envy of great Caesar;
He, only, in a general honest thought
And common good to all, made one of them.
. . . .
. . . . "This was a man!"*

—Shakespeare, *Julius Caesar*

*Envy's a sharper spur than pay,
No author ever spar'd a brother,
Wits are gamecocks to one another.*

—John Gay, "The Elephant and the Bookseller"

Envy and wrath shorten the life.

—Ecclesiasticus 30:26

*I wish that I could somehow get myself talked about as much as Wilde has
managed to get himself talked about, even now in 2005.*

—Anonymous Booth

One morning back in 2002, I received an email from my friend Homer Gold-berg informing me that the "Millennial" issue of *PMLA*[1] has a long list of selections from past presidential addresses. "And for some reason yours is just ignored." This message instantaneously provoked a silly, internal dispute:

> *VainB:* "How could they do a brutal thing like that to *me*, one of the best . . . ?"
>
> *LoverB* (chanting): "Oh, damn it man, just ignore it; to worry about fame or attention is simply contemptible. How could you spend three pages in *For the Love of It* mocking Norman Podhoretz for his celebration of the joys of 'making it' in the world and then let yourself feel miserable because *you've* not 'made it' in an issue of *PMLA* that almost nobody will read anyway?"
>
> *ThinkerB:* "Well, of course, you're absolutely right. So I'll slap the vain fool down."
>
> *VainB:* "But wouldn't it make *sense* to write the editor to find out just why . . ."

But by midmorning, LOVER had triumphed, aided by the would-be LIFER, laughing about the quarrel. I never felt any further temptation to write a complaint to that "unfair" editor. Further back,

> *November 2000*
>
> I have known, for quite a while, that *The Chicago Tribune* (now that *For the Love of It* is coming out in paperback) has been planning to feature an article about me and my celebration of amateuring. The columnist has in-terviewed Phyll and me. Two photographers have taken about 60 shots. So everything is on the way.
>
> This morning I wake at six, as usual, and suddenly find myself debat-ing with VainB about whether to go right this minute to a newsstand to get a copy, or wait until later, after getting some work done. VainB loses—for the moment—and I don't drive to the newsstand until about 7:01. I buy a copy, and glance through the load of cruddy Sunday stuff, increasingly

---

1.   *Publications of the Modern Language Association.*

worried for fear the article has been canceled. Ah, here on the front page of the BOOKS/ARTS section is my huge photo, with me looking, head raised, eyes closed!—oh, shit!—looking like someone posing as either asleep or faking rapture. VainB is crushed by the photo—why didn't they allow me to choose from the shots? I almost decide not to buy any more copies. Then, still sitting in the car parked next to the stand, I do a quick read of the article. Oh, it's quite good—all of the Selves agree. And the second photo of Phyllis and me playing is much better, though it's not the best choice either. So then I buy five more copies.

"But why plague relatives and friends with copies of that tiny celebrity blip?" the anti-vanity Selves whine [the next day]. "Why bother? Why on earth succumb to egotism like that? It's because you, you idiot, long for a bit of celebrity. You're the fool who whines to yourself every time Stanley Fish and Harold Bloom get celebrated. You want your book to sell even more copies. You are in fact feeling ebullient about this minor featuring, and you find yourself today, as you were yesterday, pleased that there was a chamber music concert that afternoon and friends there had already read the article, and liked it—and didn't mock the photo."

Before looking at the history of VainB, the slightly more defensible AmbitionB, and their struggles with the other Selves, here's what I wish were a transcription of a conversation I overheard last week. I, the LIFER, ordered them to speak frankly about their goals.

AmbitionB: Well, I want what just about everybody wants: to *be* number one, whether as teacher, scholar, husband, father, amateur cellist, or autobiographer who really *thinks* about the meaning of life.

VainB: That's fine, OK, but like just about everybody I want even more to be *seen* as moving toward the top, maybe even as number one, whether I've really made it or not. And like the author Heller in his last book, *Portrait of an Artist, as an Old Man,* I'm really upset when evidence of decline in my reputation emerges. After all, shouldn't everyone in the world still know about the ten translations of my first book, *The Rhetoric of Fiction*?

LOVER: That's stupid. What I'm pursuing is *living* today to the fullest. Make love, play some music, walk on the beach. *Carpe diem,* seize the day.

MoralB, smiling favorably on AmbitionB and speculating about whether to take the name Improver-Booth: Well, yes, but don't do the seizing just any old way. To live *right* today we've got to work hard to improve our *character* and to improve the awful world. We've got to accomplish something *good* today, even if it's only an attempt to get the *New York Times* to publish a protest letter about Bush's . . .

Suddenly a new Self plunges in, who might be called *Zen-Booth:*

Stupid, stupid! Wipe out *all* of that! Stop that Mormonish worry about self-improvement. Stop even practicing the cello and walking on the beach. Just sit down and meditate, and meditate some more, and more, until you feel your Selves disappearing into Nada. Don't seize the day; let Nada seize you.
LIFER, pursuing not Nada but a Plausible Harmony: That's absurd; nobody can do that for more than a few minutes or hours—at most. Why not probe yourself and discover the true core within? We all know that each of your cases is defensible, at least some of the time. Let's sit down and talk about it—like singing in a cantata. Or maybe we could talk one another into doing an autobiography about our conversations.

My attempts to deal with such quarrels have always been a bit equivocal, as by now you might expect. Some readers of *For the Love of It* have claimed to detect some dishonesty in it, as VainB is shoved behind the scene and AmbitionB dwells on "getting better" at cello playing: "Even as you shouted, 'live for the sake of the loving, not for future payoff,' obviously you were driving yourself to get another book out, urging yourself to practice even harder on the cello to get credit as a better player—and doing that even when your practicing was yielding no joy—and surely sometimes hoping the book would raise your reputation."

A Brief History of VainB and AmbitionB

1926

One day Mama sees in the newspaper an IQ test for young children. Ask him this, ask him that. Have him do this or that. She tries all the stuff on Clayson, her beloved five-year-old. One section asks me to consider a twelve-inch blank square that represents a weed-grown field in which a baseball is lost. "How would you walk to find the ball?" I draw a path wandering and circling in every conceivable direction, back and forth and with a lot of pointless crisscrossing.

The newspaper tells Mama that bright little boys don't do it that way: they go around in *systematic* diminishing circles or squares, lines equidistant. I have revealed myself as not that kind of bright little boy: I am a thoughtless wanderer!

"Clayson, that's very disappointing." I'm not as bright as she had thought (or hoped). Misery—for both of us.

Not long after, Mama is nursing my new baby sister, Lucille. VainB reawakens, feeling intense envy.

"Mama, can I have a little suck?"

"Of course not."

"But why not?"

"You just can't."

In tears I go on pleading, and finally Mama surrenders, sort of; she gets a teaspoon, squeezes out a bit, and offers it to me. So maybe she loves me *almost* as much as she loves Lucille.

1930

I am on my way home carrying my fifth-grade report card. I sob most of the way because I've been given only a "C" for Handwriting—the first lower-than-top grade I've ever had. Mama's confidence in me will be annihilated, and she might weep, saying again, "Oh, Wayne C., I am so disappointed in you."

She does, and she starts drilling me daily on my Palmer Penmanship.

1931

I have been caught planting the wrong seeds in the wrong part of Grampa Clayson's vegetable garden. Grampa shouts at me, "Clayson, you must learn to use your head. You haven't got the brains God gave a soda cracker!" I weep.

1933

It is my first day in junior high school, and because the gym coach has never seen me play basketball, he makes the mistake of judging by my height that I should be put on the "first team." VainB feels triumphant and plays with incredible vigor. But only for a few minutes. The coach soon sees the real, awkward me, totally untrained, and announces that I must step down to third team. VainB is humiliated—but this time keeps the sobs suppressed until he's out of sight.

1934

We Boy Scouts are camping on an "overnight," and we've been told that there will be a prize for the best-designed area around our tents. I work hard gathering moss and flowers to decorate my spot. As you have predicted, I lose; my best friend, Junior Halliday, has been declared the winner. VainB retreats into his tent, flings himself onto his sleeping bag, pounds his fists on the nonpillow, and bursts into quiet sobs that he hopes are inaudible: weeping is even worse than losing.

I could record scores more such memories, including those of being somehow *trained* to see winning as the only goal in life, allowing defeat to spoil the day. But let's turn instead to a selection from the somewhat more reliable journal entries.

The first real intrusions of ThinkerB into the diary began only after my serious four-month bout with Bright's disease as I turned sixteen. Some of the entries reveal a cheaply anxious VainB; others show me trying to escape not just vanity but all ambition. If you find yourself asking, "Why is this Lifer including so much of this?" just imagine what fun it is for this Lifer, as quester for harmony, to look back after almost seventy years and discover that self-divided kid. As his two months out of school with Bright's disease draw to an end, he soon must attend classes with students who may be well "ahead" of him and he writes:

> *April 27, 1937*
> One of my main faults is that I like to think of my own accomplishments too much. I am not exactly conceited. I don't think that I am a better person than I am but I have to watch myself to keep from talking about myself. Whoever reads my diary is going to get the idea that I do nothing but talk about myself but that is only true in this diary.

I'm pleased to see the boy beginning to acknowledge just how absurd it is to worry about popularity—and sometimes I find hints of even deeper probing. (Am I now still surrendering to VainB when I take amused pride in how the teenager continues to grapple with the problem?)

> *July 29, 1937 [after many pages about flirting with the first "intellectual" girl he has known]*
> I don't know who will read this, perhaps I should say nothing that sounds silly or girl crazy but I suppose a true account of my life should contain something of that sort. Look at the preceding account, dear reader (child be it, or grandchild or whatever you are) as the prattlings of a young boy, not near to being mature in mind (although 6'1" tall and weighing 165 lbs) and yet at times feeling that he knows more than anyone older than he is.[2] . . . Now is as good a time as any to analyse myself and what I am. I feel that to write thoughts on paper, read them over & criticize is the best way to understand which are reasonable & which are not. . . . I will endeavor to approximately every six months reanalyze myself and compare.

---

2. Note how his alternation of first-person and third-person presages his and the Lifer's later dodges. As you know, such trickery has become a cliché in fiction—sometimes used brilliantly, as in Michael Frayn's recent *Spies*.

—I will start by telling of the bad things. I am, frankly, a noisy, loud-mouthed show-off, according to some people's standards. I am inclined to voice my opinion when it is not wanted; I say what I think rather than stop for a minute and use tact. I get too much joy out of making people feel uncomfortable mentally. I waste time and thought making jokes . . . when I could be doing things of more advantage. (What a devilish hard job it is to write a journal when you don't know who will read it.)

Then, after an account of LusterB's first experience with purchased pornography, VainB arrives at a moment of triumph.

It seems that I have so much wrong with me that it would take forever to cure me, and yet I am so much better than most boys my age (no conceit intended) that there is no comparison!

Feb. 22, 1938
I'm 17 today but I don't know how old I am actually. Some of the things I do & can do would do credit to a 20 or 21 year old and some of the things would disgrace a six year old. I suppose maybe I expect too much, but I, like Benjamin Franklin, would like to become as nearly a perfect human being as is possible. (An absurd desire as far as hope of completion, yet very sane as a goal to work to.)

In his senior year of high school in 1938, VainB naturally longs to be elected "Representative Boy" of his class. He feels miserable when he loses and then writes about it.

It doesn't matter much though I wish the kids liked me more (that's what they voted for, although the characteristics listed were dependability, scholarship, all-around course activities & sociability).

1939
I really am ashamed of myself. . . . I have a hard time not to get an exaggerated idea of my self-importance. . . . I believe that the extreme joy I get from achieving minor triumphs (such as getting the highest in a test, or getting on the honor roll, etc) is not to good. I should strive to take what success I may have in my stride (to use a very trite phrase) as I do whatever failures I have.

Quite often the boy, longing for maturity, writes as if attempting to write this chapter.

May 30, 1939
Why do I write this diary? I've tried to analyze what I am trying to do, and I find that one time I write for one purpose, another time for another. For instance, occasionally I catch myself writing for the effect it will have on whoever reads this. At other times I write for my future reminiscence. . . . Sometimes I wonder if all my writing isn't just for inflating my ego (an over-used phrase).

Many destructive intrusions of VainB did not get recorded, probably because he saw them as too contemptible. One that the family has often retold and amused ourselves with occurred in the summer of 1939. Here is my memory of how Mama told it.

The family had agreed that we all should drive together to explore Yellowstone Park. But you, always criticizing almost everything I suggested those days, were nasty about it: "A silly trip." You kept saying you had too much important reading to do. I insisted you had to go with us, or else! "It could be one of the best family get-togethers ever." Well, you caved in, after I made several stronger threats of punishment. But you carried along a huge *Anthology of World Literature*, reading it not only as we drove along but as we viewed the scenes. Instead of reveling in the lovely scenes or joining our conversations, you always had that book open, reading away, or pretending to—just trying to impress us all that you were a true intellectual. The worst moment came as Old Faithful shot up: there you were, refusing to look at it, your nose buried in that heavy book!

One of my cousins recently retold a similar version of the story. She remembers—now in a friendly way—her anger and contempt at my insulting behavior. Of course, I'm embarrassed about the event (and, of course, amused by it); I wish I could believe that I was genuinely captured by the poems in that book.

In college, almost every journal entry reveals AmbitionB's and VainB's goals and his other Selves' strong reproaches.

April 15, 1940 [second year of college]
I just got my report card, and it'll put me on the honor roll. . . . I am going to become scientific if it kills me. My writing betrays my present confused thinking, I know, but I'm trying to improve my mind, along with my marks. I read more *good* books than anyone I know . . . and thus am becoming educated more than anyone I know. But boy, how I've got to work. I'm really dumb, compared to so many of the people who have been great. Constant striving is what is necessary. Lately I have slid back in my striving.

And then he almost summarizes the LIFER's quest in this book:

> I wonder if I will ever overcome my faults (lazyness, conceit, vague dis-
> honesty, crudeness, etc.) to *become a truly integrated individual.* [*Not* his
> italics!]

There we have what has been a lifetime quest for a *plausible harmony.*

WHO OR WHAT PRODUCED VAINB'S VITALITY?

Sometimes the budding ThinkerB seems to blame only Mama for the faults
of VainB, while tacitly supporting AmbitionB.

> *June 30, 1940*
> Mother . . . worries about me and her supposed inability to guide me cor-
> rectly. . . . She thinks I have the ability to "amount to something" and wor-
> ries about my reading so much, feeling that I should be preparing for life.
> I can't convince her that I am getting alot out of my reading. Of course,
> she doesn't think it's harmful, but she would rather see me work than read.
> Thank goodness she doesn't rebel when I buy books. I have such a desire to
> have a fine personal library in my head.

Then the budding LOVER describes his own contrasting picture of "amount-
ing to something"—as if to refute Mama behind her back.

> I would like to get on the B.Y.U. faculty, or some faculty of a better univer-
> sity, and learn French, German, Latin, Greek, philosophy, by taking classes
> and individual study all the rest of my life. There is that desire, but it is
> almost in opposition to my desire to be something scientifically—a chem-
> ist, or biologist, really contributing some actual knowledge to the world.
> Whatever I do, I want to be able to feel that I am doing something toward
> making others happy, because that is about the only real achievement there
> is worth having. [And on to his joy in teaching Sunday School classes.]

> *Sept. 12, 1940*
> Nothing risqué, nothing gained, I always say.
>   I see now that I will never amount to anything except a genial, lik-
> able, half-successful school teacher [which would betray Mama's hopes to
> "amount to something"]. I don't settle down to sustained effort in any one
> line, I don't do any real thinking of my own—I am a fritterer and see no
> indication of ever becoming anything else.

Then, after several rambling pages that interest me but would bore you, AmbitionB worries about losing steam.

> My worry is that I can't become convinced in myself that I am up to much. Other people . . . think much more of me than I really do, as a potentiality.

Behind all those episodes, many today would argue that VainB and AmbitionB were produced not by socialization but through genetic inheritance. Many biologists see such figures as entirely encoded in our competitive, "selfish" genes: only the winners survive, as every ancestor, all the way back to the slime, quickly learned. I'll spend no time here quarreling with these extremists. After all, though, no matter how the nature vs. nurture quarrels are resolved, we all have to agree that my competitive excesses show that I am not completely unrelated to the two deer I saw on television recently, butting each other, competing for a mate.

The second most obvious source is capitalist culture. Pierre Bourdieu, whose fame VainB envies and who detests the fame drive as much as ThinkerB and MoralB do, sees egocentric competition as inescapably constructed by our own cultures. Wasn't VainB simply echoing the drives dwelt on by Max Weber in *The Protestant Ethic and the Spirit of Capitalism*, still celebrated as supreme virtues by scores of economists and CEOs? Why should my more pious Selves blame AmbitionB and VainB for embracing what many capitalists see as the "virtue" that saves us—competition or even greed? In short, what I've reported can be found everywhere, earlier and now. To take in whatever you can by "driving ahead" is the way to live. If, as many of us lament, perhaps naïvely, our new millennium reveals an even crazier drive for winning than ever before, what's the point of worrying about it in one's Self? Doesn't every American who "succeeds" exhibit it?[3] The incredibly successful books by Steve Covey, touting Seven Habits that lead to being an "effective person," celebrate exactly what I'm worried about.[4]

---

3. This negative emphasis on American culture is surely a bit undue. We could find parallels in every "civilized" culture throughout history, and perhaps we would find them in all the "uncivilized" cultures—if only their members kept diaries and records. Hans Christian Andersen, back in the middle of the nineteenth century, said of himself, "My name is gradually beginning to shine, and that is the only thing for which I live. I covet honor and glory in the same way as the miser covets gold." (Quoted in "A Melancholic Dane," *New Yorker*, January 8, 2001.) For all we know, Andersen intended a bit of irony there—but I doubt it.

4. A recent book by Robert W. Fuller, *Somebodies and Nobodies: Overcoming the Abuse of Rank* (British Columbia: New Society Publishers, 2004) could be described as a powerful attack on VainB and, with some qualification, AmbitionB. Inventing the term

That Steve Covey is a Mormon suggests a third candidate in the list of possible causes of the excesses: Mormonism's extreme emphasis on individual progression. The Church insists that the goal of life is to "progress." Though the overt commands are usually—thank God—spiritual and ethical, there are many hints that such progress requires getting ahead in the rat race. The goal of *eternal progress*—for us males it was, as I mentioned before, progress toward becoming Gods of other worlds—can turn into the desire to outclass the others, to prove to yourself and to them that though you may not be quite Number One yet, you will reach it someday, at least in one part of the universe. God commands us to "get better all the time" and to keep a record of how we're working to get better. Onward and upward—whether in the arts, or business management, or academic achievement, or strengthening one's genuine virtues.

A recent guidebook, "counsel and inspiration for each day of the year," published by the Church President, Gordon B. Hinckley, is called *Stand a Little Taller.* As the publisher's preface puts it, "find in these pages the motivation and inspiration to follow the prophet, to make each day a little better than the one before, and to 'stand a little taller.'" To me as a boy that would have been taken quite literally: I must become taller—in fact I'm already almost as tall as Uncle Joe! I wonder how the metaphor feels to those, including most women, who are permanently much shorter than we giants.[5] In its more defensible metaphorical form, the get-taller command means "Labor to improve the quality of your soul, by cultivating love, charity, generosity, forgiveness." But again and again it turns into "Do what you can to get more credit from the world, whether you deserve it or not."

But putting it like that risks exaggeration; many Mormons I know have *not* exhibited such destructive, compulsive drives, and I can think of no other organization, religious or not, that produces as much disinterested pro bono work. Why does the Salt Lake City–Ogden region of Utah top the list of American cities in the amount of charitable giving—with the average taxpayer giving 15 percent of income?

But before looking further at the favorable side, let us return to the fourth and final likely source: the way my family often encouraged the harmful side of the Mormon drive for progress (as you've seen in some of my examples). Though I love all my family in memory, I see them as too often reinforcing VainB.

The Clayson clan, including Mama, could all be described as striving souls, worrying about getting ahead of the Joneses. All of them were

---

"rankism," Fuller does a wonderful job of deploring the ways in which aspiring to be at the top harms those considered "nobodies."

5. Phyllis says the metaphor doesn't bother her a bit; unlike me, she never felt pressed to become physically taller.

descendants of the British working class—farmhands, factory hands, weavers—and they were thus always a bit anxious about the "wolf at the door," the threat of poverty. Yet they were surrounded by evidence that in the land of Glory you could, with sufficient effort, "get ahead."

Grampa Clayson, orphaned early and having had to labor full-time from age ten, finally got back to elementary school and graduated from high school in his twenties. By the time I knew him, he had worked at several jobs simultaneously, had managed to put all but one of his eight children through college, and had produced a huge clan (which by now is loaded with doctors and lawyers and professors and rich business leaders). The family has achieved! (And yet, we often turned the religious command to *become* better into a cheap command to *look* better.)[6]

Though these four driving forces—survival of the fittest, capitalist competition, Mormon emphasis on progress, and my family's drives (what I've sometimes called "Claysonism")—hit me in especially concentrated form, I obviously can't claim that my experience was unique. My Jewish, Catholic, and Protestant friends have confessed to excessive ambition-anxieties like mine. And VainB sometimes takes great pride in claiming that, on the whole, my efforts to resist cheap vanity have succeeded far more often than my friends' have. So you see, I win.

WHO GETS CREDIT FOR THE LOVER FIGHTING BACK, IRONICALLY OR NOT?

With these four forces so strongly at work, where did my quite early contempt for such competitiveness come from? ThinkerB would like to intrude and claim that the rising critical stance against AmbitionB and VainB was a product of the drive to think profoundly—a nice paradox. But it's clear that from early on, for each kind of influence (even evolution, many now argue), I met moral counterdrives as strong as the drive to win.

Leaving evolution aside, with its recent exploration of altruism, what about American culture? Well, anyone who has read much in the literature that I encountered in my teens will find piles of contemptuous attacks on many aspects of American culture, on capitalism, on the reduction of life to mere winning. The very sources of cheap ambition simultaneously contained attacks on it. American culture and European culture, in the books and

---

6. I wonder with VainB how many of them think that I have also "achieved." And I'm amused at the pleasure I take in seeing Jane Clayson, my first cousin once removed, as anchorwoman on CBS's "Early Morning Show." My family is winning! And what, other than comical vanity, could lead to my adding this footnote?

articles I began to read, provided me with many counterspokesmen—Sinclair Lewis, Theodore Dreiser, Aldous Huxley, Anthony Trollope, Dostoevsky, and so on—proclaiming the stupidity and immorality of placing personal triumph at the top of one's list. And they had influenced the teachers I will be celebrating in a moment. (We will face a paradox every time AmbitionB is challenged: "Are you not," ThinkerB intrudes, "seeking ambitiously to be among the top critics of ambition?")

What, then, about family? Well, just as they often jumped on me for failing, they often would sermonize against such jumping. I suspect that if they read what I've said so far, they would feel it unfair. All of them—well, *most* of them—much of the time were wrestling with the very paradox I'm dealing with: the true goal was not to be *seen* as at the top but really to achieve the best possible "character." Nothing was more contemptible than *revealing* the wrong kinds of personal pride.

Sometime in High School

Some of my male friends are obviously more popular among the girls than I am. I feel especially anxious about not being the most handsome. Finally I confront my best judge: "Mama, do you see me as handsome?" She replies, without hesitating, "Wayne C., I see you as an extremely clean-cut young man." It is clear to me that the message is "Whether or not you are handsome, you should not worry about that. In our family we are above cheap anxieties about *appearing* the best. I want you to have your mind on higher things."

A more powerful example of the counterurge is the following advice Grampa Clayson wrote on the flyleaf of his daughter Ann's new journal, which she, like me, began keeping at age fourteen:

Dear Ann:—Popularity vanishes like the dew before the morning sun; reputation varies with the changing opinions of humanity, but character, real, genuine, true-blue character—grows stronger through all the storms of life. The first two are not to be despised; but the last is to be sought after, obtained, and cherished if we would know and enjoy the fullest measure of real life. Retain the first two if you can, but never at the sacrifice of the last. Your Father, Eli J. Clayson.

I can't remember Grampa ever talking that wisely to me—but surely something like that was always in the air. Despite all the drive to get visibly ahead, there was a "commandment" to become a "good person"—by becoming more *virtuous* from moment to moment.

It thus doesn't surprise me in the least to find my teenage journals full of praise for my virtuous family and of my ambition to reach their heights. "My Grandpa Clayson is surely a good man and if I can only be as good as he is when I grow up I will be satisfied."

On my father's side (the Booths and Chipmans), the points against ambition for fame and money were stressed even more strongly. My key influence was Grampa Ebenezer Booth, a farmer contemptuous of the hoity-toity. The only one of his family who didn't get a college degree, he seemed to see his main achievement as appearing clearly *against* vain aspirations, except in the matter of virtue. Violating the ambitious standards of his brothers and sisters, who were already "high" in the Utah world—lawyers, judges, church leaders—he would distress Gramma Booth by deliberately walking to the post office wearing soiled overalls and shoes reeking of manure. He loved to spend time mocking the world's achievers, especially in matters of fame and money: "Wayne C., never forget that when you meet a millionaire, you're meeting a crook."

He loved to write satirical verse, mocking the wealthy and vain. One Christmas he wrote a thirty-line spoof on the advertising of a local department store—one that I almost memorized.

> Dear Chipman Merc.,
> I received your Christmas Greetings, for which I am truly grateful. Accept the following lines as a token of my gratitude.

> Your big red store is a sight to gladden any eye.
> And to describe it properly I scarcely think I'll try.

Then, after listing the advertised items he couldn't afford,

> But my old wad has sunk so low for them, I could not pay.
> I've lost my watch and cap and gloves, which causes me to sigh,
> When I have not enough mon' left to buy a two-bit tie.
> . . . .
> And now, dear Merc., excuse me if some more I cannot tell,
> When I think of all I'd like to buy it makes me feel like—the deuce.

Thus he helped create the half egalitarian you'll meet in chapter 9.

While attacking the drive for money or fame, Grampa Booth's drive to achieve virtue and learning was intense. He would read both the Bible and the Book of Mormon cover to cover once each year. He would jump on me for spending time reading *Huckleberry Finn* rather than sacred texts. Yet much of his energy went into ensuring education for his children. As Aunt Relva put it in her autobiography, "The sacrifices both of them [he and Gramma Booth] made that we might all of us have an education can only be repaid by our lives being worthy of them."

It's clear, then, that the boy was subjected to immense pressure to rise in the world, but on conflicting paths. One goal, pursued by both clans, was for VainB or at least AmbitionB to get ahead, to win, whether in the eyes of neighbors or the eyes of "the world." But at the same time another goal, pursued by both clans, was for other Selves to win by increasing in genuine virtue.

The same division is revealed by the more admirable forms of upward-pushing in Church doctrine. The insistence on progressing eternally—achieve, achieve, achieve—was almost always put explicitly in terms of achievement in the virtues, in character. The advice (and commands) included absolute warnings against harming others in order to win—warnings that too few current self-helpers include. You gotta succeed, you gotta progress, you gotta achieve day by day, but on the other hand, as one hymn put it, "Then wake up, and do something more, than dream of your mansions above," more than getting ahead and winning all the prizes from God. "Doing good is a pleasure, a joy beyond measure, a blessing of duty and love."[7]

With these anti-VainB forces at work, it's hardly surprising that the journals soon became full of explicit self-reproach about cheap winning, along with affirmations of higher ambitions, even LOVE.

> *June 20, 1939 [age 18½]*
> I believe this is going to be the most consciously happy summer of my life (up to now). I enjoy my work [irrigating for the cóllege]. It's not hard, it's variagated [a deliberate pun, believe me], . . . it's out of doors 12 to 16 hrs a day, it's fairly remunerative [25¢ an hour]. Provo is beautiful in the summer. . . . all day long I see nature . . . at its best.

There follows a lovely description of the beauty, a list of what he's reading—and then:

> My main objective in life is to become a wise philosopher, a person who can think, and be happy in spite of (or because of) it. Voltaire said that philosophers realize that they sacrifice happiness when they become philosophers,

---

7. Another hymn that memory draws up frequently concluded with "There is no tomorrow but only today." I have to use the past tense because the current text of the hymn has been changed—succumbing to the success-drive—to "Prepare for tomorrow by working today"! That's one of the worst deliberate corruptions of text I've ever met.

and that in spite of being unhappy, none of them would willingly become ignorant for the sake of being happy again. Voltaire may disagree with me, but are not the philosophers the happiest persons if they would not trade their state with anyone less wise? . . . This happiness is what I am seeking. As yet, I'm muddle-headed. The clumsy handling of this paragraph proves that. *But, I won't always be muddle-headed.* I *will* learn to think fairly and accurately and *honestly*, if it takes the rest of my life, and it probably will. At any rate, it's a great life.

THE INFLUENCE OF TEACHERS

It was only in my early conversations with wonderful teachers—and my responses to the reading they recommended—that I discovered just how much of the "achievement split" can be found not just in my life but in all of current life and indeed throughout human history. The major authors they introduced me to, almost all of them, express contempt for those who merely want to win over others. Especially influential, memory says, were Anthony Trollope's *The Way We Live Now* and George Meredith's *Evan Harrington.*

It took me a long time reading and thinking about such books to realize, after years of blaming Mormonism and my beloved relatives for producing the anxious striver, that the whole history of cultures (particularly of American culture) was at least as much to blame—and yet was simultaneously providing resources for its own criticism.

Here's a high school journal entry about how my ambitions were already being challenged through teaching.

> *May 21, 1937*
> The two teachers that have influenced me most this year are Miss Gean Clark and Mr. Luther Giddings. . . . [Though teaching me to be skeptical about what I read, they also have taught me to believe in] love, not only of individuals but for everyone; I believe that anyone who swallows his own interests and spends his life working for others will find much more happiness in the end, not because he has followed Christ's teaching particularly, but because we are so built, our minds are so formed that it makes us feel happy to do good to others.[8] . . . I have been reading some philosophy books, some

---

8. How much pride should I take in my unconscious prediction of recent research about the brain? "Science Times" reports, as I write today, research proving that we are "wired to cooperate," that the "act of cooperating with another person, of choosing trust over cynicism, generosity over selfishness, makes the brain light up with quiet joy" (*New York Times*, July 25, 2002, D1).

novels some not, lately, and have received many ideas from them. I was somewhat surprised to find that even such sexy novelists as Aldous Huxley believe in the ultimate joy and happiness that comes from living the ideal Christian life. I have come to realize how selfish I am, how little I do for others. . . . I have decided that I will work along some scientific field and try to learn things that will benefit other people.

Thus the troubled youth illustrated how, from our beginnings, we have been indoctrinated with a split: the sheer need to win at all costs confronting a deep contempt for mere winning. (To avoid the paradox again—I want to win among those contemptuous of mere winning—let me say that the confrontation is not with Contempt-Booth but with the LOVER.)

HOW ARE "WE" COPING WITH VAINB AND AMBITIONB TODAY?

My conflicts among Selves are, as you've seen again and again, revealed most sharply in this very *LIFE* project as it relates to other projects that have tempted me recently. First, this was to be an autobiography, solicited by a New York editor and thus possibly yielding a bit of further "fame," perhaps even money. Then, after seeing that my uncolorful life didn't generate a seductive, chronological *LIFE*, it became a book *about* autobiography, one that would demonstrate to the world that even the aging Booth could still produce a first-class *scholarly* book. Then, as I saw more and more hypocritical posing in the *LIVES* I read and felt that my own drafts were really lousy, it shifted to become a critical work about hypocritical posing, valuable and destructive, in *all* kinds of writing. The drafts of that book, still on the back burner, might leave behind after my death some proof to "the world"—or those in it whose high opinion I strive for—that I was a genuinely driven *scholar*, not just a Wandering-Generalist-Booth.

Only after getting bogged down in that one did LOVER realize that what I should be writing, if anything at all, is the first one, the one I *want* to write, the one that I might even love to write: this *LIFE*. So the more defensible Selves win, sort of, with continuing conflict.

But am I not driven more by AmbitionB and even VainB as I write that sentence? Hard to judge. Ambition for what? Vanity about what? Oh, it's fairly clear: I want to write a *LIFE* that is acknowledged by the *best* readers—readers like you—to be the *best* example of one written without the slightest concern for fame or public recognition. Rising above Rousseau's hypocritical claim to write the first honest autobiography ever, a claim echoed by thousands of others, I, the humble, non-ambition-driven Wayne Booth, write the least ambitious, least pride-driven *LIFE* of all time. Anything paradoxical in that?

Certainly—VainB is still there. The mildly embarrassing fact remains (evident in these attempted ironies) that throughout it all I am still too often a "driven" man, a man who feels he must somehow be "further along" at the end of the day than he was at the beginning. Even after I've spent an hour or two practicing the cello, feeling totally freed of ambition, or after Phyllis and I have had a glorious hike up the Utah mountains, with loving conversation, I can catch myself, as I open the mail, longing for another favorable review of the last book or feeling tempted to write an angry letter to an editor who has "stupidly" turned down an earlier draft of this book, or . . .

So, as the anecdotes that begin this chapter show, silly VainB, the corrupt version of AmbitionB, still survives, hoping for more and more public acclaim. Usually I manage to hide him from the public, but sometimes I lose control.

Would you like proof that I am now above it all, that love finally has triumphed over cheap ambition? I'm tempted to list—and later will list—some of the love choices I honor most.

But why, then, ThinkerB whispers, is the LIFER concluding here with Love? The only answer I can think of is that VainB is immensely proud of being able, sometimes, to fumble toward what I—one of his brothers—am tempted to call *proud* harmony.

Chapter Five

Ambition vs. Teaching for the Love of It

To go on preaching reason to an inherently unreasonable species is, as history shows, a fairly hopeless enterprise.

—Arthur Koestler

Human history becomes more and more a race between education and catastrophe.

—H. G. Wells

Delightful task! to rear the tender thought,
To teach the young idea how to shoot.

—James Thompson, "The Seasons"

Oh, Mr. Booth, it's so good working with you—you must have had to learn things the hard way.

—Student at Earlham College, after a grueling
two-hour private conference on how to improve an essay

But where's the man, who counsel can bestow,
Still pleas'd to teach, and yet not proud to know?
Unbiass'd, or by favour, or by spite:
Not dully prepossess'd, nor blindly right;
Tho' learn'd, well-bred; and tho' well-bred, sincere;
Modestly bold, and humanly severe:
Who to a friend his faults can freely show,
And gladly praise the merit of a foe?

—Alexander Pope, "Essay on Criticism"

The true teacher defends his pupils against his own personal influence.

—Bronson Alcott

The gift of teaching is a peculiar talent, and implies a need and craving in the teacher himself.

—John Jay Chapman

Those who can, do; those who can't, teach.

—Popular adage of my youth, probably quoting from George Bernard Shaw

My lifetime choice of teaching as a vocation may at first glance seem utterly predictable, revealing no soul-splits whatever. For one thing, the entire Mormon enterprise was evangelical, didactic, preachy. Our communal task was to change the beliefs of as many outsiders as possible, and our daily encounters were full of exhortations, not to say nagging. Being surrounded by would-be "teachers" produced my lifelong impulse, often absurdly overdone, to impose "truth" on others. Even these days, as I try to resist the nagging side, I frequently offend my family, especially the grandchildren, by intruding advice when advice can spoil the occasion.

Throughout childhood I was surrounded by a family of professional teachers. Family hero Grampa Clayson's first job—except for day labor in his teens—had been as a teacher.[1] When Daddy died, he was already famous in our town as an outstanding teacher of agronomy. Mama had worked as a teacher to support us while Daddy got his degree, and after losing him she took the only open route: with a teaching certificate based on one year of college, she accepted a job teaching third grade. Gramma Booth had longed desperately to become a teacher, and she would have done so had her polygamist father supported her schooling beyond the eighth grade. Five aunts and uncles had been teachers for at least a while, though of course motherhood and other tempting careers deflected most of them after a few years of being underpaid.

I'm pretty sure, judging by how they supported me—in effect taught me—after Daddy's death, that all of those relatives had been better-than-average teachers. What shocks me, though, is never having heard any celebration from any of them, except frustrated Gramma Booth, of teaching as the ideal vocation, as a beloved calling, as *the* profession one should choose for the love of it. They all seemed to have gone into teaching because it was the only available job. The pay was scandalously low, as it still is when compared with many

---

1. Like me he had suffered the death of his father when very young. As I said in chapter 3, at age ten he was removed from school and "put out" to work to provide food for his desperate mother and siblings. His stories about how it felt later to enter high school classes with kids four years younger were always touching to me.

far less important professions. (Just compare for a moment how much good is done to the world by a really competent, devoted elementary teacher, earning maybe fifteen to thirty thousand bucks a year, and an equally competent CEO who is paid—can't really say *earns*—millions and millions.) My Uncle Eli was paid sixty-five dollars a month as a teacher before giving up and taking a better-paying job as a clerk at J. C. Penney. Mama was paid only about a hundred bucks a month for many years, until her reputation and newly earned degrees got her hired to *teach* teachers at Brigham Young University.[2]

In short, teaching was often not a vocation but a fallback, a rescuer from utter poverty—a bit like how entry-level military positions are portrayed in Michael Moore's *Fahrenheit 9/11*. Even Gramma Booth, while expressing her longing to have been a teacher, would say, "Wayne C., you argue so much and so well I think you should become a lawyer."

The result was that even though many of my elementary and high school teachers seemed genuinely devoted to doing it well, I never dreamed until college of becoming a teacher. Even the teaching of wonderful Luther Giddings and Gean Clark did not tempt me to teach; to become a teacher would leave me anonymous, unknown, far down the ladder. It would not get me *ahead of the others*, while to become a "chemical engineer" or "scientific researcher" might make me famous, or even wealthy.

Several of my teachers at BYU turned all that around. They were not famous—and never would be. They were paid poorly, just enough to "get by." They never said a word about trying to get ahead or hoping for a job at a better place. (One of them, Karl Young, a wonderful freshman-English teacher, did goad me to aspire to follow his path and become a Rhodes Scholar—but to him that didn't mean "to become a famous scholar.") They all had obviously found *the* vocation, *the* calling, that made life good. They engaged with me and other students in class and out as if that was what made life worth living.

A dramatic, unforgettable moment came when Professor Young invited about ten of us to his house for "supper" and then had us read aloud a play we'd never even heard of before: Ben Jonson's *Volpone*. We were totally carried away, astonished at our own ability to catch the subtle jokes. That evening was life to the fullest—for us and obviously also for him.

Such hours with him initiated months of debate about who I wanted to be. Karl Young and P. A. Christensen in English, M. Wilford Poulson in

---

2. What would that hundred bucks mean today, considering seventy years of inflation? Still only peanuts, compared with what you and I have been paid, right? Diverse calculations of inflation translate that $100, in 1930, to something like $1,000 to $3,000 today.

psychology (and, privately, in Church history), A. C. Lambert in a required "religion" class that he turned into a really challenging course in how to do research in Mormon history—these had me convinced by the end of my sophomore year, when I was bored silly in my required chemistry course in quantitative research, that maybe I should be a teacher and not a researcher.

But what subject would I teach? If any of the really good teachers had been in chemistry, I'm pretty sure that I would have continued on in science. But the chemistry teachers, even the one devoted, attentive teacher, Brother Joseph Nicholes,[3] led me to conclude that to teach chemistry for the rest of my life would be boring, because I'd just have to teach the same stuff year by year. But if I could teach English or philosophy or psychology, that would be a different task every day.

After long discussions with favorite teachers and, of course, with Max Dalby, who urged me again and again to choose what we all called "English," I decided for it.

When I told Mama about my choice, she was horrified. Having suffered the underrated teacher's role for fourteen years, she almost whined: "But, Wayne C., you'll always be poor; and you'll never amount to anything. You have the ability to become a doctor or lawyer or politician or . . ." Memory says that she went on to suggest I might become a governor or even president, but I strongly doubt that she went that far—even though I sometimes have dreamed of running the country.

What memory reports with great confidence—because she confirmed it years later—is my reply: "Mother, the point of life is not to make a lot of money or be famous. Why not choose a profession where you get paid for doing what you really want to do? And what I want to do is teach literature. Besides, I can make some money on the side by becoming a novelist."[4]

As you would predict, my decision did not remain unthreatened by VainB and AmbitionB. Writing to Phyllis from Paris five years later, I speculated about the rivalry between ambition and the would-be novelist.

19 April 45

No, I must content myself with being a good professor, which I think I can be; I am capable of transmitting enthusiasm for fine things, perhaps even understanding; the creation of fine things seems, as yet, beyond me, and I'm not going to worry about it, very much. As I love you . . . it doesn't seem too important to do something that gains "fame or my fortune." There is

---

3. Oh, yes, we students all called our teachers "Brother ——." Only one of those I had—one of the weakest, I have to confess—was a "Sister."

4. If you care about "creative" ambitions, see chapter 13.

a necessary renunciation, not only of money, involved in the choice to become a teacher, and frankly, I become more and more willing to make that renunciation.

Then, after discussing other possible routes, including the life of a businessman,

> I think of teaching as quite literally the noblest of professions, when done nobly. And life is too short and too final for one to risk doing anything but the very best thing there is to be done.

Today, when "making it" is much more dominant than in the Forties, I feel no hesitation in proclaiming unapologetic pride about that decision. VainB, AmbitionB, and I join for a moment in total harmony.

My account probably underrates Mama's influence in favor of the choice. After all, though she saw teaching as what would destroy her ambitions for me, she had demonstrated to me from the beginning just how much a loving teacher can mean to kids—including me. I had witnessed parents' gratitude for what she taught their kids. And AmbitionB had seen her get rewards for it; first she became principal of the elementary school, then was hired by BYU.

There was never any hint that to become a teacher like Karl Young or P. A. Christensen would yield money or fame. But was it all slightly tainted by AmbitionB's desire to dominate in argument—to exert power over students? Perhaps. The actual teaching life later revealed many intrusions from AmbitionB and sometimes even from contemptible VainB. Why would a teacher teaching "for the love of it" be upset when one student evaluation out of scores of favorable ones accused him of being wishy-washy, of not "teaching any hard facts"? And what about the envy I feel "against" my close friend Jamie Redfield because he has had *two* Quantrell Awards for Excellence in Undergraduate Teaching, while I have had only one?

Fortunately, I find in my journals (and memory) hundreds of celebrations of the sheer joy of the classroom—including the Sunday School classroom—when things have gone right. Many are, however, a bit ambivalent, especially the early ones.

January 30, 1941
I am but a shadow of my former Sylph . . .

> Today has been a rather mixed one, successes, discouragements, et al.
> Professor Young had me teach his class in 1500–1600 English literature, because he had to leave. . . . With insufficient preparation, and with

his almost illegible notes, I carried the thing off rather well, I thought. They were (the studs.) attentive and fairly contributive. I didn't get my concept of the humanity-love-taught-by-literature put over too well . . . but I enjoyed it, and at least *some* of them did.

OK, a minor success.

Considered from a "professional" perspective, my new "calling" was side-stepped by my accepting the "call" to a two-year mission for the Church and by my later being turned into an infantryman for two years. What happened to the would-be teacher during those four years? (For the problems and miseries of those Selves, see part 2.)

Well, as missionary, I was actually teaching much of the time—not in any classroom but harassing colleagues, exhorting Church members and prospective converts. Though I never consciously violated Professor Poulson's warning, "Don't try to get them under the water," I was often aggressively pedagogical, not to say pedantic: improve the world (and one's self-image as an improver) by teaching people to want to become learners. My journals often boast about this or that success in getting my "companions" to read this or that great novel or tough book about religion and philosophy.

Day by day I had to choose just how far to intrude into others' lives the "truths" I thought I had—mainly the truth that to pursue truth is one main goal of life. So the drive for learning and spreading what one has learned and producing a desire for learning more never collapsed.

In the army, chance presented some surprising opportunities for teaching. After about fifteen months slogging away as rifleman and typist, suddenly I was shipped from Paris to England to teach in a whomped-up "university" run by the army. It was designed to serve, or maybe one should say "entertain," GIs waiting to be shipped home.

15 June 1945

. . . my bad mood is gone, because my immediate future is now more bright. I'm going to England to be an academic-assistant, whatever—in the army—that is. . . .

For about five months, in Shrivenham,[5] a bunch of us lucky ones—actually now with sheets on our beds and no bedbugs!—were conducting courses designed to be *genuine* college courses. Since I'd majored in English, my assignment was to teach "composition." For the first time ever I faced a class of

---

5. Not far from Swindon, not far from London, not far from Oxford. We did lots of touring.

"college" students, mainly indifferent, all of them impatient to get out and go home. They had chosen to be there instead of waiting somewhere else, but they seemed totally bored—at least at first. Only a small number were already spontaneously engaged with learning.

So what was I to do? Well, surely the task—never mentioned by my superiors—was to turn 'em on. It was *not*, as one boss advised, to "get 'em to write fewer errors." It was to entice them into wanting to communicate more effectively.

I have no evidence about whether any of my students during those five months loved or hated my classes. All of my journals and letters stress only my arguments with fellow teachers and my longing for Phyllis. But memory sees me there working day by day, valiantly reading their "compositions" night by night, to get those guys to see education as a center for life.

The good fortune of those months continued when I was transferred to the occupation army in Bremen, Germany, assigned as the noncommissioned officer in charge of a school designed, again, for GIs longing to get home. I again taught composition, plus some literature courses, including one in Shakespeare. I think I did pretty well, though I committed one serious mistake: I chose to teach them *The Merchant of Venice*. How could I have done that in Germany in 1946, without ever a hint that we should discuss its problem of anti-Semitism?[6]

I was also assigned to teach reading to a small group of illiterate GIs. Totally green about how to deal with nonreaders, I had received what felt like a really focused assignment: teach 'em to love reading—the center of my mission. They were with me only a few weeks, and my efforts were mostly futile. I lacked the techniques, and they lacked the motivation. Nothing would please me more today than the unlikely receipt of a letter from one of them proclaiming that I changed his life.[7]

Whatever the successes and failures of those six months of teaching impatient soldiers, they somehow confirmed my vocation. Though I was even

---

6. A German teacher we had hired had become a friend, and he did have the courage to rebuke me for that choice, which had been dictated, as I see it now, by the dogmatic "objective formalism" of the time. Ethical criticism of literature was not on the scene, and it was not until decades later that I faced, in print, the undeniable anti-Semitism of that play.

7. That comment is prompted partly by my having just read a wonderful book, *Life is So Good*, by George Dawson and Richard Glaubman (New York: Penguin, 2000). It is an "oral" autobiography about how Dawson, a black day laborer born in 1898, dealt with illiteracy until age ninety-eight, when he finally fell in love with learning to read. I can't resist fantasizing: if he'd been in my army class, could I have changed his life earlier? The book has led me to sign up now to make a second attempt at teaching adults how to read.

Lucille and Mother join me when I receive my Ph.D. at the University of Chicago, 1950

more passionately committed to getting back to Phyllis than to getting back to education, my sense of a calling was clearer than ever.

GRADUATE SCHOOL

The first year at the University of Chicago did not—now to my surprise—do much to reinforce that passion. My teachers were mostly drillers intent on teaching us to become scholars, not teachers. And for them scholarship—a word I had never even thought of as a goal—was the pursuit of hard, demonstrable fact. The result? Well, a list, which I now choose to cut from an earlier draft of this book, of some off-putting, yawn-yielding courses.

I can't even remember most of them. Because I was happily married and living life to the full, day by day, no longer wondering what I wanted to "become," I didn't even keep a journal or write any confessional letters to Phyllis. All I remember is that I worked hard, got good grades, and read some wonderful but unassigned books, trying to catch up with the other students, all of them seeming more learned, some of them still now lifetime friends.[8] Fortunately, though I felt oppressed by my ignorance of scholarship, I still felt determined to earn the degrees required to get a teaching job. (The fact that nobody even mentioned our need for training as teachers—not only during that first year but throughout the next three Ph.D. years—so annoyed me that I later published a pseudonymous article condemning the department for the neglect.)

What saved my vocation was teaching in the "Hutchins College." Having received "honors" on my M.A. exam—eight hours of writing on a couple of Edmund Burke's essays and John Webster's *The Duchess of Malfi*—I was hired by the College as an assistant instructor. I found myself surrounded for three years by a gang of genuinely devoted teachers, hardly any of them concentrating on scholarly careers. Unlike any other university college in the country, the College made its own appointments and decided on its own promotions and retentions, based entirely on judgments about effective teaching. Each staff of about twenty teachers met together for two hours each week to be "briefed" by one or another on the best way to teach that week's readings. The recommended methods were often contradictory, of course, but most of them were challenging.

I felt that I was learning far more in those staff meetings—not just about teaching but about how to deal with texts—than I did in most of my classes. Though I continued to work toward the Ph.D., often quite discouraged about it,[9] my number one goal for three years was to learn how to teach as well as, and cultivate close friendships with, the best teachers on our staffs: Robert Streeter, Wilma Ebbitt, Henry Rago, and a dozen others I admired.[10] We taught one another in those staff meetings, or tried to, almost always with an implicit goal: Get those kids to love education and want more of it. (The goal actually touted in the College publicity was to produce "good citizens"—a phrase I never meet in any college's publicity these days.)

What also "rescued" my vocation was encountering, after that dull first year of graduate courses, some genuine, rigorous literary criticism. Ronald Crane's passionate revival of criticism focused us mainly on "close reading"

---

8. Hi, Homer. Hi, Mel. Hi, Norman and Mary. Hi, Dick. Hi, Walter. Too bad the others have died.

9. A standard joke on campus was that those who finished their dissertations took, on average, eight years; those who didn't finish took even longer. My four-year timing, bested only by Jim Miller's doing it in three years, still receives complaints from close friends who spent much longer.

10. Since most readers won't know these names, I should explain that there are, scattered around the country, thousands of admirers of each of them: "He/she was the best teacher I had."

to discover the formal excellence or faults of this or that work. I soon saw that when done in the right way—that is, getting the students engaged in the pursuit, not imposing your predetermined notions—formal criticism is one of the best ways to lead students into loving literature by discovering how works work.

Because of the importance of the formal criticism practiced by Crane and his colleagues, "scholarship" of that kind soon captured me, and I finally chose to do my dissertation on the "form" of a novel most often proclaimed to be formless, *Tristram Shandy*. So at least one part of the Ph.D. pursuit kept the central vocation alive.

AmbitionB Aggressively Intrudes

Once I had earned the Ph.D., teaching half-time for three of the four years, my problem, like everyone else's, was to find the right job. Where should one want to teach, even if an offer arrived? I wanted to teach the way people were teaching in the "Hutchins College." And I was elated to receive an offer of a full-time position for the coming year: 3,600 bucks!

But then an offer came from Haverford College to be chairman of a new freshman composition experiment. Haverford was said by my mentors to be "the best men's college in America," so why not try it? "And besides," one of them said, presenting to AmbitionB and VainB attractive reasons for leaving, "it has a lot of connections with the Ivy League and you might be able to move on up." I strongly suspect, without any recorded proof, that the notion of "rising on the academic ladder" intruded at that point—plus a slightly higher salary ($4,200). So AmbitionB and VainB dragged Phyllis off to Haverford, and I found myself landed in a setting of competitiveness entirely different from what I'd seen at Chicago.

There were six of us assistant professors: four like me, freshly hired for the new, wonderful program, and two who'd been there a while and had been expecting to be at the center of the tenure hunt. Without its ever being said directly, we all knew that we were competing on the tenure track. Two of the six were about the most competitive, egotistical academics I've ever met. As we gathered together almost daily to discuss our work, I more and more often found myself suffering in what I would now describe as a corrupting atmosphere. If VainB had not been so vulnerable, I surely could have refused to breathe that air. But more and more I felt flooded with anxieties about not getting tenure, not getting ahead, not being the best of the six. Contempt for such thoughts continued, of course, but AmbitionB and VainB too often won.

So even though I usually enjoyed the teaching, I had two years of increased distaste for the "profession," combined with anxiety about not succeeding in it. MoralB felt rising contempt for those, including my contemptible Selves, who seemed to be thinking too much about how to get an offer from the Ivy League rather than how to teach better. And at the same time I was troubled by deep ethical questions forced on me by having decided, during my army experience, that I was a "cynical atheist"—and one who still longed for firm ethical grounding.

So ThinkerB applied for, and miraculously received, a yearlong Ford Faculty Fellowship to study "ethical philosophy on my own." We went "back West" for a full year, and it was while we were living out in California with Phyllis's family that the conflict between AmbitionB, VainB, and my deepest vocation came to a head. An offer for a department chairmanship at Earlham College arrived by telegram.

I had already been *almost* promised tenure at Haverford, and I was obviously ranked toward the top of the six aspirers. Earlham was at that time below zero in national rankings—even in the rankings of Quaker schools. Like most of my colleagues, I hadn't even heard of it until the telegram came. When I consulted Haverford colleagues about it, they just laughed contemptuously. So it was clear to me that to accept would be a stupid move, careerwise. So why even consider it? Well, the 25 percent increase in salary and the "honor" of being a department chairman tempted me to go and at least have a brief look at the unknown place, absolutely certain that I would turn it down.

After a surprisingly wonderful first day, meeting people who seemed much more committed to teaching than were my colleagues at Haverford, I stayed on to day two. And after day three, lunching and dining and holding prolonged animated discussions about teaching, I found myself saying, "These teachers care as much about teaching as the best ones in Chicago." The four or five I lunched and dined with—all of whom later became close friends—seemed to have no fake aspirations or self-centered competitive drives. That took me on to day four, which took me on to a clear decision—my only regret now being that I didn't even bother to phone Phyllis for consultation about it. (I did soon have to have an interview with the Board of Trustees, who grilled me about whether I would resist doing evangelical work for Mormonism. At least I didn't have to practice any hypocrisy about that!)

As you've seen, LOVER (backed by VainB) takes immense pride in the decision I made: to leave "the best men's college in the country" and "disappear" into Earlham College. I had found a place where no one showed concern for rewards except the loving rewards of teaching. And over our nine years there (1952–61), neither Phyllis nor I had even a moment of regret—except perhaps on occasion when Phyllis wondered what had happened to her career. But that problem would probably have been even worse if we'd stayed at Haverford.

At Earlham College

Chance intervened to make this choice even more of a triumph over VainB—in an almost comic way. President Tom Jones had told me that the offer included tenure, so I was freed from what by then I thought of as the Haverford curse: anxiety about tenure. It turned out that the president had been wrong, or perhaps just plain dishonest, in his "grant" of tenure. About four years along, a Faculty Senate committee informed me that I had *now* been granted tenure!

Thus I accidentally was spared those years of anxiety that young academics these days suffer; no matter how well they teach, if they do not publish a book, they will not get tenure. I was freed to do what writing I really wanted to do. I went on publishing very little, collecting rejection slips, but mostly freed from any nagging by VainB. Only two other Earlham teachers were doing any publication at all, so far as I knew, and the result was that I was able to read and write and teach with never a thought about how publishing might affect my career.

That noble choice of Earlham pleased Mama even less than my choice of teaching; she'd never heard of the place, nor had any of her friends. By now she was in effect 'dean of women students' at Brigham Young University (though frustrated at being denied the actual title). She was still worried about how to needle me into the right kind of career. On her first visit, strolling about the campus, the anxious sixty-four-year-old looked critically at her thirty-three-year-old "failing" son and said, "Don't you think, Wayne C., that you are completely off the academic ladder here? You could be building a genuine career elsewhere, but never here."

Again I lectured her, perhaps even quoting Jesus, on why we should pursue genuine vocations, not money, and she politely backed down.

Did I think about how choosing Earlham wiped out getting job offers elsewhere? I'm pleased to be able to say, not that I can remember. I felt officially committed to Earlham for life, and when Tom Jones said he fully expected me to be attracted elsewhere someday, I said, "Never! I want to stay here." Even when the University of Chicago, responding to national praise for my first book, offered me a named chair,[11] I turned it down, afraid that I'd be once more sucked into the competitive scramble. I finally accepted a one-year offer as a visiting professor. The LOVER knew that he would want to go back to Earlham. (Some of my dreams recorded from those years do reveal VainB's attempting, rather hopelessly, to climb a rocky mountain—and often falling down over a cliff! Some ambition was in there, somewhere.)

But within a few months back in Chicago I felt my love of that college totally restored (and the graduate department felt better than it had when I

---

11. Or what Phyllis called a berth, since it was named after George M. Pullman.

was a student). Different as the place was, I felt as much love for it as I felt for Earlham, and we decided to stay.

Haverford did not go away; it haunts VainB still, partly because I'm sure that it was not as corrupt a place as I've portrayed. It had and has many devoted teachers. But its image still sometimes produces teaching-anxiety dreams. Dreams about failed teaching have occupied VainB's nights from the beginning: texts forgotten at home, students rebelling, empty rooms, and so on. But I can think of none more vivid than this:

> I have been hired back at Haverford to receive a glorious "named chair," the Franklin D. Roosevelt Professor of Humanities. I arrive at campus and cannot find the administrative office. Cannot find my assigned office. Cannot find a catalog telling me what I am to teach. Cannot find anything. Am totally lost. Finally do find a catalog with myself listed:
>
> Wayne C. Booth, Humanities, *Latin.*
>
> Holy terror; I'm assigned to teach what I know nothing of—and it's a subject that has been mastered by everybody who is anybody!

Earlham and the Quaker environment survive in me to this day. In fact, during my first year in Chicago, I returned once each week to teach a course, I missed the place so much. For a while Phyllis and I attended Quaker services in Chicago, having been almost "converted" to Quakerism in Richmond.

WHAT KIND OF TEACHING TRIUMPHED?

Since I could never think of myself as mastering some corner of learning that every student should be forced to inhabit (see chapter 12), I tried never to dump my learning on them or even to inspire them to pursue only my kind, but rather to inspire them to pursue learning in their own corners, always somewhat differently. From the time I first read Plato's *Theaetetus*, I had loved Socrates' description of his goal in conducting genuine conversation and loved his picture of himself as teacher.

His goal is genuine "Socratic dialogue" (of course, not his own phrase). He insists that in teaching, when you hope to stimulate genuine thinking,

> do not conduct your questioning unfairly. It is unreasonable that one who professes a concern for virtue should be constantly guilty of unfairness in argument. Unfairness here consists in not observing the distinction between a debate and a conversation.[12]

---

12. Translated by F. M. Cornford (New York: Liberal Arts Press, 1957), 167.

His metaphor for the good teacher is the midwife. Though he often reveals himself practicing almost destructive midwifery as he probes others with threatening questions in order to discover what they have in their intellectual wombs, his claim that he probes them to produce *their* offspring rather than to implant his own puts it all just right:

> My concern is . . . with the soul that is in travail of birth. . . . I cannot myself give birth to wisdom . . . because there is no wisdom in me. . . . Heaven constrains me to serve as a midwife, but has debarred me from giving birth. (150b–e)

Seeing myself as a midwife hoping to give birth to ideas I don't yet have, fighting off the temptations to implant something I already know, I've sometimes annoyed students who prefer teachers who dish it all out. One freshman complained to me after class because I had changed my mind about a poem during discussion. "My father is paying ten thousand dollars a year for this place, and you didn't even get it right!" I felt like kicking her out. A "classical" colleague once complained behind my back that the students I had taught in the previous freshman course, Greek Thought and Literature, hadn't been required to learn the three terms for Greek columns. Practicing as a midwife, I had of course failed to feed them bits of essential knowledge.

The practices produced by the midwife metaphor work at all levels most of the time, from kindergarten to dissertation supervision. But I think they work best for adolescents—those who are also ready to be impregnated with the desire for an education. That's why freshman teaching was always at my center. (Should I repress VainB's impulse to add that not only did I always teach freshmen even though it was not required of me, but I always taught *five* courses per year rather than the *three* my Pullman Professorship contract specified? Even as my various moral and thinking selves honor that choice, they are shocked that VainB entertains *mentioning* it here. That's contemptible vanity. Right?)

WHAT TECHNIQUES REALLY WORKED?

This is hardly the place to insert a textbook about good teaching or lengthy quotations from my *The Vocation of a Teacher* or even a bibliography of the essays I've published about it. I'll just offer a few key examples of teaching devices, habits, or tricks that have worked, whenever I've managed to keep my bossy self in check.[13]

---

13. VainB again has plunged in, even urging me to list the lifetime teaching awards I've received. But I have no trouble slapping him down.

Lecturing at the University of Chicago

The primary emphasis has always been on getting students to teach each other—getting them to conduct the kind of conversation that Socrates is talking about. This has meant a passionate insistence on having small classes, requiring students to become acquainted with one another quickly, and enticing them to criticize productively. Haverford had hired me to help institute a "tutorial" system that required all freshmen to criticize their buddies' papers every week, in groups of three to five—in addition to their regular class attendance. I took that method with me to Earlham (my only real inheritance from Haverford except for our lifetime friends, the Gutwirths).

Did it work? My contempt for VainB won't allow me to quote from innumerable student testimonials and, of course, the bastard censors all of the negative comments I've received.

To work at teaching those multiple small groups meant that in term time, my "scholarly" aims were often totally neglected. I got little writing done during the teaching year because I was so engrossed in reading students' papers and preparing for the next day's discussions. So, you see, once more LOVER triumphed over ambition and vanity. If my mind had been primarily set on getting the next book out in order to receive an offer from one of the Ivies, I wouldn't have had time to teach properly; and most of the time I managed to postpone the writing to summertime or to the yearlong leaves that freed me to get this or that book done. And meanwhile, fortunately, everything I wrote was strongly influenced by what I had learned in the classroom.

But the discussion method does produce problems. Often I would have to hector myself before class: How can I keep George or Kashmilla from turning it all into trashy, unfocused bullshitting? That question required that I stop worrying about my own ego and start thinking hard about George's and Kashmilla's. How can I get them to take part in order to further real discussion, rather than to show off what they think they know? How can I get them to enter in a way that will take the discussion forward, rather than just in order to earn credit?

Well, one technique was to get their minds off their grades. I would tell them at the beginning of each term that their papers would not have any grades on them when returned, even though a grade would be entered into my notebook. "I hope you won't be thinking about grades but about learning to read and think and listen and write well. But if at any time you can honestly say that my keeping your paper grades secret is harming your education, you can come to me and I'll tell you the grade." I'm proud(!) to record that over the years not a single student ever came to say, "Your concealing of my grades is harming my education." They all knew that it was helping.

Another technique that worked was imposing dramatic shifts on the daily routine. If they are to learn to think independently, they must not be subjected day after day to the same lecture or discussion style. My tacit rule was to keep throwing them off balance, sometimes with deceptions that some would consider indefensible.

Examples

When the Nixon impeachment was thought to be imminent, I convinced my colleague, the nationally famous Constitution scholar, Philip Kurland, to interrupt my freshman class to announce a package of implausible events: something like "Nixon has resigned, but he has accused the vice president of committing all the sins; he has decided to sue the Supreme Court and has appointed me as legal counsel" and so on—a list of claims that any close listener would see were phony. After I had enacted my sense of shock and Kurland had left the room, I asked them to write up what they thought of those events.

Most of them accepted the account as true, and we then had a rewarding discussion of what clues they had overlooked and of what genuine listening amounts to. They then had the option of writing up their opinion of
the "experiment" or inventing a similar hoax.[14]

In an upper-level course on rhetoric, where students were seeming a bit
placid, I privately asked the one black student to help me with an experiment. Next day he arrived late to class, following my plan. I rebuked him
mildly. He answered a bit sharply. I rebuked him more angrily. After we
sparred a bit, I began to curse him, and finally he stomped out of the room
and slammed the door.

I then invited him back in, explained that it was all a hoax, and asked
them to write up an accurate account of what had occurred. A large majority reported that it was the black student who had used the excessive exple-
tives, including "fuck you," while in fact I was the one who told him to
"fuck off." His language had been utterly "clean"—though as angry in tone
as mine. I distributed copies of all the radically diverse accounts, including one by the actor and one by me. Then we discussed not just why their
accounts were so unreliable but whether they could accept mine as totally
accurate; there were in fact a couple of differences between the cooperative
actor's account and mine.

In later years I've had students tell me that this lesson in how bias works,
both in observing and reporting, was the most memorable experience of their
college years. "I learned that I couldn't trust my own opinions about everything, even when I knew 'the facts.'"

Another "technique" is so obviously helpful that it is astonishing that so
few teachers bother about it.

May 5, 2001
The real boost to my spirits, at 5 AM, was the flood of warm memories
about the dinner session we held here last night for the students in my (our)
course, "Organization of Knowledge," "OOK."[15] I had planned the din-

---

14. The better students often developed skillful hoaxes of their own. When Peter Rabinowitz,
now professor of comparative literature at Hamilton College, was in my undergraduate
poetry course, he brought a poem to class for interpretation. We all struggled with it,
and he now claims that I arrived at some sort of implausible interpretation. Then he
revealed that the poem had been constructed by choosing every fourth word from an
encyclopedia article!

15. Three others were teaching it with me: Herman Sinaiko, Bill Sterner, and—as graduate
assistant—Adam Kissel (he also is doing a good deal of editing of this book).

ner, with colleagues' agreement, worrying about whether it would "work." And it did. Most of them came, and we had animated discussion from the very beginning, mostly in groups of two to four . . . really rewarding. After more than two hours, I called them all together for a joint discussion, and that turned out to be amazingly rewarding. I got them talking about how they now judge their choice of major field, or about the Chicago experience in general. Some began with sharply critical comments on their major field (chief victims: sociology and philosophy). But then they gradually warmed up until finally they were celebrating "highs" in their experience here.

By the end it was evident that they were feeling exuberant about the "party" itself. It was clearly the kind of fun they don't get enough of; I was shocked when several of those graduating seniors said they'd never before been in a professor's home or had any social encounter. . . . One effect of it has made me consider teaching at least one course again next year. Why not? Teaching is my bag, my center—or *was* until I stopped doing it two years ago. Why not do it again, now that my hearing aids make it possible for me to hear all that the students say? [In 2004 I took it up again, with another version of OOK. And just this winter of 2005, I taught freshmen again.]

One More Example

In a yearlong senior seminar for eight students, established as a departmental experiment by Sheldon Sacks, I was attempting to get them to be more openly critical of one another's writing. So one day I performed a trick that had often proved successful in other classes: give them a piece of your own writing, without your name on it, and invite criticism of the anonymous piece.

I gave them a draft of an encomium on the Chicago Public Library—the important role it had played in my life—to be published in a forthcoming collection of attempted tributes. Seven out of the eight said something like "It feels pretentious, self-aggrandizing, heavy-handed." When I told them that I'd already sent it off to the library committee who'd asked for it, all but one agreed that I should call it back and revise. After I had accepted their advice and showed them the revised draft, they proved much more vigorous in dealing with one another's drafts.

I am tempted, of course, to add more examples of my fantastically brilliant teaching successes as they intruded on my "scholarly" ambitions. But then, to be honest, I would have to add a collection of failures, and no room would be left for any more chapters. So—just a few words about setbacks.

The Negatives

If you consulted my journals about teaching, you would be surprised at how much less affirmative they often sound than what I've written here. Teaching is a tough job. You can't say about it what some Yoga extremists say about life or the National Basketball Association says about basketball: "It's all good." Teaching yielded so many tough problems that I often felt a sense of failure and *always* felt considerable anxiety, including nightmares, especially when my first classes approached each fall. I occasionally felt something like "The strain of trying to do this well, when your antilecturing method leaves you so vulnerable to surprises day by day—that strain is so great that you ought to take up something else." The journals tend to record those bad moments. They could be summarized like this: "Woke terribly anxious about classes today. Felt like faking illness and staying home. Phyllis easily talked me out of it. Classes went wonderfully."

The negatives were not always my own weaknesses. Since becoming a teacher joins you to a community—what I've often even felt like calling my "church"—it sometimes lands you into working with those you dislike, or even hate. Rather than dwell on those bastards (I'm sure they were not as totally awful as they sometimes *seemed* to me), how about a borderliner, Saul Bellow: my hero, as an author, but highly ambiguous as a colleague.

He and I often had good times, especially in the one course we taught together. A student came to me and asked, "If Saul Bellow agreed to give me an independent course with you, on Owen Barfield, would *you* agree to join *him*?" How could I turn down a chance like that? The three hours per week for ten weeks, just the three of us passionately discussing text after text, were a sheer delight. After that, Phyllis and I had a few lively dinners with Saul and one of his nonwives, and we both felt really rewarded by the conversations.

But quite a while later I see him approaching on the sidewalk, and I move eagerly toward him.

> "Hi, Saul. How you doin'?"
>> He draws back, refuses to take my hand, and snarls,
>> "I'm never again having anything to do with you, never."
>> He starts to walk away.
>> "Why?" I almost shout.
>> "Because you misquoted me in that talk of yours last week, here on campus."
>> "Were you there?"
>> "No. But I was told about it."

He stalks away, and I never learned whether he was actually denying having made the infamous comment I had playfully quoted. It was some years before we spoke together again.

I'm glad to be able to say that memory provides far more moments of sheer fun than fully negative or ambiguous ones. And as you'd expect, that fun reached its peak whenever I received rewards like this one.

A handsome young black man driving on 53rd Street hails me from his car; he looks dimly familiar.

"Mr. Booth! You remember me? Hanford?"

"I sure do. You were in my freshman class." I don't mention my memory that he narrowly escaped washing out in that freshman year.

"Gosh, it's good to see you, Mr. Booth. I've wanted to come in many times to thank you for that class. You know—"

Pause.

"What're you up to these days, Eric?"

"I'm in graduate school. I'm in the SSA [School of Social Service Administration]. I'll have my degree, I expect, in 1980. And you know, I *know* that I wouldn't have made it if it hadn't been for the way you worked on my writing in that freshman course. I've told lots of people about that and I hope you're still doing it now."

He notices that I am pushing, not riding, my bicycle.

"You taking that someplace to get it fixed?"

"Yes."

"Well, why not let me haul it there in my car? I'd *love* to do even a little in exchange for that class."

By this time I am in such a glow of pleasure that I can hardly contain myself. Here he is, he's *making* it; his wife is teaching at a junior college to help put him through, and . . . he is now working as research assistant at SSA, helping to revise reports. And he might well not be there if I hadn't taught that course.

Is the point clear? Teaching the love of learning, learning with students as they learn with you, is one of life's—well, I want to say "salvations" or "redemptions," but Phyllis says that will turn too many of you readers off. How about just saying this: teaching is one of the best choices I've ever made. Pursuing the bliss of learning *together* doesn't mean that you don't let your honest negative opinions show when students commit errors that really matter. But you try to dramatize, day by day, how destructive it is when a teacher behaves like . . .

(The hypocritical tongue-biter—or why not call him Generous-Hearted-Booth?—dictates that I omit my favorite example of the abominable behavior of a teacher.)

In my own view—in contrast to Phyllis's—I've usually managed to resist wanting to be seen as absolutely *right*. Though I go on trying to be as close to "right" as possible, as often as possible, my goal has been to practice teaching in a way that turns others on to the search for what is "righter," as viewed from within their own souls. And sometimes it has worked, as I've managed to keep my contemptible Selves in fragile chains.

What I hope is clear throughout this rambling account is that teaching produces many moments in which you feel totally harmonized. You experience an hour or two or even more when there is not a moment's thought of internal conflict. You've found one kind of plausible harmony.

But is that the harmony we pursue throughout this book? Hardly. A half hour later the splits burst forth again as various other Selves start nagging about the faults and failures of the LOVER.

Chapter Six

The Hypocritical Mormon Missionary Becomes a Skillful Masker, and Discovers "Hypocrisy-Upward"

He said that everybody was at home in America because nobody was. Each one of us is out there every day creating himself for the crowd. The ones that start out knowing who they are, they are just repeating what they've been told.
— The Best of Jackson Payne *by Jack Fuller*

Literary egotism consists in playing the role of self, in making oneself a little more natural than nature, a little more oneself than one was a few minutes before.
—Paul Valéry

Man is a make-believe animal—he is never so truly himself as when he is acting a part.
—William Hazlitt

Hypocrisy is the highest compliment to virtue.
—François de La Rochefoucauld

Man is least himself when he talks in his own person. Give him a mask and he will tell the truth.
—Oscar Wilde

The human face is really like one of those Oriental gods: a whole group of faces juxtaposed on different planes; it is impossible to see them all simultaneously.
—Marcel Proust

Professor Lambert hates sham, as I do (I wonder, sometimes, if I am not all show, with no real qualities—I try hard not to be a hypocrite).
—Wayne C., College Freshman, November 1938

One of my reasons for liking Bergson is the beautiful way in which he suits my recent 'conversion' back to spirituality, my reversion from materialism.
—Elder Wayne Booth, September 1942,
illicitly reading philosophy while a missionary

For several days now my left knee has screamed at me as I walk. This morning, as I limped into our university library, I saw a colleague far across the hall and quickly stopped limping—and walked toward him smiling cheerfully but giving myself much greater pain than when limping.

We had a brief, good chat about his essay on Aristotle's *Metaphysics*, and I walked away still without limping, showing no signs of the pain and aging I felt. At least I think so. Turning the corner toward the elevator, now out of sight, I allowed my more honest "Self" to limp again to reduce the pain.

Was that show of total health a masking of my inner self? Obviously—or at least I masked one of my selves, the pained one. I was playing a role, enacting a pain-free character, pretending to be in better health than I was. I did not want to plague my colleague—not a close friend but a scholar I admire—with my minor troubles. I presented to him the healthy scholar; for all I know he may have been concealing his own pains. Thus we both acted out our roles—just as we all act out our diverse roles much of the time.

Is that kind of hypocrisy defensible or a morally contemptible gesture that ought to be labeled as cheating? I have friends who think it contemptible. I think it defensible, and in this chapter I'll explain some of the origins of that defense of "hypocrisy-upward." (If the notion that some forms of hypocrisy are defensible bothers you, have a look at your classical Greek dictionary: the word originally just meant "acting out," as on the stage. And if you don't think that some "acting out" in our everyday lives contributes to well-being, have a look at the last time you shaved, or put on lipstick, or bit your tongue when speaking out would have been disastrous. You still may want to call the chapter something like "A Hypocritical Moralist Struggles to Defend Himself.")

Anecdote

When visiting American Fork in the summer break from two years of college (Mama moved us to Provo for her new job), I accidentally left my copy of H. G. Wells's *Outline of History* in Gramma Booth's house. She and Aunt Relva read it, or at least some of it. They were appalled, and they anxiously grilled me.[1]

---

1. As you encounter the flood of journal entries in this chapter, you may join some readers who have almost shouted, "Too many." Others have said they wish for even more. To

Mid-July, 1940

"The Bible is the word of God," Grandmother said, "therefore anything in disagreement with the story of creation is wrong."

Of course I was silent. I hadn't the courage to say, "I don't believe the story of creation, I believe in evolution. I admire Wells for his scientific attitude." I disliked being hypocritical, but I almost had to be silently so, as they would have thought me abandoned to the devil if I had said what I believed. . . . I hate to be around people who force me to be a hypocrite. (I don't mind lying, factually, in the least, but to have to disown one's beliefs for unworthy reasons—fear of dislike, fear of a scene, laziness—is terrible; I don't seem to be able to get away from it.)

Occasionally I find that young hypocrite writing a diatribe in his diary against other people's hypocrisy, even while providing loads of evidence about his own. (He had never even heard of Aristotle's *phronesis* or of the grand Jesuitical tradition of "casuistry" or of Machiavellian defenses of political lying, *virtù*—all three of which could be labeled as defenses of hypocrisy-upward.) On August 19, 1940, after writing a lengthy encomium of Plato's *Apology*, he laments,

I wish I had the honesty and strength to tell people what they don't know. I've tried it (that is, I've tried to point out to some people that I *think* they display hypocrisy, dishonesty, or lack of wisdom) but because of my youth, in part, and in part because of the unpleasantness of what I say, I am put down as being presumptuous. I'm going to do more of it—and I'm going to try to know a few things before I die, although I suppose I'll always be in doubt. If I can avoid becoming self-complacent, "knowing," as hypocritically as others, I will have done a lot. If I can help others to be honest in facing their ignorance, I'll have done more.

So far we see him employing the term only in its popular and utterly pejorative sense. But without knowing it, he is wrestling with the borderline between defensible and indefensible posing.

On August 26, 1941, after reading *Crime and Punishment* and speculating about Raskolnikov's immoral behavior, I recorded how my irrigation-companion and I were cheating the university with our reported hours (see chapter 2). Then I wrote,

---

me, the very quantity dramatizes one key point about my life and this *Life:* the obsession with "getting it all down." That *is* my life. So—just skip at will.

Elder Booth on a mission

Yesterday I gave the "theme thought" in the Sunday School officers and teachers meeting. I hadn't much time to prepare . . . but I believe I gave a good 12–14 minute talk, on honesty, of all things. I didn't pull punches but gave them what I thought (within minor limits of maintaining silence on some things)—consequently I had no difficulty expressing myself. If teachers only would be honest with their pupils "what a great splash that would be. . . ."[2]

I find myself inclined to let ends justify means, to a certain degree. That is, honest as I try to be to myself, I often don't hesitate to lie to others when I think it will help them, which is often. This 'concession' used to irk me terribly—it still does in principle—but I have decided one can be honest in important things, [practice] personal integrity in matters of self-analysis, etc., and still allow a little slipping at times. Of course this slipping hardly ever goes beyond saying I like your hat, when I don't really.

2. Note the parentheses: he is being *slightly* dishonest as he preaches on honesty. Obviously it has not yet occurred to the nineteen-year-old that all successful teachers do some posing; to succeed they must exercise some skill in performance.

How did ThinkerB land in all this messy thinking about hypocrisy, when he had been practicing it for most of his life and knew of so many others practicing it as daily routine?

I don't know the answer, but I do know why the thinking then came to a head. He accepted a "call" to serve two years as a Mormon missionary in the North Central States Mission.[3] That signing on shocked most of those who knew him intimately. He was not commanded to accept it. He just decided to, after internal conflict. As he put it to himself and to skeptical friends but never to the Church authorities, he was not going "out there" to "get people ducked into the baptismal water" but "to do good in the world" and "to start liberalizing the Church from within." But his days and nights were full of anxiety about how much hypocrisy such a decision entailed. His family members were pushing hard for acceptance. But his rising doubts about many Church doctrines and practices argued against it. Most painful was the internal suspicion that the decision to become a missionary was tainted by the fact that it would postpone his being drafted into the war. (Missionaries, as "clergymen," were not subject to the draft.)

> *May 17, 1941*
> The big objection in my mind is the imminence of the draft (and war?) and the questions, "Have I let the possibility of being drafted influence my decision to go on a mission? Am I using a mission, unconsciously, as a means of avoiding my responsibilities as a citizen?" It doesn't matter so much what people think, but, although I scorn to think of myself lacking integrity, I can't be sure that my decision is entirely ulterior-motive-free. I don't think it is, though. I almost wish they would lower the draft age to 20 [he's 20], to relieve me from making any moral decision.

He inevitably wrestles with that dilemma again and again, though usually coming out strongly with reasons like this, written a month later. As you read, I wish you could hear his contrasting actual words in this or that encounter with friends or Church officials.

> I hope to get, for possibly the only time in my life, the feeling which comes only to those who devote their whole time to the service of others (useful service or not). . . . I feel that I have begun to synthesize a philosophy which can prove useful to people in leading their lives. . . . I have *started* to realize a

---

3. Some of what follows is borrowed from my article, "Confessions of a Hypocritical (Ex)-Missionary," *Sunstone* 21, no. 1 (March 1998): 25–36. Responses to the article have been mixed, some expressing anger for what they see as an effort to undermine faith.

harmony between spirituality and a quest for learning, between science and religion, which has completely changed, in form, at least, my rank skepticism of a few months ago. . . . I think I can at least help a little in making available to people . . . the rather inspiring teaching of the L.D.S. concerning intelligence, eternal progression; second, the enlightened opinions of leading men, LDS & non-LDS concerning the realness of human communication with God, the greatness of human destiny, etc. [The confusion of the labels is real.]

If I cannot do even this happy message, at least I can stimulate people . . . to read and think about . . . these things. . . . If I . . . can inspire many people to a belief in the need for a working toward human betterment in this life, and incidentally preparing for improvement in a possible next life, I would have done more good than all the missionaries who spend their time trying to get people baptised.

The key moment of deciding about the mission was a long conversation with Professor Poulson:

Scene: The northwest corner of the Brigham Young University farmland, where I irrigate the farm, for sixteen to eighteen hours a day, sitting at the end of the furrows and reading my pocket Plato as I wait for the water to arrive. This evening, Professor Poulson stops his car as he sees me pulling up a headgate. As the water starts flowing, I move over to the car, put one hip boot on his fender, and we talk and talk—on through the beautiful sunset, on into the twilight, slapping mosquitoes, talking, talking, mainly about the Church.

Poulson: Don't throw out the baby with the bathwater. You keep leaping ahead into areas you know nothing about. The fact that some Church leaders are dishonest doesn't mean that the Church is valueless. Every institution, including every church, has some dishonest leaders. Surely you're not going to relapse into saying that because the Church claims to be divinely led and its leaders are clearly not divine, it must be valueless when judged in human terms.

Wayne: No, but I don't see any reason to . . .

Poulson: You shouldn't be looking only for reasons *to.* You should be looking only for genuine reasons *not* to. Here you are, raised in a marvelously vital, generous-spirited tradition, surrounded by an astonishing number of virtuous, intelligent people whose Church has helped them find ways of living effectively. You come along and ask them for reasons *to* do what they are doing! What you should ask for, before giving up anything they offer you, is really sound reasons against going along.

Wayne: But I just can't stand even *sitting* in Church without speaking up when somebody talks nonsense. Last Sunday they were talking about personal devils, and some of them really believed that stuff.

We don't bother to repeat the story of the professor's interrogation in Salt Lake City about the devils (see chapter 2). Poulson, at age fifty-five, owns what he calls "the best collection of books on Mormon history." He has surreptitiously shown me the collection, tucked away in his basement.

We talk on into the dark. . . . I can still feel myself standing there, chilling a bit in my wet socks and boots, worn out after twenty hours of work (not hard labor, admittedly), changing from one foot to the other—and exhilarated beyond description: this is what life can be, this is one of the great times. I'll stay here forever if he'll only go on.

Poulson: What you should be doing, instead of trying to undermine other men's beliefs, is discovering beliefs that you yourself can live by. And you'll find most of them being taught right in the Church by the people you're attacking. That's why I keep saying, "Show me a better Church." I'm not determined to stay with this one if you'll find me another one that does as much good and that has fewer corrupt leaders. . . .
Wayne: But that's not good enough. Don't we have the right to hope for an institution that is at least honest with itself? I long for a cause that I can give myself to as fully as believers give themselves to the Church—like my father and my grandparents did.
Poulson: Well, I'm sure you can find it if you want to badly enough. . . . *This* one could easily become *that* one to you if you want it to badly enough. This Church has plenty of members like that; all causes do. . . . What they really need is a corps of missionaries who know everything that's wrong about the Church—and who yet don't care because they know that it can be an instrument for good in their hands.

In the dark now, the moon not quite ready to rise, the stars brighter than most of us ever see these days, the "old" man's gray hair is faintly visible inside the car. When I ask whether he is suggesting that a half-believer like me should go on a mission, he answers sharply.

Poulson: Why not? If you could work not to get the people under the water in the greatest possible numbers but to tune in to them where you find them and help them to grow—why not? Can you think of a better way to spend two years than setting out to help other people with no concern about your own welfare? That's what the missionary system is, at its best.

. . . If you worked hard, if you thought hard, and if you could keep from worrying too much about your own reputation—you might make a real difference for a lot of people.

After following Poulson's advice and announcing his acceptance, the internally divided young man continued to get complaints from those who knew he could never honestly say, "I *know* that Joseph Smith is the only true modern prophet," or, "I *know* that the Book of Mormon was translated from gold plates given to Joseph Smith by the Angel Moroni."[4] Actually the budding hypocrite revealed those doubts to only a tiny percentage. And he naturally worried about whether he would be able to endure many more of the hypocritical moments he was facing.

> *Sept. 24, 1941 [still three months to go]*
> Will a mission be an endurable thing for me? Will I actually help people or will I only make them unhappy? Can I serve two years in an organization such as the missionary system is, doubting as I do, and not have irreconcilable differences arise between my mission presidents, my companions, and me? If the differences don't come to a head, will I be spoiled as a thinking being . . . as thousands of missionaries have been? Will the insidious self-hypnotism ["conversion"] get me, too? Will I start out by making concessions for the sake of peace, and end up believing in the things I have conceded to? Or will I come back bitter against the church as now functioning?
>
> These are important questions, and they have me worried: but I am determined to work out a harmony without compromising my integrity or antagonizing my colleagues. I believe the missionary system needs me.

It was not long before he discovered that he had landed himself in more turbulent waters than he could have predicted. Even Poulson, who had served as a totally unhypocritical orthodox missionary before doing the historical research that destroyed for him the divine origin of Joseph Smith's golden plates, could not have foreseen what this "second-generation liberal" would encounter. Unlike the devout younger Poulson, I became a missionary only *pretending* to be committed to the *official* mission.

As I lived every hour with companions and supervisors, including many who took literal acceptance as even more important than love or charity or

---

4. Note for non-Mormons: Joseph Smith founded the Church on the claim that God had led him to a holy text recorded on gold plates—a history of some of the "Twelve Tribes" who came to America many centuries before Columbus (some by submarine!).

any of the other virtues, I became submerged in the daily task of translating my internal language into public language that would not harmfully offend either my missionary companions or the non-Mormons they addressed.

Sometimes my behavior then appears now as quite impressive hypocrisy-upward: balancing inner beliefs and external goods. But often it was not just dubious activity but downright cowardice or fraud. Many moments of hypocrisy can hardly be defended as constructive, as "upward." How could I ever defend my having acceded, in Cincinnati, to the local Mormon practice of refusing to allow blacks to partake of the holy sacrament in the chapel? We were ordered to deliver the "sacred bread and water" to the only family of black members, *at their cottage*, rather than allowing them to partake of it in the chapel. I did protest, mildly, to supervisors, with no effect. Why didn't I organize a real protest? Even now I fantasize about doing that and, of course, then being renounced and sent back to Utah to be drafted. What a hero that would have been, in a *LIFE* I could now take pride in writing! Instead we meet a coward, a "pious" cheater—only occasionally "doing good in the world."

The waffling, posing, sweet-talking ranged widely, going far beyond the everyday, unavoidable masking that most, maybe all, missionaries practice in order to project total piety from the podium. For me it was a daily, even hourly, suppression of my own true beliefs, intellectual and sometimes moral. It entailed systematic probing for rhetorical devices for defending or explaining this or that doctrine in ways that I could accept, *metaphorically*, while hoping to lead literalists to deal with it more thoughtfully.

RHETOROLOGY DISCOVERED

What interests me most about all that now is the training it gave me in the kind of rhetorical probing for sufficient shared ground that allows genuine dialogue to take place. Whatever we call it, this is not the mere practice of persuasion (what the rhetor does, honestly or dishonestly) and not the mere study of how people persuade (what the academic rhetorician does) but the study and practice of how to interrelate conflicting rhetorics: "How can I reconcile their rhetoric with mine, their surface codes with what I am sure are shared beliefs that are more important than all those literal claims? How can I get each side to understand the other?"

To practice that extreme effort at dialogue requires, of course, a lot of skill in hypocritical posing, especially when the speaker knows, for example, that the very words "Book of Mormon" carry opposite meanings for him and for his audience. "Inwardly I disagree with you strongly, on many crucial points, but outwardly I must seem *not* to, hoping that we can move closer and closer to some point where we *really* agree—and thus can make some progress together."

I gradually got better and better at that form of posing. Sometimes it was still in ways that many a devout Mormon would damn as just plain fraud, but often it deserved my adjective "upward"—as do the posings of leaders of all churches whenever they leave their "everyday" world behind and present a persona far more pious than the one who shopped for cars yesterday.

It's true that the young hypocrite accomplished little in pursuing his goal of "liberalizing the Church from within." But he learned how to pray in public in a language that joined the literalists while not violating his own meditations. He learned how to give sermons that woke people up, undermined their clichés, and led them to dwell on the central virtues and limits of Mormonism, without leading (most of the time) to angry attacks against him for heterodoxy. He learned how to conduct official funerals without producing annoying and pointless debate about whether there is literal life on "the other side." In short, he learned from the orthodox what was really valuable in their orthodoxy.

He did so well at all that posing that the mission president chose him (to VainB's great pride) as number one missionary: mission secretary at headquarters in Chicago. And he was all the while training himself, without knowing it, for a lifetime pursuit of rhetorical inquiry and the ethical borderlines it always lands us on.

That cheerful account of what he learned is much simpler and more affirmative than the picture he often gave in his journal. Reading the journal entries now, I often see him as totally discouraged, deeply depressed—never suicidal, but often thinking about giving up the mission.

Yet he managed to slog it out for two squirming years, wrestling almost daily in his journal over the question of just which religious ideas, if any, he could embrace. Like the history of many probers through their youth, his account reveals great swings from almost total rejection of all religious belief to excited recovery of ways to reconcile reason and faith. Sometimes his reports strike me now as silly or clumsy, sometimes as a bit pathetic, sometimes admirably insightful. Though he often defends his hypocrisy-upward, he never thinks very hard about its difference from harmful fraud.

And meanwhile his commitment to Mormonism constantly felt challenged by his commitment to "scientific" truth and to political service. It's always as if his Selves were challenging one another: "If you really care most deeply about genuine, rational truth, you ought to quit; *but* if you care most deeply about human welfare, now or in the future, you should continue." "If you want most strongly to avoid the sin of deceiving others, you must quit; *but* if you care most about improving their lives, even while you are posing, you should continue."

One comfort came from the discovery of how many great thinkers supported religion, denying the hard clash between reason and faith. As he read more and more in philosophers and mystics and religious psychologists—Plato, Henri Bergson, Aldous Huxley, Carl Jung, and so on—he experienced what he called a "feeling of oneness and sympathy for all life and especially all human life, the feeling of a creative and impelling force greater than oneself." He was especially grateful for Jung's saying "that he has never known a psychological problem that was not essentially a religious problem." What a relief, he writes, to "find that religion can actually be defended by fully rational thinkers."

But the threats of "hard reason," according to his narrow definition, were never far removed. In entry after entry he struggled to reduce the cognitive dissonance between "religious belief" and "rationally defensible belief." As he went on reading—Joyce, Kafka, Whitehead, Santayana, William James—he inevitably continued to wrestle with his critical view of the Church. As his first long year drew to a close, he had the idea of organizing Church liberals.

> If all the so-called liberals . . . could organize . . . some beneficial changes could be wrought (might even be just plain made, without having to be wrought, but I'm sure it would be much more effective if they were wrought).

But then, in a long fascinating paragraph, which I shall spare you most of, he described the differences among the liberals and concluded that

> the group who think as I do probably numbers no more than twenty at the most (and of course this is the *right* way, and all the others will eventually come to our position: of course!). Yes, we [the larger group of "liberals"] are a hodge-podge of mal-contents, and we'll probably never get together.

While engaging in these inner intellectual battles, his external behavior mainly remained "pure." He complied publicly—most of the time—with all of the commandments. Only rarely does he mention actual violations of Mormon codes, though there were quite a few. One brief example:

Sept. 5, 1942
We went [four missionaries taken as guests] to a highly picturesque place called the Beachcomber . . . the food was delicious and exotic. . . . Tea was served—and drunk only by me and Mr. Burgener [our host]: I was not going to let a foolishly specific interpretation of the word of wisdom spoil my enjoyment of the meal. If the other missionaries had not been along I'm sure I would have accepted Mr. B's invitation to join him in a delicious rum preparation, but I could not. (The tea was enough non-conformity for any Casper Milquetoast, anyway.)

His decision to take a few classes at the University of Chicago could be considered a much greater violation of Church rules than any glass of wine or cup of tea could be: it was going off into threatening territory. While he complied with all the physical commandments, the hypocrisy-upward was almost always totally intellectual.

> *January 31, 1943*
> Santayana, withal his naturalism, says more favorable things about religion—even dogmatic religion—than I would be able to. What is worse, he convinces me of the justice of his comments, thus making me apologetic for all the time I've spent condemning my religion and my people.
>
> How to know where to draw lines, that is the goal of the Life of Reason, and because S. has never had to break away from a conventional belief on his own initiative, he doesn't realize the difficulties involved in drawing lines; he acts as though any halfway sensible person would be able to work out his compromises gracefully and quietly, without fanfare even in a diary.

Naturally the feeling that even his hypocrisy was wicked often almost choked him.

> *March 16, 1943*
> In trying to detect any particular theme running through my dreams, I find only one: I am a fake and in danger of being found out. One night I am back at my irrigation, doing my usual half-hearted job, not knowing where to go next nor when the water will get out of control, cheating the university (which, in reality, I did); next night I am claiming five pictures in an art gallery as my own, when in reality they are not. I stalk through my dream trying to avoid questions about my methods of work, knowing I cannot answer them intelligently. I even forget which are "mine" and am in fear that someone will ask me, and so on. Another night I am a crook going to high school, and I get discovered and have to shoot my way out.

> *April 6, 1943*
> One possibility [in explaining these dreams, considered, rather belatedly, after trying out some other interpretations] is the essential hypocrisy of my present position.

What I find most revealing about his daily record of inner turmoil is how all of it slowly began to resolve itself: in more aggressive and self-aware practices of rhetorology. Without quite knowing it, the young man was discovering the new passion (call it a "religion," if you please) that informs so much of my professional and private life today.

October 2, 1943

I neglected to mention, I believe, the speech I gave at the Northshore Ward last week. I was in my old stride, at my best: perfectly at ease and composed, I yet had them intensely interested all the way—one can tell such things—and I *think* that I really made them think. My subject was, "Some of the faults which prevent Mormons from making what they could of themselves." (It was never thus expressed, but that's what it was.) I gave it to them straight, and I believe there was only one member who did not like it; and even he seemed interested. I am a little disappointed with myself for not having given more such good accounts of myself while on my mission. . . .

I hardly ever mention my mission and my opinion of it here [in the journal]. That is, I suppose, partly because I am generally quite discouraged about the little I have accomplished. I enjoy myself around my Mormon associates—more now than ever before.[5] I think the Mormon people are good people and I think that I am what I am, including the good parts, largely as a result of the Mormon environment. Yet I have been discouraged by the difficulties in the way of intellectual improvement among my people. The Mormon ideology is so firmly rooted in superstition that it seems impossible ever to separate the two: despite all my apologetics, one is simply not a Mormon unless one believes in the divinity of the Book of Mormon, any more than one is a Christian unless one believes in the literal Christ Jesus. . . .

In general I would say that I am glad I came on the mission, though it has been far different from anything I expected. . . . [But then] the last year or so of any active life always seems very valuable in retrospect.

I still have in mind doing a book about and for Mormons, analyzing our faults, proposing future attitudes, clearing away dead beliefs. . . .

My big problem now is: shall I continue with my people as a hypocrite, shall I openly express my doubts and take my chances with my group, or

---

5. My favorite memories about such enjoyment involve "Elder Duff Hanks"—Marion Hanks, who later became a Church official. As I wrote to Phyllis from Paris, on December 8, 1944, the subject of redundancy somehow came to mind, and I recorded a memory: "At a conference, someone said, 'Nobody likes an arrogant missionary.' And I mumbled, hardly expecting anyone to hear, 'Don't be redundant,' meaning, of course, that Arrogant and Missionary meant the same thing. Duff looked at me and said, 'I don't know what you mean,' and I tried to explain and failed. . . . After we became good friends he still accused me of being a man who enjoyed too much throwing big words around without bothering to have them mean anything." That certainly wasn't good rhetorology, if Duff was right.

Missionary companions (Marion "Duff" Hanks, *left*)

shall I completely break away . . . ? As I see it now, the last named is completely impossible: I love too many Mormons.

He fails to add, "And am loved by too many."

With the "highly successful" mission drawing to a close, the inner conflict intensified. He went on reading and reading and reading, hardly ever in the scriptures. He fell in love with and memorized Blake's "London" and quoted it entirely in the journal, commenting on the mind-forged manacles that he felt still binding him.

In every cry of every man,
In every Infant's cry of fear
In every voice, in every ban,
The mind-forg'd manacles I hear.

Jan. 7, 1944
"We are all conscript minds, but in different armies. And none of us are striving to be free, but each to make his own conscription universal." Santayana is right; Blake is right. Yet there are some who work at least most of the manacles free—some who become conscientious objectors in the conscription of the mind. (Block that metaphor!) If I didn't think that I had, in part, cast off some of the manacles, I would have less hope of ever achieving any degree of greatness of spirit. But the distance ahead is indicated by nothing more than by my own "complicity" in the Jewish matter [the news about the Nazi atrocities was getting clearer and clearer]. With all my sincere horror and sympathy, with all my subscriptions to Refugee societies and my talking and debate, with all my reiterated concern about a society that allows mass brutality and does nothing until attacked, I find myself guilty, as I have found myself guilty a hundred times before, on the score of personal selfishness of the sort that has caused the war, personal desire for acclaim of the sort that breeds politicians and Hitlers, intolerance of the sort that persecutes Jews. . . .

Musing in this way leads one easily—unless one is careful—into nonsense about original sin. . . . Very few can ever maintain a true central position: man is neither good nor bad; he is good and bad. He is eternally damned and he has eternal possibilities of "salvation." Mankind as a whole will not go down to bestiality tomorrow, to please [Albert Jay] Nock or [Alfred] Kazin. . . . Nor will mankind achieve tomorrow any sort of Brave New World, with everyone being super-human, not even with social ills eliminated, not even with war eliminated (I'm afraid). But I know empirically that men can improve (I have actually improved, myself). They can learn; they can sublimate their selfish desires (to use a corny phrase). They can, in short, progress, whether they have done so or not in the past.

And with this, the young unbeliever who still believed in the Mormon doctrine of "progress," yet also in "the validity of the scientific method" and the continuing triumphs of science, in "the possibility of development of a beautiful spirit of man," in "free will" (though "science" would seem to threaten this one especially strongly), in the moral truth that "it is always in all cultures wrong to hurt others," and in the claim that with all its faults the Mormon Church was still one of the best, one of the most "true"—that young man, radically confused not just about the problem of original sin but about almost everything, completed his assigned two years and was belatedly drafted into World War II.

For two long years, then, he was learning what it takes to practice benign hypocrisy on an intellectual and emotional borderline. Most other skeptical Mormons he knew either gave up their skepticism and returned to orthodoxy or pushed it further and broke with the Church. He chose, as I still choose, to pursue the ground *shared* by the orthodox and the doubters, living daily with troublesome soul-splits. Just as he "prays" to "God" with full "devotion," hoping for "salvation" (grant him his definitions all the way), so I am now a "devoted" "Mormon"—violating some of the codes every day and almost always practicing hypocrisy-upward when I'm with Mormon friends or relatives.[6]

AFTER THE MISSION

The borderline straddling went on, inevitably, even when the two years of totally imposed hypocrisy were over. A few weeks after returning to Utah, he wrote the following entries.

Feb. 4, 1944, [home from mission]
Chronological table of insignificant events:
Jan. 19, testimonial for me at mission home [in Chicago], with everyone pouring out praise in completely unbelievable quantities. Acutely embarrassing, even to think of it now.
Jan. 31, homecoming address, conciliating all forces quite successfully— and compromisingly. [Obviously he's thinking of hypocrisy-upward but naturally employing less troublesome language.]

Feb. 5, 1944
B.Y.U. would like me to teach here after the war. . . . I remain completely undecided, as there are so many advantages and disadvantages. I think

---

6. The ambiguities I see in all religious commitment are dramatized by the "prayer" I have for some years had pinned on the shelf above my desk: "ALLOW THE DAY TO *FLOW!* LEAVE THE FRUITS IN THE HANDS OF A (RELATIVELY INDIFFERENT ABOUT THE DETAILS, BUT IN THE LONG RUN [THE ETERNAL RUN] GENUINELY LOVING) *GOD!*"

Christensen [who was recommending me] was a little put out at me when I suggested that I was afraid of working at B.Y.U. I implied that I thought it would be hard on a man's integrity, to say nothing of the stifling effect on his intellectual abilities. I didn't mean to have him take it personally, but of course the implication was there, and he did not miss it. However, he is too intelligent to take offense at anything as well grounded in truth as my expressed fears of BYU influence. Finally he confessed that he *sometimes* felt that he *had* been poisoned by his many years here. I really don't think he has been, but I might be, since my moral courage is still unknown, if not proved deficient, already.

Do you need more evidence that you're dealing here with a lifetime hypocrite? I could go on quoting, into my thirties and forties and fifties—and on to the smile I put on for a grocery clerk yesterday when I felt that she had really insulted me. Or I could use, as further evidence for my case about the universality of hypocrisy, "totally honest" Phyllis's professional behavior. She sometimes poses, with a client, as totally cheerful when in fact she's feeling blue.

Back to the young hypocrite: Why did he not feel guilty—most of the time—about the hypocrisy implied by the "accommodation to the audience" required to survive as a missionary? Because, I think, he unconsciously had discerned that hypocrisy-upward is one of the essentials that makes the world go round. From Aristotle on through Quintilian and into modern times, rhetorical theorists have discussed—almost always superficially—just how much accommodation is ethical. The short answer is this: accommodate your means, hold fast to your ends—your convictions and purposes. But every rhetor knows how hard it is to draw a clear line between accommodation and selling out.

Why do I not feel guilty even now—except sometimes—about the innumerable other "accommodations" to the audience that my rhetorological inquiries have required? I think it was and is because that young man and I have been simultaneously "worshipping," or at least trying to serve, the deepest of all human values: understanding—sympathetic, serious listening to others—which almost always requires at least some biting of tongues, some posing. It is the rhetorological attempt to enter the spiritual domain of other human beings. Nothing we ever work at, I came to believe, is more important than the drive not just to maintain peace with rivals or enemies or misguided friends, not just to tolerate them generously, not just to condescend to them with a benign smile or hide something they would hate, but to understand them, to learn to think with them while assisting them to think with you in return.

That faith abides, and it informs many of the best moments of my life. It often enables me even to forget, for a while, my many divisions of Self.

And the role of Mormonism in that faith continues. Just as your deepest faith—whether "religious" or "atheist" or "agnostic"—penetrates all that you do, so what I sometimes call "the good side of Mormonism" penetrates my life and will be with me till I die.

Chapter Seven

The Puritan Preaches at the Luster While the Hypocrite Covers the Show

My mind and my body hate each other.

—Charlie Brown in *Peanuts*

Our souls are hideously subject to the conditions of our animal nature!

—George Meredith, *The Egoist*

The expense of spirit in a waste of shame
Is lust in action; and, till action, lust
Is perjured, murderous, bloody, full of blame,
Savage, extreme, rude, cruel, not to trust.

—Shakespeare, Sonnet 129

[In eternity] . . . worms shall try
That long preserved virginity:
And your quaint honour turn to dust;
And into ashes all my lust.

—Andrew Marvell, "To His Coy Mistress"

Make me chaste and continent, but not just yet.

—St. Augustine

You don't have to be taught that you feel desire. You do have to learn what to do about it.

—Eugene Goodheart, *Confessions of a Secular Jew*

I often have wondered whether the fact that I've had only one "consummated affair" in my life—my marriage to Phyllis—should just wipe out this chapter. How can full monogamy in two descendants of polygamists be anything but boring? Or does the fact of my having had "real sex" with only one beloved woman grant the chapter an interesting escape from the floods of boring accounts of *unloving* sex? Probably not. My hope is not that my routine masturbative escapes from doing harm can prove interesting but that the perpetual battle between Puritan-Booth and LusterB will prove at least representative of this book's theme. I can't resist imagining that even the most aggressive womanizers have experienced some dim echoes of my conflicts.

You decide now whether to skip forward.

Like every "normal" male, I experienced sexual arousals and lustful temptations early on. And like all those raised in Puritan cultures, I was hectored from the very beginning to believe that to be lustful was a sin—"naughty." As Christ and President Carter put it, to *think* lustfully is as sinful—well, maybe *almost* as sinful—as to act it out. No one even hinted when I was a boy that, after marriage, sex would be not merely OK but almost divine. I can't remember ever wishing to have been born a few decades earlier when the Mormon polygamy doctrine would have taught me, implicitly, The more the better. No. From earliest memories on, the message was: *All sex (and thought about sex) before marriage is sinful, and after that it's purely for procreation.*

> *Age Four (most of what follows is memory; the journals are silent until late teens)*
> Mama is drying me after bathing me in the round, zinc-plated tub in front of the kitchen fire (we have no bathroom). She stands me on an old trunk and dries me, coming to my balls.[1] I giggle, delighted. She rebukes me sharply. I have done something very naughty, something I must never do again.

---

1. My word for them then? I'm pretty sure it was.

Age Four-and-a-Half

I am playing with neighbor kids—one boy, two girls—in a shed behind our apartments. We begin exploring our crotches, some of us pretending to be doctors. Mama somehow catches us—and I am in the doghouse for what feels like weeks.

Age Six

Grampa Booth and I are peeing together in the police station toilet. I lean forward hoping to see his penis—the first (except mine) I've ever seen. Even Daddy has kept his parts private. Grampa snarls at me, "What you think you're doin'?" and twists his body away.

Age Seven

I am playing with Cousin Lucy, one year younger, around the vegetable cellar at Grampa's. She is visiting from Idaho—I always long for these visits, with the intense games and quarrels she and I engage in for hours at a time. I am coaxing her to let me see under her dress, under her panties. She won't. I still coax. She resists. I playfully try to pull up her dress. She gets angry. I stalk away, trying to look proud but knowing that I have been very naughty.

From Age Five Until Phyllis Turned Up

Throughout my childhood and youth, I can remember trying to catch glimpses of the vulvas of naked babies and of the breasts of women. (I don't think I then had any term for what I was seeking to see. Crotch? I don't think so.)

Some women back then still nursed their babies openly in Church services, and I couldn't resist twisting around to stare at them, with Mama jerking me back straight. Was I actually aroused? Can't remember. In fact, I can't remember having an actual erection at any time until my teens, though there are many memories of mysterious feelings in my groin.

Age Nine or Ten

I ask Mama why I sometimes, when I squeeze my knees together lying in bed, feel a funny feeling "in my stomach." Can't remember what she said, but her manner was embarrassed, dodgy.

Ninth Grade

Two friends and I have figured out a way to get our first full view of female bodies. Our gymnasium has an attic. We sneak into it when no one is around and grind out a peephole over the girls' shower room. Then, at the right hour of the day, we crawl together and peer down at the girls as they shower. What a revelation!

Would the longing to see breasts and genitals have been less if I'd been raised in a culture that permitted nude statues and paintings in museums and television? I think so. At least I'd have known what other people's bodies look like.

Knowledge about Sex

Unlike almost all American kids these days, the Mormon boy was given absolutely no information or instruction about sex—except that even to mention it was forbidden.[2] But then things started to happen, breaking the silence.

Age Ten

I have noticed that my Aunt Zina seems to be wearing a pillow under her dress, on her stomach. Is she ill? A bit later I learn that she has just had a baby, her second child. Could that pillow have been it? I feel that I must now find out about all that, and I corner Mama in her bedroom (which she shares with six-year-old Lucille). "Mama, am I right in thinking that babies are not really delivered by storks?" She is fairly frank about it: babies do indeed come out of their mamas' "tummies." Nothing is said, though, about how babies are really made. God creates them.

Surely by age ten I should have heard enough even from other kids to know all about it. Maybe I had, but I certainly had no sense of knowing anything about *human* birth until that day. On the other hand, I must have been fully informed, in a sense *unconsciously*, since we were in a "farming culture"; I had witnessed the birth of calves and piglets. How could my mind fail to relate that to childbirth!

The passion to learn what one couldn't talk about lasted a long time. Why, for example, is the following memory one of the most vivid of my entire life?

Age Eleven

Uncle Joe is to take our cow Blackie to the bull, and after I coax a bit, I am allowed to go along. We walk her three blocks to where the bull is, with me

---

2. When I was writing the first draft here, I assumed that the suppression of sex talk would be surprising to anyone not raised in an enclosed culture like mine. Instead it's been surprising to hear reader after reader report similar silence; one, a Catholic, reports his ignorance as lasting much longer than mine.

wondering all the way about what is going to happen. I watch in utter amazement as the bull mounts her, all of us stooping and squinting to see how the huge penis enters; this is my first sure knowledge of how impregnation takes place.

ADOLESCENT DISCOVERIES

A key example of what it's like to be an *ignorant* male virgin comes when my first pubic hair appears. Had I ever expected it? Don't know, but think not; males' bodies were as hidden as females'. What I'm certain of is that when the first hairs appeared, I soon took a razor and shaved them off. When I told Uncle Joe about it and questioned him about the hair, he again mocked me as a knuckleheaded idiot.

But here's a far more striking example of ignorance. Imagine if you can an ignorant Puritan who had his first wet dream without knowing that males produce semen. (Actually two readers of this chapter as manuscript have reported similar ignorance until puberty ambushed them.)

Age Fourteen
I wake up and as I start dressing I'm suddenly aware of some large caked spots on my underwear. (I never had a pair of pajamas until perhaps five years later.) I examine the sheets and see not just dried cakes but some moist spots. Alarm! Am I ill? Have I issued some form of colorless blood? I leave my basement cubbyhole, go to Mama's bedroom, and ask her about it.

The only thing I can remember is the embarrassed look on her face. What did she tell me about it? A while later she insisted on a "serious conversation," and she told me that Daddy before he died had said to her, "Lillian, I do hope you can warn Clayson against sinning the way I did when I was a lad. Tell him that I have always regretted some of the things I did." She never explained what those "things" were, but it is all clear to me now; I was supposed to understand that any effort to produce the kind of flow my wet dream had produced would have been considered by my beloved father as the ultimate in sinfulness.

As every reader will expect and everyone except for some extremely rare orthodoxites will forgive, masturbation soon followed.[3] I can't reconstruct

---

3. I know that many who have indulged in masturbation will still be disturbed by open discussion of it. When I was being prepared for my two years of total "purity" as a missionary, our supervisors did not mention masturbation even once, except with the oblique allusions again and again as they advised that we must "come home clean." I wonder if any young men manage to do it?

how long afterward, but suddenly my journals reveal that the young hypocrite—in public, pure as the driven snow—was grappling with irrepressible lust. Somehow by sixteen, the journals suggest, a genuine "man" should feel free to discuss masturbation directly—even if behind everyone's back. Obviously I felt that I was maturing fast and could reveal some of the embarrassing facts I recorded about the last two or three years. That sort of surprises me, even now when historical studies of masturbation reveal that in ancient times masturbation was taken for granted as in no way immoral. Oh, how I wish I could have read such a study back then.[4]

That's not how it had felt to the earlier diarist, who first reveals only superciliously that something new is going on: "After dinner took a nap." "Fooled away most of the day, instead of accomplishing anything." But suddenly the sixteen-year-old decides to be frank.

July 27, 1937

I think I am a normal human being. I have, for quite a while, over a year & a half, been developing sexually, with the normal (I think) sexual desires to suppress. I have periodical sexual excretions, coming up to about a month ago, of natural causes. At that time, it was in what you would call a moment of temptation or weakness, I purchased, in mother's absence, a licentious, suggestive, sensual book of stories, with pictures. I don't know why I was so dumb, but I read it, got in more of a sexual condition of passion as I progressed until finally, unable to resist, I, by violent physical agitation, produced the flow of the fluid (I still don't know whether I should write this or not. I wish that I had a more adequate brain to be able to know what to do.) Immediately after I gained control of myself, I felt ashamed of myself. I cannot blame this sin on not knowing of its being a sin, because I knew it was so, I had held in contempt boys who had admitted of the act to me and yet I succumbed. I have heartily repented and have tried & succeeded to keep from repeating. Another thing I have stopped is thinking before going to sleep of suggestive scenes & acts [with girl friends I felt desire for], a practice which I almost acquired a habit of. I am going to, I hope to, live to be able to warn my boys [sons] against such practices. If I had had a father to tell me not to do such things I would, out of respect for him, have refrained.

Mother talks to me freely but of course knows nothing of many of the practices that go on and that have to be guarded against. [Where did he get that notion?] I sometimes wonder why our gospel doctrine, Word of Wisdom or something does not contain a warning or command against bad

---

4. Thomas W. Laqueur, *Solitary Sex: A Cultural History of Masturbation* (New York: Zone Books, 2003).

sexual habits. Maybe they do. . . . I hope whoever reads this will look at it in the right way, will realize that this is an age of temptation, that girls deliberately try, at least it seems so, to make boys look at them wrongly, by wearing scant clothing, etc. . . . It seems that I have so much wrong with me that it would take forever to cure me, and yet I am so much better than most boys my age (no conceit intended) that their is no comparison.

Does he mean that he is less lustful than the others? Or does he know that others were not resisting?

The masturbation inevitably continued, with increasing frequency and always with strong attacks from PuritanB and continuing successful efforts by HypocriteB to keep it secret. On August 28: "After dinner played one thing or another till 6:00." A day later: "Laid down most of afternoon." Only rarely does he provide more direct clues. Sometimes he writes at the top of the page, "J.O." for "jacked off." How could he ever have thought that God, who ordered us all to keep honest journals, wanted a record of *that*?

1936 or 1937

I have been on the toilet, reading a pornographic magazine and masturbating; have cleaned up the semen. I leave. Suddenly remember that I've left the magazine on the floor. I rush back to get the dirty rag (and it was indeed dirty, in two senses—"soiled" with semen marks and full of what memory sees as cruelly chauvinist images, the male as seducer or near-rapist. I'd bought it from Virginia Thornton at her father's drugstore; they kept the copies out of sight in those days, but poor Virginia, fat, unloved, sold them to us boys, with a leer.)

To my shock, I find the door locked; my sister, four years younger, is in there. Panic! Terrible sense of disaster looming. She'll see it, she'll learn from it what I am. She'll report me. Utter misery.

"Lucille, come out."

"I'm not through yet."

"Well, hurry up." Pacing the floor, desperate, blushing with shame. She'll tell Mama; she'll surely tell Mama. Misery, more misery.

She comes out, not carrying the magazine, looking absolutely normal. No reproach, no blushes, no special looks.

She leaves, I scramble into the bathroom; the magazine is on the floor, apparently on the precise spot where I'd left it. Has she seen it? How will I ever know?

Many decades later I ask her about it. She has no memory of the episode at all.

1937

I had been "chosen," as my proud diary put it, to go to the National Boy Scout 25th Year Jamboree in Washington, D.C. Actually, all it took was a parent's willingness to pay the fee, $125![5]

Feeling honored, important, enjoying a public reputation as a model boy, I felt guilt ridden about many things, but especially about the frantic and frequent masturbation. Twice a day, thrice, I pounded away, often dangerously close to being caught. I felt quite certain that the genuinely pious boys were not guilty of this sin—only we bad ones. (Would my life have been improved if I could have read Philip Roth's *Portnoy's Complaint*? Who knows?)

As the Washington trip approached, I swore to myself that it would bring masturbation to an end; I would turn over a new leaf. The oath was soon broken (you surprised?). In my one-boy tent in Washington, perhaps a week after leaving home, I one night had a wet dream and the next night once again flogged away, no doubt with a memory of the kind of magazine that I had been using in the bathroom at home.

I can still remember some of the fantasies derived from those magazines—comically bland by current standards. What appalls me now is the effect of those stories on the young male's attitude towards women. I unconsciously imbibed from them a sharp division between two kinds of women: the saintly pure ones offered by my religion, suitable as wives, and the sinful nymphomaniacs I met in the magazines, the kind a true male really desired, worthless as human beings, useful for lusters.

Such a memory might lead you to a sharp question, Why, Booth, do you not have a separate chapter entitled something like "The Male Chauvinist Pig vs. the Defender of Feminism"? Well, yes, I was for a while in many ways a chauvinist. But I have become an ardent defender of feminism. Phyllis and Kathie and Alison were crucial in my steady learning about just how show-vain-istically I had sometimes behaved.

It's hardly surprising that almost all of HypocriteB's entries about girls are on the completely "pure" side, with no mention of lust.

April 27, 1937 [age 16]
I have never really liked one girl any more than several others. In other words, I have never suffered from "puppy-love." The reason that I take Maxine whenever I take anyone [out] is that I respect her more than any

---

5. How could Mother possibly have afforded that, more than a month's salary? Did she ever do anything comparable for poor Lucille? I'm painfully sure that she did not.

other girl of the school, that is, she is more conscientious and intelligent, higher in character than any girl I know. However, I intend to change off before long, as I don't want to stick to one girl yet.

The remembered situation was utterly different. LusterB was pursuing many other girls—phoning them flirtatiously at night, discussing "biology" after their biology class (I never took the class), reading pornography with the wilder girls and fondling them in the school halls, dreaming of them, night after night. And meanwhile PuritanB was flooded with guilt about all that "sin," yet always trying to project to the girls the image of a powerful lover. LusterB was proud of wearing swimming trunks reduced almost to a jock-strap, exhibiting himself on the edge of the pool—like some medieval knight or Renaissance dandy with a prominent codpiece. PuritanB would later pray for forgiveness for that sinful display.

Yet through all that, HypocriteB was officially dating Maxine—as the most "conscientious, intelligent" girl and of the highest character. Actual-ly, she was the girl who aroused me least, and I was *using* her as a screen. I'm pretty sure, now, that she thought I was seriously interested in her, even though I hardly ever kissed her—and kissed her "seriously" only once. We did talk, one time, about what marriage would be like, but the talk was totally sexless. Meanwhile I was fantasizing about sex with girl after girl.

The battle between PuritanB and LusterB became more and more trou-blesome as the years went by. Just before my seventeenth birthday, I revealed myself almost torn apart by the conflict, though in language that disguised the lust problem by calling it "uncontrollable, masterful passion."

[Age 17]
There are many minor things which I don't like in books; heavy love sen-timentalism—probably arising from the fact that I have never been in love and consequently don't believe in there being such an uncompromising and masterful passion—I hate to think that there is such a thing uncontrollable; I want to be able to use my head instead of my heart, as the saying goes. I don't mind the thought of falling in love, but I hate to think of marrying an inferior girl just because I am blinded by love so as not to be able to see her faults; while another girl, superior and probably as likely to be a good wife, goes unnoticed. I realize that in my extreme inexperience I may be talking through my hat; preaching what I wont practice, but at present, I doubt it. However, I am proceeding on the assumption that there is a passion which hits you between the eyes when your not looking, and am associating only with those girls whom I would not mind being in *love?* with or marrying. In that way, I think I am safe, barring stories of love on first sight. Right now, I

believe I could fall in *love?* easier with Nan[6] than any other—she is the prettiest, sex-appealingest (to me at least), likes me more (I think) than anyone else, but her background is different than mine. She isn't a Mormon, her mother has been divorced etc. I'm not saying she or her folks are not as good as mine, just born and raised under different standards. So I am, while not avoiding her, being careful not to encourage any association with her, and still am trying to remain a friend. Maybe I should just let things come as they would (If I'd let myself I'd have a date with her every night) and chance the consequences, but I don't know.

Thus, to maintain his image as a pious Mormon, HypocriteB conceals his true interests and goes on dating Maxine.

The journal entries are full of promises of total chastity. The most amusing one was written on my seventeenth birthday, after PuritanB read Benjamin Franklin's unfinished autobiography.

> Like Benjamin Franklin, [I] would like to become as nearly a perfect human being as is possible. (An absurd desire as far as hope of completion, yet very sane as a goal to work to. . . .) Franklin's plan for self-improvement was one of the best to be found. He listed thirteen virtues . . .

I then wrote out a description of each virtue as an explicit exhortation to myself—for example, "*Chastity:*—Stop sexual-abuse in the form of forcefully bringing about the ejection of the sexual fluid. Avoid bad thoughts." Then I constructed a full chart, for a day-by-day grading of my achievement on each virtue. Like Franklin, I was to concentrate for one full week on each of the thirteen. At the top of the chart I explained that inserted X's would indicate a "falling down" in the virtue.

In the only full week that I recorded (in which "Temperance" was designed by Franklin to get the most attention), there are failure X's for all the virtues except Cleanliness (the blank must have been a deliberate lie), Dependability (probably a lie), and Chastity (no X's, and scribbled in is the word "Unnecessary"). A really comic bit of hypocrisy.

> *Sept. 19, 1938 [half a year later, when we've moved fourteen miles away]*
> Maxine has been going out [with others] some recently (not much). When I was in Idaho she went several times with Lyle Tregaskis, and I approve very heartily. . . . I like her more than any other girl I know.

---

6. Nan Chipman, with whom I'm still sort of in touch because she married my second cousin, T. Y. Booth, now dead.

Others excite me more but I curb myself from ever going with those that do, as it is dangerous, I believe. As I look at things now, I don't want to get at all serious with any girl for at least 7 years, but if I did want to, Maxine would be the one, & I believe with more constant association, I would love her, although my ideas about what love is are very vague. It can't be anything more than something built up in the individual's own mind, by himself and fed by constant association and encouragement from the one supposedly loved. It doesn't worry me, however, and won't until a long time has passed. I firmly believe I can stay out of love as long as I want and when I get ready can regulate conditions so as to fall in love.

Despite the rigorous Mormon code, "absolutely no sex before marriage,"[7] the actual practice was complex and, to me, often puzzling. A fair number of the girls in my class had dropped out before graduating to get married—many for "shotgun weddings." A careful study done at BYU in the late 1930s in my county found that 60 percent of first births occurred within the first seven months of marriage. So, while all of us were pretending to be virginal, many of my buddies and girlfriends were, like President John Adams and Abigail (though unlike me), going all the way. All of us were hypocritical, especially those of us Puritans who barely managed to draw the line. Just what is it about PuritanB that at this point, in 2005, resists reporting some vivid memories of . . . ?

HypocriteB intrudes steadily, not just here but again in his "private" journal. The daily masturbator steadily expresses the desire not for sex but for a virtuous (but beautiful) wife. Here's how the male chauvinist put it just before turning nineteen.

Jan. 6, 1940

I would like to find a wife, (or rather, at present, a girl friend) who could and would meet me on my own ground, who would be good looking (not beautiful), sensible, a piano-player, an inveterate reader of good books, etc. etc., a good cook . . . a *clean*, morally & physically (this includes an absence of gum chewing) girl, yet not a prude, a girl who would unintentionally make me want to love her physically and yet make me respect her enough to cause me to hold back, of my own accord, etc.

---

7. The standard definition of "having sex" (only behind the barn called fucking or screwing) was—as for President Clinton—not just orgasm but full penetration. Oral sex? I never even heard of it until after marriage, and "blow jobs" were never mentioned in public, as I remember, until the Clinton fiasco.

And PuritanB always finally triumphed.

> *August 19, 1940*
> I have just been attacked—one of Lucille's 'friends', an over-sexed, boy-cra-
> zy, bold, brazen, senseless, and ripe young woman, just came in the house.
> My bedroom door was open, and I had jumped up and closed it when
> I saw her enter the front door. Nothing daunted, she opened my door,
> backed me (in the silliest kind of confusion) into my chair and proceeded
> to ask me what I was doing. . . . I suppose she must have observed my obvi-
> ous distaste, but she continued questioning, moving toward me, with only
> mumbled answers in response, until finally, satisfied I suppose, she jauntily
> walked out of the room and closed my door. The huzzy—she was clad
> in practically nothing—a sun-suit, I believe it was—bare-back, bare legs,
> practically to the crotch, and breasts accentuated shamelessly or shamefully.
> Horrors. She *is* sexually attractive, but I would like nothing better than to
> spank her hard, or, best, to apply a rifle bullet to an appropriate place. How
> is it that such a positive abhorrence can exist in company with such animal
> attractiveness? Phooey—what a come-down from the Plato I was reading
> when she arrived.

His anxieties about similar experiences led him a few days later to attempt a
poem:

> My dear, dear girl,
> I'm sensitive.
> Not only that, I'm delicate,
> And I like to pride myself a bit
> On being sensible.
> This being true,
> My dear, dear girl,
> I'd just a little rather
> That you make a slight attempt to hide
> Your amorous intentions.
> In other words, and far less kind,
> Hands off, until I say the word.

CONTRASTING INTIMACIES, MALE AND FEMALE

For a year or so, through the five years at Grampa's starting at age seven, I had
played more games with girls than with boys: jacks, jump the rope, roller-
skating. As a weeper one year younger than everyone in my school class, I

somehow didn't fit in with the male gangs. But then there quickly arose a series of close male bondings, a bit puzzling, considering my steady lusting for females. In fact, until Phyllis, almost all of my closest friends were male. As I read journal entries about my friendships now, it's striking to see how my affection for the men is accompanied by endless sexual fantasies not about them but about more than a score of girls I was "almost in love with."

My two closest friends through almost two decades were male: the somewhat feminine Junior Halliday—the "best friend" whose death at fourteen I reported in chapter 3—and then, as top of the lot, Max Dalby, with whom I exchange frequent emails and still meet at least once a year. Max, who became central to my life in my second college year, was not at all "feminine," though some machos in Utah might have called him that because of his intense interest in art and music.

He was in fact my first *real* love—without a hint of homosexuality. As I turned twenty, the diary reveals entry after entry about my longing to be with him every day, all day. I'll trouble you with only one report, which would probably be interpreted as gay by most readers these days.

August 23, 1940
Yesterday was one of the important days of the Summer, or of my life. I visited Max on his 20th birthday—even wrote him two pages of poetry as a gift.

It was wonderful; we discussed everything. . . . He played the Firebird Suite, Stravinsky ($6.50) which he just recently bought. It was extraordinarily beautiful.

Max is so fine. As I went in to meet him . . . the blood rushed to my head and I felt giddy; it is like I want to feel with the girl I marry.

We burnt at fever pitch all day, riding, talking, eating. I don't suppose I'll ever forget any of the details of the day. We practically wept at parting—it sounds silly but it wasn't.

And I later even wrote about that relation as "almost like a love affair"—even as I began serious courting of possible wives and continued fantasizing about sex with girl after girl.

The Rescue

It was only after the two totally virginal (though often longing) years as a missionary that the battles between LusterB and PuritanB achieved a kind of truce: *genuine love took over*. As soon as missionaries return home, pursuit of a mate, licit or illicit, almost always takes over. Young puritans deprived of all

Phyllis Barnes in Long Beach, age 16

sexual contact for two straight years are desperate to find a legitimate mate.[8] Most returning missionaries are either married or guilty of unmarried fornication within about a year. (Can I prove that claim with a scientific study? Hardly.)

Returning to the BYU campus, I found myself surrounded by hundreds and hundreds of girls longing for dates; all of the "qualified" men had by 1944 been drafted. I dated and dated, fondled and fondled. And then one day I attended a chamber music concert, and there she was on the stand, the most beautiful girl I'd yet seen, even among the hundreds of "availables." And she was playing the viola in a Mozart flute quintet. After the recital, my sister introduced me to Phyllis Barnes, and the three of us chatted a bit. A day or so later Phyllis played a violin solo at my missionary homecoming, and we went for a walk on "lover's lane." I quickly realized that I'd found the idol of my life. (It took her a lot longer to see me as her unbreakable choice.)

As I courted her and as she became more and more interested, there was no full sex, only "petting" and "necking" and "pitching woo" (we, of course, didn't have later terms like "smooching" or the British term—what is it?—snoggling?). Though I was constantly nagged by PuritanB about the temptation to "go too far," LUST and LOVE were finally in harmony. When we parted, I declared myself fully "engaged," while granting her the privilege to do whatever dating attracted her while I was away.

Within six weeks I was drafted, and I managed to visit Phyllis only a few times during the next few months before being shipped overseas. Soon I found myself in Paris, surrounded by sexual invitations but determined to be faithful to Phyllis.

The conflicts for a virginal soldier in Paris were a lot sharper than for a missionary in Chicago. The streets were lined with prostitutes; my buddies were commenting daily about this or that successful or botched bit of fucking. Our officers were taking it for granted that all of us guys had to have our cocks checked regularly for foul consequences. And all I had, really, were my daily letters to Phyllis, which I filled with sexual allusions and jests. Fairly typical are these two from the spring of '45.

March 15
Dearly Beloved,
. . . . [yesterday one of my buddies said] "Now, what *I* always say is, how will she look when she wakes up in the morning. No use going to bed with a china doll and waking up with a rag one.". . .

---

8. As you'd expect, there are many violations of the rules even during missions, sometimes confessed only forty years later.

The four volumes of the pornographic "My Life and Loves," by Frank Harris, now sell in Paris for 100 francs each. Harris moved among the celebrities of England and the continent several generations ago, and wrote up all of his seductions of the great ladies and ladies of the great in livid detail. As I see it, the main attraction of the book is the announcement on the front cover, "This book not permitted in the United States or England." Being banned lends a kind of dignity to a book. . . . Incidentally, remind me when I seduce you to use the Harris technique.

April 15 [following a discussion of differences between American and French sexual mores]
For the fellows who are out for what they can get, the situation [here] is marvelous; the girls who can be had can be had quickly and without tedious preliminaries. "Mais pourquoi pas?" the cleaning woman at our billet said to me when I declined her kind offer to sleep with me [in exchange] for three bars of soap. "C'est bien naturelle, pour vous aussi bien que pour moi. Je vous aime beaucoup." ("But why not? It's very natural, as much for you as for me. I like you very much.") I had seen her three times before this, and talked to her all of five minutes; yet she is not exactly a whore, exactly, because she obviously was considering the pleasure more than the three bars of soap.

I resist repeating the heavenly bliss of returning to Phyllis and marrying within two weeks; it would read like the climax scenes in thousands of novels these days. Nor will I bother you with a list of women who, over the years, have aroused my "interest"—especially when Phyllis was pregnant and not wanting any sex. Just record again the miracle, perhaps puzzling to many of you: fifty-nine years of genuine, mostly blissful monogamy, with LusterB and PuritanB united. (Anyone feel envious? VainB hopes there are a few among you.)

How ThinkerB Intrudes with Irresistible Reflections

What do I think now about how I might have lived or should have lived during those years of unconsummated longing? Would I now prefer to have been out seducing girls during high school, as many of my buddies did, some of them then trapped into "shotgun weddings"? Do I wish that I had accepted the "offer" of X, Y, or Z, and had thus been more sexually skillful when we married? Do I wish that I had been in the culture some of my friends have reported, in which uncles or older friends or even fathers take the boy to visit a prostitute to learn the best ways of quenching unquenchable adolescent fires? Would I prefer to have avoided masturbation by living as promiscuously as many do these days? What kind of life would it be to screw 1.2 women per day, as the famous basketball player Wilt Chamberlin has claimed, with a total beyond twenty thousand? How would it feel in later life to look back on that and consider what effect you had had on the lives of those women and their other lovers?

Considering it now, I think that the effect of such a life would be tragic or, at best, pathetic, marked by the loss of what it has meant and still means to have a lifetime loving companion—not to mention what it would have done to those one-night, cast-off girls.[9]

Such moralizing talk seems increasingly out of fashion, except in the more conservative religious circles. Everybody knows that the explosion of talk about President Clinton's affair with Monica Lewinsky has shattered many of the rules that once governed public discussion of sex, and many fear that that discussion has lowered even further the standards of what's acceptable—both in discussion and in behavior. A few years ago it would have been unthinkable for *Meet the Press* to discuss the question of whether Monica experienced orgasm. Before the scandal, the "respectable" media had never explicitly mentioned oral sex or semen spots. In earlier decades it was unthinkable to discuss in any "respectable" publication how many women President Kennedy had sex with or to ask whether President Johnson or Governor Bush committed adultery. Though the word "fuck" still cannot appear in *The New York Times* or the *Chicago Tribune* or on most national TV channels, it's now on every fourth page of *The New Yorker*—according to my most recent painstaking survey.

Such changes deserve and receive endless moral speculation about the effect of public discourse on private life. Resisting a full chapter of speculation about the radical differences between the lives produced by my puritan culture, including the guilt and hypocrisy, and the lives our so-called free culture encourages, I offer just one final bit of sermonizing.

I can't think of any fully coherent way—other than happy marriage—to reconcile masculine lust with what is for me the supreme moral commandment: thou shalt not, in pursuit of your own current pleasure or profit, harm other people or your future Self. What I do not question—what produces not the slightest Self-Splits (except, the Honest Self intrudes, the many times

---

9. In most current novels I read these days, there's not a hint of anything wrong with "sleeping with" whoever is available. In John le Carré's *Our Game* and Jane Smiley's *Good Faith* all characters, male and female, do comfortable one-night stands with no hint of any moral judgment against it (except for mild suggestions that sex *with love* is a bit better).

when LusterB's eye has been momentarily distracted)—is my slow discovery that monogamy, *sexually faithful* monogamy, is a much neglected rescue from life's many threatening disasters. In other words, the nagging from PuritanB has helped me, over almost six decades, to avoid "affairs" that might very well have destroyed our marriage as they have destroyed so many others. That fifty-nine-year harmony (not yet quite the harmony sought through this book) seems, as I wait impatiently for Phyllis's return from conducting a weeklong workshop in Finland, the greatest rescue from dangerous cultural indoctrination that any man could ever experience.

Would Phyllis's and my polygamist ancestors scoff at that claim just as vigorously as promiscuity celebrators will? Possibly.

Chapter Eight

The Lover Becomes a Trapped Army Private

An army marches on its stomach.

—Napoleon

I never expect a soldier to think.

—George Bernard Shaw, *The Devil's Disciple*

"You must not tell us what the soldier . . . said, sir," interposed the judge; "it's not evidence."

—Charles Dickens, *Pickwick Papers*

But we are soldiers;
And may that soldier a mere recreant prove,
That means not, hath not, or is not in love!

—Shakespeare, *Troilus and Cressida*

They're changing the guard at Buckingham Palace—
Christopher Robin went down with Alice.
Alice is marrying one of the guard.
"A soldier's life is terrible hard,"
Says Alice.

—A. A. Milne, *When We Were Very Young*

November 1944

As a private, trained as a "clerk/rifleman," longing for undelivered letters
from my true love, I was for quite a while just idly, miserably waiting for
assignment. We were stationed at a "replacement center" in Givet, France,
the "prick that France sticks into Belgium," sleeping on the ground on straw
ticks. One day a sergeant snarled at us, "All right, get it out of your fuckin'
heads you're going to be clerks. You're gonna be fuckin' riflemen, see?" We
could hear the bombardments in the distance; we believed him. Then, a few
days, maybe even a week or two later, they lined us up to get into trucks that
would move us to the front.

"Anderson!"

"Here"—and buddy Jim goes towards the truck.

"Banderzinsky!"

"Here."

"Booth!"

"Here."

"You're not goin'. You're goin' back to Paris to be a fuckin' typist."

Somebody had seen on my record that I could type eighty words a minute. I was taken to the officers' headquarters and granted not only a typewriter day by day but—oh, bliss!—a bunk bed. But my buddies were gone; even
the few who for some reason weren't shipped seemed more distant, perhaps
angry because I had dodged the bullet.

After lying around for a few days, doing a bit of office typing for the
Center, feeling more and more guilty about the contrast between my buddies' fates and mine, I was trucked back to Paris. On that cold, rough trip I
meditated a lot about God, chance, and choice, and recorded my thoughts a
bit painfully.

November 22, 1944

It appears that Bob [a buddy with a wife and two children at home] and
Dean [with a wife and child] will probably go into combat as riflemen. . . .
I always had a superstitious faith that "something would happen" to keep

me from combat—that "my abilities would be recognized.". . . Mack Cun-ningham [a high school friend] would say, "There is some power overseeing your destiny, or this would not have happened." Poppycock! I'll admit that I had one brief moment—may I never cease to be ashamed—of thinking, "This is what I deserved." . . . But immediately I recovered myself and felt ashamed for allowing my ego to play such tricks on my sense. The thou-sands of men—better men than I—who have died in this war should be given a special assignment to haunt me for eternity. . . . It is arrogance of the most unforgivable sort to think God would preserve me, without wife & children, and allow to be killed men with families. . . . I feel guilty about it, undeserving, disappointed about not being able to observe myself in danger—and exuberantly happy at being out of the worst part of the mess.

That entry understates what I dwelt on in other entries—the absolute, final decision to conclude my inner debates about God's existence: there is no God, because no God deserving our worship would commit an act like that. I had no choice but to pronounce myself an atheist. Pronounce? Well, not out loud, not in letters home, only in my heart and diary. HypocriteB still knew how to bite his tongue.

That painful, true story underlines a curious fact about being a soldier landed into training; you've lost all free choice about what you are to do hour by hour. You are left with puzzles about where the wild "chances" are coming from. Every moment is decided by this or that officer's order, whether stupid, cruel, or wise. You are thus in one sense freed from the Self-Splits that faced you day by day when you were free. In training, as you sit on the ground wait-ing for an order or conduct a four-hour hike or practice with your rifle, you tend to think of only one split, and it's not *within* your Self. Instead, it is "I am trapped and I want out; I want Phyllis."

It's true that you're never tempted to escape; you are doing your duty. When you're told to do something, you don't debate with yourself about it; you do it. Hearing the corporal's shouted order at 5:00 AM to "Drop your cocks and grab your socks," you wake up, jump out of bed, make it up so neatly that if the inspecting lieutenant later drops a quarter on the blanket the coin will bounce. And then you go through the day doing whatever you're told to do.

Inner voices do intrude frequently: "Fuck you, lieutenant—my neck is as clean as I could get it in two seconds!" "What an idiot you are, Corporal, for saying, 'No, you don't have to file 'em chronological—jes do 'em by date.'" But such voices don't even get recorded in your journal, let alone in letters that might be seen by a censor. You simply obey. Most of the time you just "shit, shower, and shave," and then—as often happened to me long before the

Paris assignment—you may spend the morning assigned to clean up the crap room where the other GIs have shat, showered, and shaved. If the inspector finds any cleanup failures, you don't get your weekend pass. The slightest bit of neglected shit and I'll lose my visit with beloved Phyllis, two hundred fifty miles south in Long Beach, California.

Here's how I put it in a poem, in letters to Phyllis, other friends, and my favorite BYU professor.

The Witching Hour

The hour of decision comes apace.
Impending doom? We ask. Impending grace?

We mutter incantations over toilet bowls,
And wave the magic brush above the urinals.
We waft the witching broom with curses soft and low;
The sacrificial mop is wafted too and fro.

The Great God comes, inspects with gloves and glasses—
Our demons do their work: we get our passes.

Even when, after training, you have many idle moments because army life consists of "hurry up and wait," you simply read whatever book is available or listen to whatever records the Red Cross room provides or write letters to the loved ones you long for. (My strongest memory of the good that such drifting can yield is reported in *For the Love of It*: the "freedom," as I waited for assignment, to listen again and again to Beethoven's *Grosse Fuge* and then write at length to Phyllis about how it had transported me, on my way to almost certain death.[1])

In a curious way such freedom from choice liberates you for daily speculation about what it all means—if anything. Most of your deep Self-Splits disappear, especially after the Mormon within stops believing that some God is responsible for at least part of what you have to do. You can't debate "should I do this or do that?" You can't blame yourself for doing something stupid that your officer ordered you to do. You do, however, find plenty of time to engage in the flowering of *thought*-splits.

ThinkerB actually wrote endlessly about them—and lots of other matters—in diaries and even more in letters to Phyllis and friends. CheaterB practiced the cheating I reported above, typing letters to Phyllis while

---

1. See *For the Love of It*, 33–35.

pretending to do my dutiful copying of GIs' letters; by using carbon paper, I could type the secret letter underneath what looked like the official letter. No supervisor ever caught me at it, and I could type fast enough to get my other jobs done as well.

How the Longing for Phyllis Worked

The one Self-Split that in a way plagued me most through my two years was between the Luster and the Puritan—no, not really the Puritan, now, but the Lover who longed for Phyllis and was determined not to betray her. A few weeks after arriving in Paris, I wrote her one of my long daily letters, ending with the following.

> Speaking of blessings: Sunday evening as I was standing in line for tickets for "Sacre de Printemps," a French civilian came up to me and said, "Are you alone?" "Oui." "Would you care to join the party in my box? I think there are no more of the other seats." My little man was more than solicitous. . . . After the concert, he took us all to a bar, and seemed surprised and a little hurt when I asked for ginger ale to drink while they drank champagne. While the ladies were talking together, he said, very matter-of-factly: "Would you like a woman to take care of you while you are in Paris? I understand most of the soldiers want one, and you should have a clean one, if at all." Hastily weighing the relative—no, what am I saying?—I immediately refused, thanking him for his kindness, and explained that I had a fiancée to whom I was remaining "fidele." This seemed much simpler, and was certainly easier to get across to him, than to try to explain about my voluntary virginal state. He immediately understood. "When I was in the first war, I was engaged to my present wife, and I was—what you say?—true, fidele. It is the best way." . . . The upshot of it all is that he is going to take me to "many concerts," because it pleases him to please the Americans.

One could argue that such a choice was determined strictly by my being raised a sacrosanct Mormon. I can't argue that there was no quarrel between PuritanB and LusterB; there was, for about one second. (The episode could well belong in chapter 7.) But no matter what it was that produced my resistance to the whore offer, I can never resist boasting, to myself and to others, about the rightness of all that and the result of it in our later lives.

Am I suggesting that if I had taken up with one or many available prostitutes, we later might not have had as happily sustained a marriage? Yes, I am suggesting that again, with no solid evidence whatever. What I'm sure of is that the excessive guilt of the young Mormon screwer would have changed his life a lot, often for the worse, perhaps up to right now.[2]

Even though I did some half-dating after that with women who in effect offered themselves, I lived with masturbation (always a bit guiltily), reveling in the dream of getting back to my dream mate. And my letters miraculously kept her interest in me alive so that we could marry two weeks after my return in June of '46—neither of us, so far as we can reconstruct, experiencing any sense of doubt as we embraced at the wedding ceremony.

The journals through the two years show endless speculation about "what it all means" and "how to deal with my sense of guilt." I didn't quarrel with god (lower case!) any more; he was as dead as Nietzsche had declared him, and he no longer deserved a capital on the pronouns. (Another "God" returned eight years later. See chapter 17.) But I did feel frequent guilt about not being able to "do any good in the world today"; I debated a lot about whether to volunteer back into combat—but the coward always won.

> *December 20, 1945 [letter to Phyllis]*
> I talked to a couple of combat soldiers, in Paris for a 48 hr furlough, the other day. They complained less in an hour than the desk-soldier [like me, in the Intelligence office] does in 10 minutes. Yet they had been losing buddies and officers, talked calmly about half of their unit being wiped out in one battle. I felt very guilty and depressed. . . . My conscience is rather weak in some respects. I can tell a lie without having it bother me for months, if I think the lie justified by events. I have little difficulty in maintaining a hypocritical attitude toward most devout members of the church. But when I see unfair distribution of suffering, I invariably feel guilty. I felt guilty when I saw those fellows who were to go back into

---

2. I have to resist speculating about how much other soldiers' lives were harmed by the prostitute-rich life. I'm almost certain that many who had been raised more or less "virginal" became prepared in the army for the sexual revolution. After writing that sentence, I learn, reading in James Atlas's *Bellow: A Biography,* about how strongly Wilhelm Reich's sexual theories influenced Saul's and my generation after the war. Reich actually preached that promiscuity was essential to good health—or so Atlas claims—and it's scarcely surprising that men who had been "offered" prostitutes throughout the war would buy into Reich's comforting, self-destructive thesis. I can remember laughing at Reich's orgone boxes back in the Fifties, and now I learn that Saul Bellow actually bought one and did his "exercises" in it.

    Can you forgive my moralizing? And can you understand my deep pleasure in coming across an editorial in our student newspaper today arguing that the widespread "hooking up" that students engage in (what I would call sex-without-love) has "disastrous consequences"?

Thinking about Phyllis in the army, Bremen, 1946

combat within a few hours, leaving me warm and dry and safe in Paris. . . .
I feel guilty when I think of the suffering in America, and more guilty
when I think of the suffering in all the war torn countries. There is something perverted about this guilt: why should I feel guilty about things I
have no control over, and not guilty about those things I do have a chance
to regulate? Perhaps it is not guilt at all, but something else: a feeling of
futility, of impotence—perhaps even of disapproval of the universe and the
way it is "run."

"The universe," my nongod, had trapped me into impotent guilt.

With lots of free time to wander about—sometimes no duties for three
full days in a row—ThinkerB writes to Phyllis about "the problem of the
spirit of giving." Giving a few bits here and there is his only available way to
"do good in the world today."

February 28, 1945
For some months now I've been giving away my weekly allotment of candy,
cigarettes, gum, and cookies[3] (yes, and here is a good place to confess that I
gave away the pineapple and half of the cake you sent . . . .)

(a) There is little or no pleasure derived from giving an inadequate gift.
To give only a candy bar to a cold and hungry child is more painful than
pleasant. It is as unpleasant as dropping a small coin in a beggar's cap, and
it embarrasses me terribly. I see some fellows doing the same thing, and assuming a look of the great big beneficent American giving alms to the poor
little French children. All I can do is feel helpless, and it becomes more and
more a task to drive myself to distribute the miserable allotment we have.

(b) . . . It is momentarily fun to see the light in the eyes of a little girl
when you give her a piece of candy, but again I feel embarrassed; it is obviously a gesture of selfishness and arrogance, comparable to a millionaire
saying, "Keep the change."

(c) Perhaps the difficulty in both cases is that I am giving nothing that I
really need, and also that I am too conscious of my role as giver. . . . I rather
think that many who believe they are getting the genuine pleasure of giving,
who believe they are practicing Christian charity, are a long long way from
the kingdom of heaven, even as I am.

---

3. Actually he's exaggerating. He had often used the cigarettes as "cash" to purchase mu-
    sic, books, and etchings. One original Whistler, still prominent in our dining room,
    cost two cartons of cigarettes. And one first edition of Joyce's *Work in Progress* (actually
    Finnegans Wake) cost one carton. So where was the Giver at those moments of pur-
    chase?

The point in this chapter, again, is that throughout those two years I find far *less* of that kind of self-probing (and self-loathing) than I find in my journals and letters before and after the war. Most of what I recorded and remember is about one sharp pain: the miserable separation from Phyllis. The soul-split torments fade into a single longing but never with a hint of having any choice about it. I won't desert; I have to obey, but I want to escape. I have to stay, but I want to leave. I have to be my non-Self here "typing away, eight hours a day," but I long to return to my true Self, the one who will find ultimate happiness with Phyllis.

How do I decide what to quote from the four hundred or so love messages? Here's one, just after we debarked from the Isle de France and traveled through Britain, headed, we were told, to Normandy—long after the very word "Normandy" spelled PROBABLE DEATH![4] At some moments I *knew* I was doomed to die and would never see Phyllis again. At other moments as I wrote the daily letters, I *knew* that they were keeping our love alive and thus assuring our future.

> *[No date]*
> Dear Phyll, of the I-surely-hope-the-war-doesn't-last-much-longer-so-that-I-can-return-and-marry-her Phyllises:
> We are "Somewhere in Great Britain," and if they [the censors] don't cut that out I'll be surprised.
> Going for long periods like this with no chance of our letters being mailed for days or perhaps weeks is not at all conducive to any creative urge. . . . When I finally get set for writing you, after fighting hoards of crap shooters or poker players away from my bunk, I sit and think and think about the distance between us . . . and I have to resist writing simply, "I love you, I miss you. I want you. I love you. I am lonely for you. I miss—" and so on.

Even such longing did yield its ups and downs that might be called splits, especially between the optimist and the pessimist—moments when, after reading a letter from Phyllis, I imagined the bliss of being with her at last, followed immediately by utter despair. Though I kept trying to sound optimistic to her, I often blurted out the lamentations.

One of the worst moments came relatively early. Letters from home were irregular, scrambled in delivery. Some never got to me, and many arrived in an order reversing the order in which they were written. One of Phyllis's delayed reports began by almost crushing me, received after about two lonely months in Paris. Here's my reply.

---

4. My close cousin, Jim Ross, was killed in Normandy.

December 12, 1944
[After declaring lonely love]. . . Now for your letter, written on the 23rd
and 26th [of November]. . . . You said, in case you have forgotten, ". . . for
one horrible minute there I had the thought that I couldn't remember you!
I couldn't think what you were like, what to write to you, a stranger. . . ." If
that was a horrible minute for you, think what it was for me, over here and
unable to do anything about it but be frightened. Yes, fear is what it was,
fear of losing you, of having you forget our plans and our hopes, fear of time
and what it can do to any love if not carefully preserved.

My fear, like your minute of strangeness, was soon gone. After all, it is
natural that you should have moments when I seem hard to remember. I
haven't as yet had that trouble remembering you, but I rather expect it, as
the time since our last closeness lengthens into a long stretch of weary war
months. . . . Anyway . . . I consoled myself, calmed my aching heart, so to
speak, and read on—to learn with gladness that you had, after all, remembered that I am by far the best matrimonial bet of the season, even over here.
But please, please don't let time have its way with us. Don't forget, even for
brief minutes, the wonder of the things we have known and felt together
and the greater things we shall feel and do together—after the g.d. war.

Always a bit anxious about the relative rarity of her letters, I naturally was
thrilled by them when they came. Many buddies were receiving "dear John"
rejections from lovers back home, and the fear of rejection returned again and
again. (A standard joke about that situation ends with a GI getting a letter
that reads, "Dear John: I'm sorry, but I've decided to marry the mailman.")
Even my generally optimistic letters show that I felt desperate to portray a
"self" that would be too appealing to resist, despite often feeling worthless.
Here are some brief excerpts from letters, which were always at least two pages
long, single-spaced.

March 17, 1945
I love you and want you and curse the Goddamn war and its evil, when I
sit over a sad typewriter and beweep my state. But I love you and want you
a thousand times more (rough estimate, made rather quickly) when at a
fine concert or when looking at the Seine. The positive enjoyment of things
becomes in itself a refined sort of torture, infinitely more healthy than inactive sorrow.

April 4, 1945
. . . my subconscious has discovered a refinement on the regular . . . dreams
of you. Today as I dozed in the Red Cross, you came and woke me, and I

explained to you that it was very peculiar, but I had been dreaming that I was dreaming of you, a dream within a dream, and you came and woke me. We both seemed to think that very clever, to have dreamed that I was dreaming of you, so you can imagine how much more clever I thought myself when I really did wake up and realized that I had been dreaming that I was dreaming that I was dreaming. That sort of thing is what you're going to have to contend with, sooner or later.

April 6, 1945
Pfc Wayne Clayson Booth, ASN 39928483, draws himself down to his most depraved posture, hands sloppily in pockets, stomach out, chest in, chin at a 45 degree angle with the ground, and makes the most despicable pun of his career:
"Darling, I love you so much that for me you are a walking Phyllic symbol."

April 8, 1945
Bob has tickets for us to the Folies Bergere tonight. I promise to close my eyes every time there is a nude woman on the stage, cross my heart. Why should I want to look at anyone else's body, when in my mind's eye—but we won't go into that.

When the Germans surrendered on May 9, I at first expected to be home soon or thought I could perhaps work out some way for Phyllis to come over and work with me in the occupation forces. But soon it became clear that because of my "low points of service"—not drafted until April of '44—I was among those who would go home last. In fact I might well be shipped as a "clerk-rifleman" to fight against Japan. So the loneliness and anxiety did not diminish.

17 May 1945
[After a page and a half, single-spaced] It seems almost certain that I shall be going into Germany with the occupation administration, at least for a while. I'd almost be willing to go to the Pacific just to get a thirty day furlough with you, but not quite, especially when there is a chance for working out some sort of deal later on. . . . I am unhappy without you. . . . About tomorrow I shall break into your dormitory and carry you off on my ectoplasmic charger to my metaphysical castle on my eschatological estate. Better get your guard up.

18 May 1945
Fellow in the office next door offered to bet $150.00 that if I was away from you another year, you would be married to someone else. "With veterans

returning, no girl will be faithful to anybody. I don't know your girl, but I've got a safe bet." But when I smiled in my beard and agreed to bet him, he backed down. If I could only work out some way to create doubt in peoples' minds and then bet them, it would be an efficient means of increasing our nest-aig. Trouble is, I always give myself away in situations like that with a smug, this-is-different air that puts them on their guard.

19 May 1945

[After a page and a half, single-spaced] You will be interested to know (or else!) that when I'm with a girl I know (Nina and Nicole, in other words) the sexual frustration that is so strong at some other times disappears completely; I am as a boy scout talking with other boy scouts, a lamb talking with other lambs, or something. Really, it's a kind of obscure tribute to you (and, from what I can judge of the other men's behaviour, a blessing for both of us, that whenever I am alone with another girl (about five times now . . .) nothing is quite so present as the adverse comparison with you; somewhere in the process of thinking of you, my abstract desire for you drowns out any specific desire that one would expect for them.

June 15

Since you insist that I be honest about everything, I will confess right out that I've been the saddest of young men for about four days—no, three. I'm not going into details—when I get home and you read my diary you'll find out about them . . . . All a matter of complete disgust with myself, with the Army, with the way world events are going, and even with life itself; an equally complete inability to drive myself to work or read or write letters or even smile at my associates. Everything I've done before the mood or during the mood has seemed futile and inept; I seemed ignorant, hypocritical, and unable to find any redeeming feature about myself, except perhaps that I loved you, and that didn't help any, either. In the blackest of the mood (still being perfectly honest), I counted up the number of days since I had received a letter from you, and cursed you silently for being unworthy of all the time I spend writing you. (Only in the blackest of the moods, you understand, after having rejected the alternatives of jumping in the Seine, picking up with one or another of the prostitutes who kept accosting me as I walked along the lonely street, or going back to the billet and bumping my head quietly and desperately against my wooden bedpost.) Probably I shouldn't mention how your not writing for—I believe it was fourteen days between the [two] datelines on your letters, a perfectly understandable delay at the end of the [academic] quarter, or so it seems to me now—for fourteen days had a part in the matter. It was not that that caused the mood. . . .

It sometimes seems that my former buoyant optimism is slowly leaving me; that if I don't get in a different environment soon I shall become sourly cynical. The only different environment I can think of that will serve adequately to prevent the catastrophe is you.

Reading that now and thinking about how it must have felt to Phyllis, trying her best to write frequent loving letters, I cringe. How many nineteen-year-olds, separated by now for over a year from a man who writes that way, would hang in there? But she did. In my incomplete collection of letters from her, I find none revealing any offense at such outbursts, only apologies for not writing oftener. Here is one of her many apologies, just a week or so after receiving my note of despair.

June 25, 1945
Dear Wayne, of the much neglected, much loved, much wanted Waynes,

It is unforgivable that I should have left you for such a long while, end of the quarter or no end of the quarter. It was a terrible time, I can assure you. I was tired & cross & busy and all I did was study and bore myself with my dullness. Never have I spent such a time. I wanted to write and instead of taking time, I just got more busy with other things, till I couldn't write. I don't want to suggest that you try such a thing, but you have no idea how difficult it is to get down to writing letters after you haven't written for such a long time. But here we are back home & writing semi-regularly and things are looking onward and upward.

Except I do get a little lonesome without you. After all, I'm still a young girl. You'd think a fellow in Paris could find something thrilling to buy for a girl at home. Especially when she is the one who is supposed to be sending things to the service man overseas to keep him happy. I wish you would tell me what you would like soon. The money will be just rolling in, so to speak, and I would like to send you something. [By now she's making ninety-three cents an hour for teaching in a nursery school, which to both of them seems high pay!]

I will come over as soon as possible. Just wait & see. I know that's the trouble, but "he also serves," you know. I wish he didn't. Wouldn't it be fine if we changed our policy and decided he doesn't really serve at all. M[ilton] did, why can't we?

Neither of us suspected that it would be almost a full year before I was finally sent home. As the months went by, her letters left me less and less worried about losing her. Definite plans for marriage became more and more frequent. For a while we planned seriously for her to come to England so that we could both attend universities there. So it could hardly surprise either of us when we were married in the Salt Lake Mormon Temple just two weeks after I was shipped back. Ecstasy—to repeat—ecstasy: the best, the luckiest, the most blessed marriage in the history of . . . well, how about the history of primates?

Did the Self-Splits that had been largely suspended by two years of sustained, unified, unquestioned longing return after marriage? Silly question with an obvious answer. Freedom of choice flooded back in. Conflicts about right choice were met every day, with no army officer to simplify matters. Though the marriage from then to now has never for a moment been considered in doubt by either of us, the diverse ways of handling marriage and the rest of life yielded, as the other chapters here reveal, sustained continuations of the divisions I had inherited and imbibed from birth.

The first choice-free interlude was over. But another radically different one arrived about twenty years later, postponed now until chapter 10.

Chapter Nine

An Egalitarian Quarrels Scornfully with a Hypocritical Bourgeois

The men of culture are the true apostles of equality.

—Matthew Arnold

The moral regeneration of mankind will only really commence, when the most fundamental of the social relations is placed under the rule of equal justice, and when human beings learn to cultivate their strongest sympathy with an equal in rights and in cultivation.

—John Stuart Mill

Democracy means Equality; but what does Equality mean? Obviously it does not mean that we are all alike in . . . any faculty. . . . But as their bodily needs are the same their food and clothes and lodging can be rationed equally; and they are all equally indispensable. The cabin boy needs more food and wears his clothes out faster than the aging admiral; but the same income will provide for either of them. They are both equally necessary to the work of the fleet.

—George Bernard Shaw, *Everybody's Political What's What*

Poor naked wretches, wheresoe'er you are,
That bide the pelting of this pitiless storm,
How shall your houseless heads and unfed sides,
Your looped and windowed raggedness, defend you
From seasons such as these? O, I have ta'en
Too little care of this! Take physic, pomp;
Expose thyself to feel what wretches feel,
That thou mayst shake the superflux to them
And show the heavens more just.

—King Lear, addressing the world's billionaires

They all shall equal be!
The Earl, the Marquis, and the Dook,
The Groom, the Butler, and the Cook,
The Aristocrat who banks with Coutts,
The Aristocrat who cleans the boots.

—W. S. Gilbert, *The Gondoliers*

167

As I came out of our drugstore this morning, a man came toward me to sell a copy of *StreetWise*, our Chicago newspaper sold by the homeless. As usual, I took a dollar from my pocket and accepted the copy of the journal. Then he said (almost predictably), "Sir, you know, I'm in real trouble this mornin'. Nobody wants to buy any papers, and my family at home is hungry, jes like me here. Could you gimme a couple more dollars?"

Since I wasn't in a hurry, I subjected him to some of the skeptical questions that I usually ask before succumbing to such hackneyed appeals. (For the source of such skepticism, see chapter 11.)

His answers were much more plausible than I often get—and he did actually *look* hungry. Well, I happened to have three hundred dollars in my pocket, just obtained from the cash machine. The thought occurred to my egalitarian self (or if you prefer, call it my half-Christian or half-Mormon self): "Why not for once do something really generous—startle him, change his day, maybe his life? Give him the whole pile! To do that won't affect your standard of living one whit, next week or next month."

I reached into my pocket and pulled out a twenty, said "Good luck—and I hope you find a job," and walked off, moved by his tearful thanks. But the egalitarian (I'll label him Egalitarian-Booth) was a bit troubled by the knowledge of how little that twenty would actually do for the man.

The very act of writing a *LIFE* can be called anti-egalitarian. The LIFER can be described as aspiring to join, in the very act of writing, an elite. All of us LIFERS have had at least some education (unlike billions of brothers and sisters from today back to the moment when humanity emerged from the slime). Archaeologists all agree that before "we" learned to write, something like five thousand *generations* had gone through human life, coping, inventing, competing, triumphing—but all of 'em just plain illiterates! We precious few have somehow learned to read and write. And by the very act of attempting to write a book, we show that we have, unlike a vast majority of our siblings, enough escape time from the survival struggle to write.

And then there are the writers we might be tempted to claim are themselves in an elite class. I bet that 99.99 percent of Homo sapiens have never even *thought* about *writing* about having *thought* about how to *think* what their life means; that vast majority, the lost souls "down there," haven't ever even *read* a book about it. Though perhaps 99.99 percent of all human beings have differed from our animal ancestors by consciously *thinking* about what life and death mean, those who do not write or read *LIVES* are simply cast aside by us LIFERS. They give us no clues about how to live because they have kept their thoughts unwritten. So you and I are "up here," as I write and you read about it; we may even be *thinking.*[1] So we're immensely superior to most of the others, right?

Even though that elevation of LIFERS is intended ironically, the fact remains that behind the sarcastic attack on Bourgeois-Booth is a forceful challenge to EgalitarianB's passionate belief that "all men and women are created equal."[2] I am absolutely certain that my life is not inherently worth more than that of a totally illiterate peasant working for a feudal lord, or an enslaved whore in Babylon, or an illegal immigrant earning less than minimum wage, or some beggar I meet on a Chicago street. Oh, yes, the actual life that has been *granted* me, especially the material comforts and the amazing fortune of Phyllis and family, can in many ways be called far better, but that's where the unfairness paradox comes in. The circumstances of birth have mistreated those sufferers all the way, as circumstance has most of the time "blessed" me. But "in theory," EgalitarianB still passionately believes that we were all created equal—or *should* have been.[3]

---

1. What a difference between my ironic, self-mocking speculation about our billions of nonwriting ancestors (did Adam ever write a word?) and the picture created by those who wrote the Bible. I wonder what the author of Genesis was thinking about how to write the opening, as he sat down and started the account we now have. Was he tempted to put it this way? "In the beginning was the Word, who invited me to bear witness to the Light He was creating, that all *men* through him might believe." Could he have put it like this, as Joseph Smith did in his "Inspired Version"? "And it came to pass, that the Lord spake unto Moses, saying, Behold, I reveal unto you concerning this heaven and this earth; write the words which I speak." (Published by the Reorganized Church of Jesus Christ of Latter Day Saints, Independence, Mo.: Herald Publishing House, 1944.)
2. Equality was never *fully* embraced by our founding fathers (consider the granting to blacks of a three-fifths vote), and it's actually practiced by hardly any leaders these days. And it's violated daily by BourgeoisB.
3. But, ThinkerB intrudes, consider those who are mentally or physically maimed at birth. My passion for full equality will never cope adequately with *incurable* inequalities at birth. Mormon doctrine copes with the inescapable paradox by declaring—often quite cruelly—that how we are born is determined by how we behaved on the other side before birth. My father's "patriarchal blessing," an official message given when he was newly married, told him that in his life before birth he had chosen and deserved his wonderful parents and his new wife. The standard blessings don't refer to that quite so frequently these days, but they often stress that preexistent behavior is what produces birth inequalities.

Nobody claims to know when the ideal of *universal* equality first cropped into some thinker's head. But as it did—as some scribe suddenly began to wonder about full human justice for all—that thinker immediately joined one kind of elite, already contradicting his brilliant new idea. His (oh, shucks, I catch myself assuming it was a male!)—*her* mission then became, "I must convince those proud, selfish defenders of injustice that my views are superior. And I wonder whether there are any other thinkers anywhere bright enough to join me, 'up here.'" This paradox is thus inescapable.

For more than sixty years I've been consciously and unconsciously wrestling with it. We were taught by the Constitution that "all men are created equal" and that we lived in a "democracy" where everyone's opinions counted equally; taught by Christ that God cares at least as much for the one lost sheep as for the ninety-nine in the fold; taught by my family (thank God) that when a depression "bum" (oh, yes, we called them that—but never to their faces) came to the door we should feed him (it was never a woman) and also that blacks and Indians are really our equals and would someday be recognized as such by the LDS church; taught by Grampa Booth that all the wealthy were criminals. Yet we were also taught that Mormons are inherently superior to non-Mormons and that "the glory of God is intelligence"—a quality not given to everyone.

Taught in such conflicting ways, I was thus a prime target for elitist messages, most of which now seem not just paradoxical but absurd: the true elite are the religious folk who get the message straight; no, the true elite are the atheistic Socialists and Communists who fight for total human equality; well, yes, but the true elite among those elite are those who obtain the most education; but obviously the true elite are those who get the *right* kind of education, being taught by VainB.

I have spent a lot of time in life trying to join the only true, genuinely defensible elites: those few who have really thought hard about those paradoxes. No, actually, the *genuine* elites are those who don't misread an ironist when he uses words like *true, genuinely,* and *defensible.*[4]

In WWII, I met many draftees who, by their contempt for the "dummies," got me thinking about my own elitist pride. Here's how I put it in a letter to Phyllis in March of '45.

---

4. My life is full of misreadings of my attempts at irony. Phyllis claims that most of them, when I intend to mock some stated view, actually betray the fact that the view has occurred to me and is therefore a thought genuinely—and thus shamefully—in my head. I deny it, but maybe she's right. When I played the game here just now, hoping you would join me in mocking anyone who sees ironists as an elite, had it not occurred to me that successful ironists *are* superior to nonironists or those who fail at it? Of course we are. Oy vey. And isn't it true that the true elite are those who know just a bit of Yiddish?

It is surprising to me to notice how many people think of themselves as more intelligent than "most people." The average GI [here in Paris] is always saying, "Now you take the average GI, and all he does is ———." The average college student, when he gets in a bull session, says, "It's too bad there aren't more students who get together and discuss things intelligently like this. But the average student is not concerned with such things." Indeed, most pretensions to intelligence, including my own, are made up largely of scorn for the ignorance of others. More and more I try to pin myself down to something specific when I start classifying others as ignorant: "Just what is it that I know and they do not know?" "In this particular instance, is my 'intelligence' tangible, or is it just something I've conjured up to protect myself and my pride?" "If the task of teaching them were mine, what do I have to teach that would genuinely improve them?" "Are my 'intelligence' and their 'ignorance' merely circumlocutions for differences of opinion or emotional background?" Generally, when I ask these questions, I manage to squeeze some sort of answer out of the situation.

Any careful reader so far will have uncovered in my Selves at least two branches of the paradox: (1) the conflict between morality-driven, left-wing EgalitarianB, pursuer of political justice, and a cowardly nonactivist, protecting BourgeoisB's academic and family territory; (2) the conflict between EgalitarianB as writer, wanting his work to address everybody, and the "intellectual," especially VainB, who wants to be admired at "the top."

And what about political inequalities? My family was politically divided, though all were more sympathetic to the impoverished than most Americans seem to be today. Grampa Clayson was an ardent Democrat; once he had risen above poverty, he actually won an election to the Utah State Legislature. Gramma and Grampa Booth were ardent Republicans.[5] As I moved more and more strongly to the Democratic side, I can remember being very angry at Gramma for her claim that the "abominable President Roosevelt" was so awful that she sometimes felt like moving to Argentina.

Hovering behind these differences was a Mormon history of radical communalism, or communitarianism, usually referred to as the United Order. Joseph Smith had received revelations from God dictating the "laws" of "consecration" and "stewardship." All members should deed *all* property to the leaders, receiving in exchange a "stewardship" of the property consecrated unto God. The ideal was total communitarian sharing—total equality among all members (except, of course, the leaders). Though the inescapably egotistical leader never quite managed to practice total financial equality with other

---

5. The Republicans were not quite as dominant in Utah at that time as they are now.

members, he always insisted that every last penny of anyone's property is God's property and that it all should be shared equally with all of the other righteous. And Prophet Smith actually worked out several possible community plans for realizing that dream.

In increasing conflict with America's rising capitalism, the dream survived in various weakened forms after the Mormons fled to Utah. Not long after leading the emigration to Salt Lake City, Brigham Young, while growing increasingly wealthy himself, established more than two hundred "United Order" villages, one actually named Orderville. They were considered to be a first step toward the time when all property would be placed in God's hands. In those villages every member surrendered every penny to the community leadership and then was given an *equal* share back, day by day, week by week.

Today such "communistic" views are hardly mentioned by the Church, as the devout Steve Coveys build their mansions and the Church invests more and more millions in thriving companies. A fragment of the dream does survive, as I've reported above, in the commandment to give a full tenth of one's "increase" to the Church and thus to God. But I never see the ideal of *total* sharing even mentioned. Yet the ideals of equality and full justice still survive in the beliefs of many, including me: equal sharing is the—no doubt hopeless—escape route from current exploitations and from the woundings of democracy. And the Church does engage in vast international charity enterprises.[6]

Fairly early in my teens I found myself converted to various versions of communitarianism: total equality of opportunity. Living almost next door to our town's only millionaire family, the Firmages, envying them, sort of in love with their daughter, Edna Fae, humiliated about being ordered to knock on their door trying to sell some ears of corn from Grampa Clayson's yard, I quickly came to detest their wealth and to imagine what our town would be

---

6. For a witty satire underlining that word "hopeless," see the novel *Facial Justice* by L. P. Hartley (1960, now out of print). He portrays a society whose dictator tries to enforce full equality, including equal physical beauty. To no reader's surprise, it just won't work. For recent, careful probings of the complex and troublesome issues and paradoxes faced by us egalitarians, see Keith Hart, *Money in an Unequal World* (London: Texere Ltd., 2000); Brian Barry, *Culture and Equality: An Egalitarian Critique of Multiculturalism* (Cambridge: Harvard University Press, 2001); Simon Blackburn, *Being Good* (Oxford: Oxford University Press, 2001); and Nick Hornby's novel, *How to Be Good* (New York: Riverhead Press, 2001). See *Daedalus*, Winter 2002, for an excellent collection of essays exploring both the history of inequality in our so-called democracy and the reasons for its increase.

like if that wealth were really shared equally. Grampa Booth's slogan about the millionaire "crooks" made more and more sense to me. I remember a fantasy, after getting a hamburger in our one snackbar, about an ideal future when all of the cooking would be done communally, all of us taking turns at it, so that only on a few days of the month would any one family have to cook—or do dishes. These days, on the rare occasions when I take a bite at a fast-food place, I'm amused to think just what a parody of my young dream these joints provide; I don't have to do any cooking, and I don't have to do the dishes, while these slaves go about their underpaid jobs.

No doubt my reading of Mormon history about communal sharing was a prime source of early interest in diverse versions of Socialism and Marxism. Through my late teens, I was reading steadily in various leftish journals—*The New Republic* (totally different from today's rag), *The Nation, Partisan Review,* and books by Socialists and Communists. I longed more and more for a country where everyone was treated not just kindly but equally. George Bernard Shaw's *The Intelligent Woman's Guide to Socialism* totally converted me to the notion of absolutely equal pay for all. What possible argument could be offered against it, other than the desire for triumphing over the poor by hanging on to one's fortune?[7]

Meanwhile I was irresistibly acceding, every day in multiple ways, to the American pressures that obviously and often viciously violate equality. Various competing Selves were creating BourgeoisB, the hypocritical aspirer to join the financially comfortable. (At the same time ThinkerB loved Mencken's coinage, Booboisie, but that love didn't quench the others' aspirations.) While professing hope for a Socialist revolution, I often behaved like an aspiring full-fledged, commercialized "American." For example, though EgalitarianB was strongly pro-union, he somehow didn't find time to join a single strike demonstration. (ThinkerB was too busy working toward his Ph.D.—hardly a Socialist aspiration.)

The only time I came close to genuine political action was in the 1948 election, when sort-of Socialist Henry Wallace was running against Truman

---

7. On the day I wrote that sentence, a new issue of the *Boston Review* arrived, with a powerful argument for a *universal basic income* (UBI)—a guaranteed survival income for every one of the earth's billions (Philippe Van Parijs, "A Basic Income for All," *Boston Review* 25, no. 5 [Oct./Nov. 2000]: 4–8). I immediately joined the small minority of his sixteen respondents who embrace the idea—but then, after a bit more reading in his respondents, I had to join those who claimed that it simply could never be worked out. The paradox between the desired and the realizable is alive in me right now, as in many of those respondents. What is not paradoxical is my contempt for those among the wealthy who spend energy and money to get a less "progressive" tax system or to kill all moves toward equality.

and what's-his-name. I hated what's-his-name—ah, yes, it was Tom Dewey—and I was contemptuous of Truman, so I campaigned to get Wallace on the Illinois ballot. Phyllis and I went up and down the streets of Hyde Park, knocking on doors and depositing leaflets in mailboxes.

But in the election booth, Booth faced the same dilemma that supporters of Ralph Nader faced in 2000: a vote for the tiny minority will be wasted—and it is likely to help the even worse candidates win. So at the last minute I changed my vote to Truman, and the following morning I shared in the celebration in our college hall; at least we had helped defeat the GOP. But EgalitarianB was not at all elated; a country that would give so few votes to Wallace, a country full of people like me who would sell out and vote for a dummy like Truman was doomed.[8] (I should add that, as with millions of other Americans, my opinion of Truman's presidency has risen considerably over the years.)

Before becoming a wishy-washy Socialist, I had gone even further and become, for a while, a surreptitious, secret "Communist sympathizer," a kind of half-assed Trotskyite who most of the time posed in public as just a liberal. The move to the left began early in my missionary years when I stumbled on some persuasive Communist authors—some Stalinist, some Trotskyite. After reading Anna Louise Strong's account of her intellectual struggles in converting to Communism, I felt myself half-converted and spent two diary pages going back and forth on the issues, feeling "completely upset."

That strong temptation toward a full joining of the left was reinforced by an astonishing coincidence in the army. I found myself bunked for a couple of months with Harold Rosen, then an ardent British Communist. (His level of commitment was revealed when I asked whether his wife was also a Communist. "You think I would ever marry a *non*-Communist!") He did not break with the party until the Hungarian disasters in 1957. He is still as close a friend as one can manage cross-Atlantic; we still debate what to do about the world, now that Stalinism has totally tainted the very idea of Communism.

I was immensely impressed not just by his passionate commitment but by his learning and wit. He took me to some of the public Communist meetings, where I was surprised by the quality of the speakers and their debate. How could intellectuals as bright as Harold and those speakers be wrong in their devotion to a cause that so clearly supported my desire to work for ultimate total equality? So EgalitarianB decided that when he returned to the U.S., he would consider joining the Communist Party there.

---

8.   Phyllis and I heard Truman give a campaign speech in Provo, Utah. I was shocked that the media ignored a goof he committed: "Now I've embarked on this campaign trick—I mean trip—to . . ."

A year later, settling into graduate school, he attended a couple more Communist meetings. ThinkerB found these speakers far inferior, in both style and content, to the British intellectuals Harold had introduced me to. Then, after some internal debate among Selves, I took part in a *public* debate with Party members about the movie *The Ox-Bow Incident*, which I loved and they hated. I found them totally unwilling to engage in real debate: it was all obediently predetermined by what their "superiors" had decided. So it was clear that I couldn't have anything to do with a party that echoed the Mormon notion of blind obedience to authority.

I was still, however, a socialist, lowercase and deep down. As I played the double role of conventional scholar/subversive socialist, I remember often thinking of myself as a lifetime "subversive." For more than a decade I had been a "subversive" in Mormonism (I was still teaching classes in Church—teaching what I would assure myself was the *genuine* form of Mormonism), and now I was a subversive in the classroom, teaching *genuine* American ideals—full equality—as opposed to all the major politicians in all parties. I even said in my journal, violating what I would now describe as the teacher's true goals, "All good teachers must be subversives: that's their role, to undermine the conventional beliefs of students." Though I never openly told a class, "You should vote for X, not Y," EgalitarianB was always subversively trying to turn students toward this or that version of "the left wing"—not in terms of political membership, necessarily, but in terms of fundamental beliefs about the primacy of social and economic equality.

Meanwhile—to stress again the hypocritical edge to that belief—I was usually silent in public about my inner commitments. Though writings of Marx were sometimes on our course reading lists,[9] I would *try* to reveal no more commitment to him than to other authors on the list. I had embraced the pedagogical commitment of my favorite mentors: "Teach every thinker's works as that thinker would want them to be taught." Like my teachers Ronald Crane and Richard McKeon, I was pleased when students complained about my having been dogmatically committed to two authors who were obviously in flat conflict. But I'm willing to bet that the more perceptive students detected, beneath that effort at fairness, my actual biases.

A clear example of what now appears to me as *indefensible* hypocrisy is my failure to take any active part in the civil rights movement of the '50s and '60s. As a lifetime-committed antiracist, angry at the Church for its refusal to grant full equality to black members, I was envious of those who went south

---

9. I've been told that today's best-known Marxist thinker in America, Fredric Jameson, says that I introduced him to Marx when he was in my freshman class at Haverford. I wonder if that's true.

and demonstrated. But I didn't even come close to going. Though I gave a bit of cash to this or that organization, HypocriteB didn't wear badges or carry signs or take part in marches.

I also curse myself for the mild, self-protective form of my protests about the Vietnam War. I was certain that it was an awful mistake, as it now appears to almost everyone who studies it. So what did I do about it? Nothing but cautiously support student protests, quietly sign some letters of protest, privately argue with supporters. Why didn't I join protest marches? Why didn't I wear angry buttons or carry placards or threaten dishonest presidents and legislators with more angry letters? (The extent of their lying has become big news these days, as some careful studies have emerged. But we knew about most of it from the beginning.)

I just lived with my conflicts day by day, in effect protecting myself from troubles that strong protesting would have produced. And these days, as the troubles in Iraq mount, I find myself saying, "Why are you wasting your time on that book when you should be joining public protests about our inhumane and grossly unfocused retaliations and preemptive strikes?"

There was one amusingly bland defeat of HypocriteB a bit earlier, in about 1957 or '58 when the Kresge drugstore chain was being rightly attacked all around the country for its racism. I was walking home from a visit to my dentist in downtown Richmond, Indiana. I saw across the street a line of protesters—some of them my students—marching in front of the Kresge store. I was almost torn apart: HypocriteB knew that Earlham College, while proclaiming political neutrality, would want nothing to do with any public protest. EgalitarianB knew he should join; the protesters were justified. So finally I walked across the street and joined the march.

Next day I was called to the president's office.

> "You realize that you probably cost Earlham a lot of money yesterday—your marching in that parade got featured on local TV last night, and I've had protest calls from members of the Board."

We discussed it, with him insisting that I promise never to do it again. I can't really remember what I finally "promised," though it was probably something like "I promise never to do it again without thinking very hard about it." What I do remember is that I did nothing further to support the causes I deeply believed in—except for, again, those tiny annual cash gifts.

Am I still a socialist, lowercase? BourgeoisB answers sharply, "Of course not." Even those who, like Fredric Jameson, still consider themselves Marxists admit that totalitarian top-down socialism can be dangerous. We all "know" that *total* bureaucratization, of the kind to which Socialist aspiration has so often led, just does not work. Managers with no attention to marketing and competition do a worse job of devising production rules and controlling costs than market competition does. Right? And don't the atrocities of Stalinism prove the disastrous effect of destroying competition?

If Socialism had come to America, I might not have been able to buy a pen this week or perhaps my brand of toothpaste or toilet paper. Right? Who knows? As one satirist has put the problem, "The Socialist's dream was that everyone should be equally deprived."

But EgalitarianB is still uncomfortable with that picture, as he considers the fat-cat CEOs who receive four hundred times the income of their workers. Do my other Selves join him in hating those bastards? Absolutely—unless, like George Soros, they donate *most* of their excess to the increase of justice and fairness. Do I still believe that the government should impose an even more progressive tax law that would pass much of that wealth down the line? Absolutely. I'm still longing in my heart for some sort of financial and social equality—equality of *opportunity*—in our increasingly commodified, competitive, rise-to-the-top culture. I can prove that longing by reporting my response when I recently read a favorable review of a new book, *It Didn't Happen Here: Why Socialism Failed in the United States.*[10] I bought the book as soon as I could, wondering, "Why *did* the socialist aspiration to justice and equality fail, not just in American culture but even in my soul?"

Well, an answer I like better than the marketeer's is this: We socialists have sold out to the comforts of getting ahead, the pleasures of owning houses and cars and yachts that others cannot afford. We hypocrites surrender daily to violations of the ideal of true equality; I'm typing here on my expensive computer, sitting on a costly ergonomic chair. We're just back from a lovely vacation in Utah at our second home, having been able to afford a third "senior citizen" seat on the plane for my cello. We've each paid more than $4,000 recently for hearing aids, without thinking very hard about what $8,500 would mean to this or that impoverished family.

The egalitarian is still alive in me—I wouldn't be writing this chapter if that were not so. I still believe (does the belief come from the Jesus I meet in the Bible and the Joseph Smith I read about in mostly ignored historical records?) that I can be *fully* defensible to my better Selves only when I follow the directive to "sell all that thou hast and give it to the poor." St. Francis is surely the right model for a "saved" world. I believe that—while,

---

10. Seymour Martin Lipset and Gary Marks (New York: Norton, 2000).

simultaneously, Phyllis and I make (somewhat shaky) plans to take all of our family for a week in the Bahamas at Christmastime.[11]

"Stop that squandering," EgalitarianB shouts. "You must give those thousands of dollars to some charity—or, perhaps better, to some political cause." Does BourgeoisB have a persuasive response? Not really. And so my Selves go on quarreling, one enjoying the pleasures of full inequality, another pontificating against the fat cats up the line, while pitying—but doing little to aid—those below.

Through all this, ThinkerB works hard to exonerate my Selves by making the obvious point, daily, that the real problem is not me but our commercialized societies and the fantastic complexities faced by anyone who tries to combat the increasing inequalities. Unless we find large-scale measures to fight back, democracy is doomed. At which point I hear a voice shouting, "Why, then, don't you drop this silly book and get out there to work with organizations that . . ." But a chorus of other Booths silences him.

Meanwhile, how does the egalitarian face his aspirations to academic success? How does he face the Booth who has hoped to be admired most by the "top" minds?

A while ago I read a report of the annual conference of Mensa, that bunch of elitists who boast to the world that they have an IQ score above something or other. I found myself laughing about their false pride. How could anyone be so stupid as to think that scoring high on an IQ test makes you somehow a Somebody, looking down on the Nobodies?[12] Even if you believe that, how could you be so stupid as to declare *openly* that kind of absurd pride? And how could anyone with any sense want to associate for five minutes with a crowd whose yardstick of human worth is such a test?[13]

Ten minutes later I was making out a check for the annual gift to the University of Chicago, which could almost be called my true church. Why? Because it's inhabited by the truly elite, the intellectually "saved." Because when I walk down a campus sidewalk, I can count on meeting friends and strangers who have really studied Aristotle and Plato, Aquinas and Spinoza, Kant and Hegel, not to mention the history of literary criticism, of rhetoric,

---

11. The plans were never realized, in part because of worries about travel after September 11, 2001. Fortunately the debates about the vacation were never as troublesome as those dramatized by Jonathan Franzen in *The Corrections*.
12. Again I'm obviously referring to Robert Fuller's book, with his attack on "rankism." (See chapter 4.)
13. Some months after writing that draft, I read (in February 2001) that Mensa was putting some energy into charitable activism—with a hint of equality-drive in it. Bravo.

of England in the year 1819, critiques of T. S. Eliot's anti-Semitism, and on and on. I can count on a conversation about ideas with almost anyone I meet, anywhere on campus. When I meet strangers in the bookstore, students or faculty members, they are buying interesting books, and we can chat about them. Colleagues can read my manuscripts and tear them apart productively. What a place! We almost chant to one another the slogan: "This is *The* University, the one place where pursuit of ideas counts more than anything else."

If that isn't elitist, what is? And if you believe, as I do, that every person on this earth is as important as any other person, that teaching high school or elementary school in the inner city is more important than teaching undergraduate students and graduate students, that teaching a nonreader how to read a newspaper is actually more important than teaching a grad student to read Jacques Derrida or Homi Bhabha, how can you defend your having sold out to the most intellectually elitist university on earth?

I can reconcile this conflict only with self-centered language like "LoverB chooses what he loves to do." There is simply no way to argue that more is done for the "good of the world" by teaching where I've taught than is done by a devoted teacher in the inner city. I've sometimes claimed that if I could have been paid an equal salary and given an equally light teaching load in a high school, I would have chosen to teach in public high schools. But is that really true? I doubt it. For reasons already clear to you, early on I joined the "intellectual elitists," the kind who look down on Mensa for having the wrong notion of what intellectual quality is: "It's not IQ, buddies; it's ideas, thinking, probing, inquiry—call it what you will." And VainB adds, "We genuine thinkers are at the top of the intellectual pyramid."[14]

It's hardly surprising that I find such inner conflicts irresolvable. If you believe Christ is right in his exhortations, how can you spend your life concentrating on "improving the lives" only of those whose lives are already "at the top"? You should concentrate on the "least of these," right?

Absolutely. Maybe if this book sells a few copies, I can afford to raise my annual charity commandment from 10 to 15 percent.

---

14. EqualityB, feeling a bit oppressed, now whispers, "Every member of Mensa is absolutely equal, in the eyes of your God, to every other human being. It's stupidly elitist of you to feel contempt for them even while you wonder whether, if you had taken the IQ test at the right time, you could have been invited to join. Besides, haven't many of them read Aristotle or Heidegger? Surely they do real thinking—occasionally?"

Chapter Ten

A College Dean Struggles to Escape

December 1965

Edward Levi, Provost: It seems to all of us that you are by far the best qualified of our candidates for the deanship.

Professor Booth: But Mr. Levi, I just don't think I *am* qualified. For one thing, I'm not good at handling paper-clip details.

EL: Nobody qualified for real administering of a university is good at handling the paper clips. You can hire somebody else to do the boring details.

June 1966

Psychotherapist: But just what is it that has led you to come to someone like me for the first time in your life?

WB: I feel trapped—and I feel more daily desperation than ever before.

February 1968

WB: I really must resign, much as I know it troubles you. I just can't take it any more.

EL: That would be a major betrayal. With all of our rising threats of more demonstrations, we just cannot manage without you. So I say, absolutely, no. I will not accept your resignation.

To obey is better than sacrifice. . . . For rebellion is as the sin of witchcraft.

—2 Samuel 15:22

May 14, 1967

I'm at Berea College, Kentucky. Having given my lecture, I'm now having a bad, restless night, worrying about the sit-in problems back in Chicago. Phone rings at 2 AM. Edward Levi, provost, has called to "order" me to return to Chicago immediately to help him cope with the sit-in. He is trying to sound calm, but his voice reveals that he is clearly seething below the surface as he says, "Maybe we've come off not too badly so far—I can't tell."

On the plane very early in the morning, I have the following wild fantasies: I'm chatting with Ed and say, "I'm tired of pulling your chestnuts out of the fire." I'm asked to take over on Levi's resignation. I'm fired. I'm back again, telling off the students for betraying the university—defending them against excessive reprisal—then standing them off—persuading them to drop it, with my superior rhetoric . . .[1]

Except for the two years in the army, the only sustained period when a single longing dominated almost all of the splits was my five-year term as dean of the college at the University of Chicago (1964–69). I began with an exhilarated sense of a terrific opportunity to make a difference; I would restore the sense of excitement and innovation and intellectual quest that had marked the so-called Hutchins College when I taught in it for three years (1947–50). But I soon found that I had infinite responsibilities and almost no authority or power or skill for carrying them out.

It took me a while to discover the trap I'd landed in. But I did quickly see the inadequacy of my ability to correlate the complex demands of the job with the surprising lack of authority to impose decisions. The authority was mainly in the hands of department chairs and division deans—and on up the line. As mere *college* dean I was, much of the time, only a smiling public image.

Edward Levi,[2] whom I greatly admired, had most of the power and "gave me no rope," as I put it after more than a year of disappointments. Even the

---

1. See my journal entry on the plane.
2. Not long after, he became the president, and then Attorney General of the U.S. under President Ford—said by some today to have been the most important, and certainly the most passionately committed to integrity, of any of the Attorney Generals we've ever had.

Dean of the College, 1964

5411 S. Greenwood, the house we lived in for almost forty-five years

chairmen of minor departments had more actual effect on day-by-day decisions than I had. I was mainly a showpiece, even from the beginning. And to
put on the show, my main assignment seemed to be deciding which mask I
should put on for this or that occasion. Unlike the masking I had done as a
missionary, these hypocritical moments seemed always imposed by . . . well,
not by an army exactly, but by a collection of external forces.

The hopelessness of my effort was revealed in my first dispute with a department chairman about an appointment. The history department had chosen to
appoint a young man whose specialty was Japanese naval history in the late nineteenth century. Protocol required that I interview him about how he would meet
the requirement to teach in the college core courses, especially History of Western Civilization. After two hours probing his interests, I could see not only that
he was indifferent to and ignorant of western civilization studies; he was opposed
to the requirement that he teach beginning undergraduate courses. So I had a
long argument with William McNeill, the history department chairman, appealing to his decades-long commitment to the college. And, of course, I lost.

June 13, 1965
Effect of the conversation: depression. Prof. McNeill so clearly represents the
new mood of indifference to undergrad. education. He reminisced proudly

about the great days (late forties) when he and five others developed the Western Civilization course. "We really gave ourselves to that, almost thoughtlessly, you might say; we paid no attention to whether it was valuable to our professional advancement. What you ought to try to do—well, maybe it's impossible, but if you could find a similar group of young men now and turn them loose to develop their own course, that might get more of them involved. . . ."

Nobody can predict what will happen to undergraduate education in the next ten years. Will the grotesque rush for graduate positions continue? [Of course.] What can reverse it?

The discouragement soon moved to moments of despair about the entrapment.

July 20, 1965 [about six months in]
Still working, with a sense of desperation, to complete what we call the "team" of [five] Associate Deans, or "Masters." And every morning, as I try to get myself down to work, I am filled with a revulsion for my job that is stronger than anything of the kind I can remember—except my sense of being trapped when I was a missionary. [Somehow he fails to mention the entrapment of the army.] I can tell no one how much I hate my present situation, not even Phyllis (because it depresses her needlessly); to tell anyone at the University that I hate it would automatically spoil my chances of success—and might make it more difficult to obtain a replacement when I quit.

Why do I not quit now? In theory, hating a job must ensure failure. Why not admit to myself (and others) that I made a mistake and get out? Well, one difficulty is that I don't feel steady revulsion: once I get down to the work I enjoy perhaps half of it, and there are even moments when I have fantasies of staying at it by choice, not necessity. I even (God help me) have occasional fantasies of being offered other administrative positions and accepting! There is something really curious about my character, something that I do not see clearly yet: I impress others as suited for administration, I inspire confidence, I can do what is required (some of it even with flair), but I have not the central drive, the central pleasure in power—*something* is lacking that is a necessary part of effective leadership. One trouble is that I simply detest giving orders, yet orders must be given. . . . What I enjoy are the surface moments, the speaking, and the rhetoric of the job. What I hate is the substantive, day-by-day decision making.[3]

---

3. It's amusing to me now to see so little in my journals about the negative side effects of being a preoccupied dean. I don't mention the loss of time for playing chamber music or the neglect of Phyllis and the children. (See chapter 14.)

Then, after some thoughts about "the panic of middle-age" and not knowing what he really wants to do with his life, the trapped dean rounds it off:

> Have I ever used the word "despair" about myself before? It is wrong, even here, because it is not my temperament (or so I tell myself) to despair as many men despair. But what other word is there for the empty-gutted feeling I have as I think, now, at 9:30 AM, of having to face that desk and the [promotion] decisions about Irving Kristol and Don Levine?

A week later he thinks he's surviving.

July 26
Since that last despairing entry the mood has gone generally up. Why? No good reason. A talk with Ed Levi, whose air of competence no doubt accounts largely for my sense of incompetence, cheered me, for once:
   "When do you think we should appoint the committee to look for my successor, in two years' time?"
   "Oh, you don't want to quit in two years." [Obviously his refusal to describe me as a failure is what kept me going for the full five years.]
   "But I don't have the temperament for this job."
   "Nobody does. Who could have a temperament for academic administration? . . . Anyway, you're doing beautifully, beautifully.". . .
   Even on this fine clear cool Sunday morning (after a heat wave) I cannot really understand how I could have "done this to myself."

Within a very short time, I became so depressed that I went, for the first time in my life, to a psychotherapist.[4] It's hardly surprising that the main themes in my sessions with him were fear of failure and embarrassment about resigning. After three months I wrote this:

October 21, 1965
My sessions with Eugene Gendlin, a "non-directive counselor" [trained by Carl Rogers], have been extremely helpful:
(a) my fears of failure are not only contemptible, which I have long known them to be, but they are explicable—in the sense that they have a long history. I have feared failure from earliest memory, often when I was succeeding very well—and there's the comforting thing. My history, talked over in four sessions, reveals that fear of failure, for me, bears no relation to the external facts of success or failure.

---

4.   The only other time was after Richard was killed.

(b) I am unusually dependent on the judgment of "the world". . . . long years of dependence on father figures [he then lists them] . . . and Edward Levi.

My chief hope, before I had quite realized my utter powerlessness, was to recover for the college something like the full intellectual brilliance of the "Hutchins" curriculum. Robert Maynard Hutchins and Richard McKeon and others had constructed what many of us saw as the most profound and coherent basic curriculum in educational history—four years of requirements culminating in a capstone yearlong course putting it all together: Organization, Methods, and Principles of Knowledge (OMP).[5] I had become deeply converted to that college, particularly because of learning so much in our weekly staff meetings.

Through the preceding decade the curriculum had been, from my perspective, grotesquely mutilated,[6] and it was time to restore at least some of the lost coherence. And so, working with the five new "Masters" of the "Collegiate Divisions," we developed a plan for reducing the first-year requirements in order to redistribute some of them into the third and fourth years, including a genuine capstone course pursuing how the greatest of educational philosophers had attempted to organize all knowledge.

The plan still seems to me almost brilliant. We did not then, and I would not now, commit the folly of claiming that there is some one complete and unique way to organize knowledge; the plan was "pluralistic" in ways that, if understood, would harmonize with many "postmodernist" efforts to discredit various dogmatisms. But the proposal, with its genuinely challenging intellectual quality, was defeated—perhaps mainly because of my political naïveté as an administrator. In our passion for a challenging change, we six completely ignored the political problem that no administrator should ignore: the need for elaborate "precinct work." We failed to consult in advance with all of the factions. We worked the plan out privately, quickly printed it up, and mailed it to all the professors. They must have felt that it just came out of the blue, as an authoritarian effort to take charge, and it was immediately attacked—on all

---

5.   That impulse to help students put together what they've learned through four years survives strongly. Two colleagues and I developed a pale imitation of that "OMP" in 2001, now designed as an elective for seniors: Organization of Knowledge (OOK), using Plato, Aristotle, Kant, Comte, and some modern thinkers' efforts to "put it all together." Many students said, "Best course ever," and nearly all of them wrote in their anonymous evaluations that we should do it again. (We did, in 2004. See chapter 5.)

6.   I had written from Earlham College in 1954 or '55 a protest letter, telling the president that his abuse of "my" college had led me to decide never to give any further donations. A few weeks later I received his response: "Dear Professor Booth: We think we can manage without your $25 per year."

sides. We had *intended* to produce discussion and only afterward a vote. But to those receiving the mailed proposal, the discussion was already over; we six had done the discussion, and they had been ruled out, their interests ignored.

A passionate movement against it arose quickly, with very few taking the trouble to do an actual study of what the proposal was about; some professors openly refused even to read our plan. It was soon voted down, with no serious discussion. I was shattered. Here's how I recorded the protests:

> A petition from the philosophy department, protesting that the plan was too philosophical. A petition from the Jr. English teachers, protesting that it would make them work too hard. Radical misreading all over the campus. . . . some active politicking. Delegations from students—they had not been consulted. . . . Why haven't you done this? Why haven't you done that? . . . Home to bed, bowels churning. Hardly any sleep; endless arguments, counter-arguments, pleas, angry letters. Just as I would get to sleep, cramps would wake me; and I would lie twisting the whole thing over again. Two AM decided to resign. . . . Felt sense of betrayal, to self and others. Whatta mess. An unfair mess. Why me?

My next plan had more success. I managed to persuade the faculty to close *all* classes for a full week of "free inquiry"—a week of widespread, informal discussions of "The Knowledge Most Worth Having." With scores of faculty members volunteering discussions of why *their* knowledge was worth pursuing and with our characteristically engaged students joining enthusiastically, we had a fabulous week.[7] I felt that we were on our way to a genuine Hutchins-style revolution.

I must ask those readers here who are teachers, have you ever seen a college cancel all classes for a week in order to have scores of somewhat chaotic discussions of what education is about?

Despite that success, the misery, the chained-down misery, continued.

> *February 15, 1966*
> One morning recently, as I walked to my office, I found myself thinking, over and over again, "This is the worst period of my life. This is the worst period of my life.". . .

---

7. This memory is one that receives confirmation still today, more than three decades later. A junior colleague recently wrote me a full page of praise for that week: "The Conference was the first thing to help clear up my dark edges [about what my education was about]. . . . People were explicitly talking about the meaning of education . . . saying things that had direct personal meaning. . . . For the first time I felt I might be able to belong to the University community."

Dream: Someone is drowning, someone jumps in to save him, is grabbed, begins to drown. I jump in to save them both, but the second man, already dead, has grasped my hand in an unbreakable grip. We go down, down; I realize that I cannot save myself except by cutting off my own hand. I take out my machete and am just about to hack at my wrist with it when I wake up.

. . . My misery is really caused by my knowledge that as a dean I'm a fraud: except for making speeches and being cheerful, I'm no good at it.

On through to the end of my mostly miserable five years, I felt I was "accomplishing nothing"—partly because of the sit-ins we come to below. I often tried to resign, but Edward Levi would "plant his foot on me," as my journal put it, and talk me out of it.

Do I now think of those five miserable years as a total waste? Of course not. They taught me the strongest lessons ever about my own deficiencies— my total ineptitude in political matters and my ignorance of how social improvements can be managed. Somehow sticking out the five years and being pressured to take a second term, I resigned as a considerably less arrogant guy than I had been at the beginning. And as I escaped from my hated office, I swore never to become another administrator.[8]

The point here is mainly, however, to dramatize how those five years, like the army two years, somehow transformed the whole pattern of my division of Selves. Most of the time I was faced with only one debate about what to do with my life: resign or not. Circumstance, not the free agency that Mormonism had promised me, controlled every moment of every day. I was facing conflicts between "impossible" dean-demands and my duties to family; I was plagued by getting no writing done, by accomplishing nothing as a "scholar." Though I did teach one course every term, the classes became more and more routine heirs to what I had managed to invent earlier. In general I felt chained to my circumstances and thus—most of the time unconsciously—freed from any need to grapple with my divided Selves.

But was I really freed? Some of the journal entries reveal a deeply divided self.

July 24, 1966 [after reporting how miserable Phyllis was, working on her dissertation]
Deaning absorbs me without transforming me. Or if it transforms me, it is into something I don't like. I no longer really enjoy sitting down to the

---

8. I had actually turned down several direct offers, including the presidency of one of the Seven Sisters in the Ivy League: no more administration for me!

typewriter. I can't write letters, I can't read steadily. When I listen to music, as I just listened to the Brahms Cello Sonata (which one? which one?) I fiddle with other things—munch food, glance at the comic strips, think about things to be done. . . . I am so scattered that this morning, when I had planned four hours of solid work . . . I am instead writing here, a bit tense, blue, unable to face any one of my immediate tasks.

And on I go, with a "definite decision" every few months to "resign now."

At 10:30 AM, after talking with my assistant, I decided that I will definitely resign on or before Dec. 10, 1967—one year from now. . . . Like Huck Finn, I immediately felt washed and cleansed of sin.

February 22, 1967 [my birthday; a letter to a friend]
On the phone you said I sounded dead. Phyllis dreamed night before last that I *was* dead, and she felt very bad about it indeed. I have recorded that I feel "destroyed" by the job; sometimes it has indeed felt like a kind of death, though more often it feels like a depletion or emptying—a probing into an empty container. Today I decided . . . to get some counseling with a [second] psychologist who will see me next week and explore why I can be ok one minute (as this minute) and destroyed with self-loathing and a sense of incompetence and/or *acedie* the next. Won't he? Surely he'll be able to say what was/is wrong with a man who is overwhelmed with a job that is, objectively speaking, intolerable!

Actually the counseling worked—at least for a bit. Three months later I wrote my sister:

Talking my fears out each week with Dr. Lipkin and Phyllis . . . has proved tremendously helpful: after our Thursday morning hour, I go to work with real bounce; all of my thoughts about resigning have disappeared, and I'm really looking forward to the summer in which I can make solid plans for the last two years of my term.

Then, two months later, I sent a formal letter of resignation to the president and provost—and again Levi talked me out of it.

THE EFFECT OF THE PROTEST GENERATION

No doubt my response to all of the pressures would have been much different if we had not suddenly found ourselves dealing with a series of threatening sit-ins. Not long after the success of the "Knowledge Most Worth Having" conference, we began to have sit-ins—three crises (and other threats) over four years. These became my obsession, and all possibility of serious curricular improvements disappeared.

The first administration building sit-in occurred over the issue of the government's using college grades to determine eligibility for the Vietnam draft. I found myself mainly on the students' side, though often troubled by their extremism. I attempted a lot of negotiation and was accused of fence straddling. I openly joined the students in opposing the Vietnam War and the unfairness of the draft policy, and yet I was often seen by them as only an "administrator," a member of the detested establishment who wanted nothing but to get the students out of the building. We found ourselves endlessly engaged with meetings and demonstrations, the faculty and administration inevitably divided on how to get the students to clear out.

Now there you have my memory as of May 2003. Today I happened on the following penciled journal entry, written on a plane flying back from St. Louis on May 14, 1967; it's a much more complicated version:

> The "troops" occupied the adm. bldg. at about 2:30 on Wednesday. That morning at 10:30 about nine faculty members came to my office, hoping to "stop the sit-in"—all but one clearly meaning "to get the adm. to change its mind" [and side with the students]. Kim Marriott, who had been at the Council Meeting, had a different view—"find some way to get the two sides together." It was reported that the students had, the night before, "moderated their demands," now insisting only on postponement of the provision of ranking [for the draft] until the fall.
>
> It was proposed that I meet the students at the door and "plead" with them—or as K. M. said, explain how slight was the difference between their demands & what the administration statement meant. I said I was willing—but could not think it would do any good. (I *was* willing, too.) [Richard] Flacks agreed [that it would be useless], & we decided not to. This now seems to me to have been a mistake (perhaps)—is there a chance I could have stopped them? So slight as to be meaningless.
>
> They wondered if a further statement from the adm. would not be a good idea—if only to clarify. (Some were insisting that the adm. change— all were opposed to the draft policy [as of course I was].) I tried to explain the nature of the present decision, including the Council's role. . . . After they left I phoned W. Blum [Professor of Law]—he was absolutely adamant [about any compromise]: "just smile and tell them to go to the students and talk *them* out of it.". . .
>
> I cancelled my lunch and went on talking w/students and faculty—always trying to defend the adm. while making clear that (a) protesters had

not really understood the adm.'s position, and (b) that the position could not be changed under threat. (Am I sure we are right in this? No—only that we must not appear to change out of fear of the threat. To change, as we should, *regardless of the threat*, could be an act of magnanimity.)

At 2:30 I was being harangued by a hysterical young man who somehow expected me to stop the whole show by some kind of last minute phone call. I phoned [W.] Blum twice to see if he would talk w/the student; he would not. And by then the students were in the bldg anyway.

I phoned Jeff Blum later in the afternoon to see if I c'ld not get thru to him that the "exploration of alternatives" promised in our statement was really intended. It was clear that if he and I had been able to deal together no sit-in would have occurred. Earlier Peter Rabinowitz [protester who was one of my favorite students, now a "lifelong friend"] had said, "If you were in charge the whole thing wouldn't have happened. I hope you don't give up, lose yr. faith."[9] I also talked with . . .[etc.]

W[arner]W[ick, professor of philosophy] & EL said I should feel free to go [give my talk] at Berea—nothing to do here. So I got on the train, feeling guilty, and had a beautiful night's sleep—next day was advised not to return, by WW; speaking for W. Blum and C[harles] Daley [presidential assistant]. WW's talk was full of EL's anger, threats against the College, against the students. Redfield phoned me in St. Louis Friday evening to say that EL had talked of cutting College to 500—"what would it matter"—talked of resigning. Very angry, very disgusted. Redfield thinks we should—now that main group is out (leaving perhaps 25 in) work at convincing the moderates to abandon threat of another sit-in. I'm disturbed at EL's anger, his threats of reprisal against faculty & students.

EL waked me at 2 AM to ask me to return [from Berea] for meeting at 10:00 this morning. I gather that the purp. of mtg. will be to agree on punishment—for me about the last pt. we sh'ld be working on now.

My mind is churning w/fantasies: I am resigning, w/a flourish. "I'm tired of pulling your chestnuts out of the fire."—I am asked to take over on Levi's resignation.—I am fired.—I am telling off the students for betraying the university—defending them against excessive reprisal—standing them off—persuading them w/ superior rhetoric—

EL was calm, at 2:00 AM, but clearly seething below the surface— "Maybe we've come off not too badly so far—I can't tell."

What line do I take at that meeting this morning?

---

9. I'm pretty sure he couldn't have had in mind the multiple meanings the word "faith" would carry for me.

The outcome was ambiguous. The students did not carry out their threat of another sit-in. The administration held firm—for a while, but within a few months the Senate faced the moral issue of basing draft status on grades and cancelled it. The student *position*, backed by many faculty members including me, had finally won. But that's not how it felt just after the sit-in.

> *Saturday, May 21, 1966*
> At no point [in the meeting of administrators, where I was expected to make a speech but did not find any way to fit it in] did we ever arrive at a clear administrative line. Our meetings [have all been] horrible examples of how not to arrive at staff decisions. Whether this was [President] Beadle's fault . . . or Levi's, the result is terribly wearing, and no doubt it is what made us all finally so snappy and—the last two days—so depressed and apathetic. I've managed to keep going, with far more energy for action than I normally have, but Edward is utterly defeated—talks of resigning. . . . I *think* of resigning, but cannot do so if he does. His resignation in itself would be disastrous. His and mine together at this point would be, for me, unthinkable, much as I have hated my entrapment.

The second sit-in, the only one that yields me any pride, has never been reported until this moment, so far as I know.[10] Black students, of whom we had only a shamefully small proportion (and still have; my student assistant has told me that in his class of graduate students in English "there's not a single African American or Latino!"), were organizing a protest. The administration, in the aftermath of the first sit-in, was preparing both an elaborate disciplinary code for protest movements and a document promising improvement on all "black" issues. I was sitting as an official observer at a large public protest meeting when word came that the black students had already occupied the sixth floor of our administration building. I ran out and across campus, found the elevators closed and the stairs blocked by a huge male student. I convinced him, somehow, that I was hoping to help, and he let me climb the six floors, where I found about fifty students chatting, lunching, wandering about. Nobody would speak with me. So I simply sat down on the floor, uncomfortable, wondering what I could do.

Suddenly two white policemen came in from the stair entry. I jumped to my feet and accosted them.

"Why are you here?"

---

10. When giving a talk about this event recently (June, 2004), I was told that some people did learn about my "secret" event from reports in some fringe newspapers.

"We were called because of this sit-in."

"Well, I'm sorry, Sir, but this has nothing to do with needing police help. We are handling it ourselves."

We argued, I won, and they retreated down the stairs.

I returned to where I had been sitting on the floor. A woman student who had been in one of my classes and who had looked a bit embarrassed earlier about not greeting me came up to me and said, "Mr. Booth, would you like an apple?"

We chatted and finally agreed to have a meeting to talk over what could be done. As the whole group met, I gave as forceful a speech as I could muster, pursuing two lines: "What will you gain if you continue this sit-in?" and "What might you lose if you continue?" I explained that simultaneously across campus a disciplinary committee was preparing an indictment that would lead to suspension or expulsion of everyone identified with any sit-in. I then gave a detailed account of the University's plan for improving the lot of black students, a plan that none of them had yet seen. I described it—I hope honestly—as designed both to improve relations with black students and to increase recruiting.

I like to think that it was one of the best extemporaneous speeches of my life. They voted to leave the building, and the whole event disappeared.

So the troubled dean did have the power of rhetoric. But that was not of much use through the next months—ending in the third sit-in, the most prolonged of the three, in the winter of 1969.[11] I won't bother you here with the many journal entries about how we managed, day after day for fifteen days, to avoid calling the police (our decision committee was always divided, with Edward Levi always agreeing with my side that this should be an internal matter, not one for the police). The behavior of some faculty members was atrocious. One arrived at most meetings wearing his army uniform with all of his badges. Another suggested, before the students actually got in, that we leave some cash distributed about the office desks so that we could have students arrested for theft.

After the students' fifteen days of increasing frustration (and some vandalism), they left the building, confessing defeat. Then we had endless disciplinary

---

11. No one has ever been able to offer a precise single cause for the huge sit-in. One version had it centered on our not offering tenure to a Marxist woman, Marlene Dixon; as time went on, student views of how good she had been as a teacher shot up, while faculty views shot down. Another explanation was, of course, the Vietnam War. And another has been cultural analysis of that generation of students. What I am sure of, having known many of the protesters personally, is that some were genuinely, deeply motivated by wanting to "improve the world."

hearings (in which I was not involved), ending in punishment, excessive in my view: total expulsion of about thirty-six students who had refused to appear before the committee to defend themselves, along with innumerable "suspensions" of those who did turn up.

Whether or not social historians approve of that sequence of decisions—recent accounts have reported it as the best handling of protest by any university—the effect on my hopes for college reform was again disastrous. There was nothing but "how do we deal with this protest mess?"

My deaning ended with an episode that could almost be called comic. I must report it because it provides a bit of semiviolent drama for a book where too much of the drama is merely internal. At the time of graduation, after those students had been expelled, many seniors, perhaps a majority, either refused to attend the graduation ceremony or wore black armbands. We feared the kind of open violence that had occurred on other campuses.

As we administrators gathered in a side room, preparing to march into the chapel, we heard from a security officer that someone had spotted a machine-gun among the students who were gathering downstairs. Levi hastily reorganized our scene; instead of my being on the west side of Rockefeller Chapel, calling out the names of the would-be graduates, with him on the east side handing out the diplomas, I would move over beside him, with someone else calling out the names. My job was to scrutinize the students' hands as they walked toward us, to see if any gun appeared. HypocriteB stood facing the marchers with a broad smile, trembling inside. I had put on the mask of utterly cheerful innocence.

Sure enough, one young man did begin to pull something out from under his robe. An automatic rifle! I leapt forward, and quickly realized, as I grabbed the gun, that it was a toy. The student whispered to me, "Mr. Booth, it's just a fake!" I tucked it out of sight, Levi gave the student his degree, and the ceremony went on, with HypocriteB still smiling as I scanned for any more guns.

Only later did I learn that a security guard standing behind me had a *real* gun aimed at the kid, with me actually in the line of fire. Wouldn't this *LIFE* be a hell of a lot more interesting if I'd actually been shot at that moment?

Instead, after five years of distraction from my split Selves, I escaped—back into the conflicts of "real" life.

Part Two

The Splits Multiply—in Somewhat Less Torturous Form

As I've explored my many "splits," it's been hard to rank their importance. At times this or that one feels most important of all, and then, once ThinkerB intrudes, it seems trivial—not worth including. As I now introduce some that I feel are "less torturous" than those we've met so far, one or another may seem to you more important than some you have already read about. In any case, none of them now feels to me really trivial; they're just slightly less threatening to the hope for final harmony. At least I deserve some credit for omitting some trivialities, like the split between SpeederB, who—as one student said of him—never loses a minute, and ReviserB, who almost never allows hasty production of a manuscript, as well as ZenB, who feels deep reproach of anyone who spoils the day by pushing too hard to get things done fast.

Readers of drafts have been almost comically contradictory in their advice about cutting and adding and placement: "You surely don't think that your dealing with lust is more significant than your failure to be an ideal father!" "You should not downgrade your desire to become a novelist by placing it here, while playing up your obviously insignificant impulses for political reform in chapter 9." "Why have you left out the conflict between the Skinflint who has always struggled to save every penny and the Squanderer who once bought a Mercedes-Benz?"

Thus the ranking of the splits constitutes another split: just which of my various "Voices" or "Selves" gets top priority and which need never be mentioned? From the beginning you have been receiving contradictory hints about possible answers. In the final chapter I move toward a bit more clarity. But meanwhile, as you exercise your judgment about my choices, keep in mind the question "How do my divisions of Self, major or minor, compare with yours?" I'm willing to bet that you have some that I've never even thought of.

Chapter Eleven

The Quarrel between the Cheater and the Moralist Produces Gullible-Booth

The most positive men are the most credulous.

—Alexander Pope

Want of tenderness is want of parts, and is no less a proof of stupidity than depravity.

—Samuel Johnson

Man's gullibility [is] not his worst blessing.

—Thomas Carlyle

Work on,
My medicine, work! Thus credulous fools are caught,
And many worthy and chaste dames even thus,
All guiltless, meet reproach.

—Iago, just after gulling Othello about Desdemona's sex life

Never give a sucker an even break.

—Popular saying through twentieth century

There's a sucker born every minute.

—P. T. Barnum

If the world will be gulled, let it be gulled.

—Robert Burton

Anyone who cannot be gulled by a clever beggar is obviously not a Christian.

—Anonymous

You might expect that being an (almost lifetime) cheater, I would have become unusually suspicious of cheaters. But for some reason, it's been the opposite. I've turned out to be gullible to many con artists. People who know me intimately—no names, please—claim that I am often just plain dimwitted in response to appeals *they* see as obviously fake. MoralB and EgalitarianB sometimes answer with an angry outburst, "Even if they're conning me, isn't it better to risk that than to ignore the possibility that they really need the cash—that they may be genuinely suffering?" "Don't they need this cash more than I do, even if they're conning me?" To which the others respond, "You're not *helping* them when they con you. You're *enabling* them, encouraging them to continue with their alcoholism or drug addiction or sheer daily thieving."

So the splits remain strong and will never go away. One Self says I'm absolutely right, driven to do what I can for "the least of these," but ThinkerB knows that the attackers are also absolutely right: "You don't help someone by letting her con you."

The sources of these splits are clear from previous chapters—my Church, my family. As I've said, Mama always responded with food when a Depression "bum" came to the door, and my grandparents always gave something to the Indians who came each fall with their pine nuts. But the family also issued plenty of warnings about how the "world" is full of cheaters. Mother once even went so far as to say, as we quarreled about it, "Practically anyone will cheat you or drive a hard bargain if they get the chance." I answered quite gullibly, as my journal reports at age twenty-two:

> Few people will cheat you, and one is happier when one forgets there are cheaters in the world. One will be cheated occasionally but the amt. will be small. One doesn't need to be foolish about it, but this eternal suspicion is terrible. . . . The world is improving—people are getting more honest, kind, chaste, humane, social-minded all the time. I am going to try to make myself be *good*, & without being pious, make others good. Man has a long way to go. There is much dishonesty. Man is still human, but there is no cause for general discouragement. . . . I wish mother was happy, or at least happier. She feels sorry for herself, in many respects.

As I see it now, the skepticism and sorrow were largely about having been cheated by God with Daddy's death. But the young optimist doesn't mention that.

For now I select only three of many episodes when my optimism about "the world" and AmbitionB's desire to become more virtuous, with VainB's desire to earn virtue credit, produced Gullible-Booth.

1943

As mission secretary in charge of the mission office, I have a small "charity fund." A uniformed GI comes to the door, explains that he is a "devout Mormon," displays his worn Book of Mormon, and tells an elaborate account about having had his pocket picked the night before while sleeping in the railroad station. He needs $45.70 to get to his uncle in Hammond, Indiana.

Feeling immense sympathy, I immediately succumb with cash from the fund.

A few months later I receive a call from "the American Red Cross in Gary, Indiana." "We have a down-and-out guy here, says he's a devout Mormon, and he is desperate to get to his home in Texas. Do you have a charity fund?"

"Yes, of course."

"Well, he says he needs $95 for his transportation and food—says he's almost starving. Could you possibly meet him in the railroad station just south of the Loop? We'll pay his train fare."

I immediately agree, without a smidgen of doubt, and drive downtown. At the station, I suddenly recognize that the man coming toward me is the same man I had previously "rescued." He glances at me, shocked, and quickly ducks around a corner. I try to catch up to him, but he outruns me.

If I had caught him what would I have done? I felt both anger and sympathy.

Winter 1965 (quoted from a long letter to several family members and friends)
Scene: Bedroom of Professor & Mrs. Booth. Heavy snowstorm outside.

Phone rings. Alison answers [from other room], calls: "Dad, it's a collect call from somebody named Trorie." WB goes to phone.

"Will you accept a collect call from Edward Trorie?"

"Never heard of him."

"He says it's desperate."

"Well, if it's desperate, I'll accept a call. Where is he calling from?"

"Phoenix."

"Oh. Well, OK, I'll still take it."

"Professor Booth, you don't know me, but I've long been an admirer of yours. I'm calling you, I don't know, ah, it doesn't make sense, but I have no place else to turn. It's just that, knowing your *Rhetoric of Fiction*, it's been an important book to me, I'm a writer, you know, and here I am, 61 years old, and I'm absolutely desperate. I just don't know where to turn, I—oh, this must all sound confused and implausible, but you're my last hope. I've phoned my uncle—he's the only one I have left who even knows me, and he didn't answer, and . . ."

"Now wait a minute. What is your trouble?"

"Professor Booth, I've had the most incredible run of bad luck—my writing has never succeeded but I've always got by until now, but here we are, my wife and I, stranded in Phoenix, on our way to California, absolutely out of money. She has been blind, or nearly blind, most of the past four years, though she recently had an operation that restored partial sight in one eye, and I've been trying to get to LA where the Association for the Blind has promised further aid. I just have *got* to get there, but my wife felt sicker yesterday and we had to stop off, and now we don't even have enough to go on with."

"Well, Mr. Trorie, I'm afraid that your brilliant story doesn't sound very convincing. I've often been conned before, and this sounds like a con game to me."

Sounds of sobbing. "Oh, I know it must sound weird and unconvincing, but if you don't help me, I don't know what I'll do." More sobbing.

"Is there anybody I could phone to check your story?"

"Yes, there is, there's my uncle I tried to phone today, in Kent, Ohio. T. S. Trorie, Kent, Ohio. You could ask him about me. But I couldn't get through to him, today; you might have trouble."

"How much do you need for bus fare to LA?"

"Just $23.60. We've not eaten all day, but that doesn't matter, if we could just get on the bus tonight, tomorrow we'll be all right."

Booth still suspects that he is being conned, but he does not have the presence of mind to ask such useful questions as what parts of the *Rhetoric of Fiction* Mr. Trorie has found especially profitable. After more sobbing, dreadful to hear over the night wires, he asks,

"Have you tried the Phoenix traveler's aid or any other charitable group?"

"Oh, you don't know Phoenix. These people out here, they don't care about anybody but themselves. This town is so unfriendly . . ." More sobs.

So Professor Booth agrees to phone Kent, Ohio, and to send money if the story is true.

There follows a brief discussion between the professor and his wife. She is deeply skeptical. Booth phones Kent, Ohio: no T. S. Trorie listed. Phones bus depot. Fare from Phoenix to LA for two is exactly $23.60. Booth curses. Booth moans. Booth decides that it is now only 90% likely that Trorie is a con.

Booth curses again, puts on his coat and snow boots, walks through the deep snow to the Western Union at 63rd and Ellis, and sends $27.00—they've got to eat, too.

The thinker in me feels a bit ashamed of himself for being a gull on that one, but MoralB comforts him for having a heart of gold, while VainB assures him that he does *appear* to have such a heart.

Scene II, two weeks later
Denver, Colorado. Five professors are dining in the Denver Hilton. Subject of conning comes up. Booth asks, "Have any of you ever heard the name Edward Trorie?" Professor Robert Gorrell laughs.

"Have I heard of him? Have I *heard* of him? He phoned me, talked me into seventy-eight bucks—but now I remember, he took Robert Clark [son of Walter Van Tilburg Clark] twice, for a hundred dollars and then for a hundred twenty-five. And he took Ray West. With Clark he pretended to be from Clark's hometown . . . and to know relatives, relatives Clark said had never been listed in any biography so the story *must* have been genuine. With me he pretended to be from near my hometown in Indiana. And he was an English teacher. I don't know what he said to West. That s.o.b.—I swear, that s.o.b. was *so* effective!"

Booth and Gorrell almost fall into each other's arms—with laughter, with mutual admiration, and with only mild self-contempt. They feel they have established a lifelong bond.

I later learned that Trorie had made a similar attempt on Saul Bellow, but Bellow caught on quickly and just hung up.

1999, Chicago
A tall, macho black man rings the doorbell, asks if we need someone to shovel the huge snowfall. We do. I pay him, at about ten bucks per hour. Joe does a good job. Next snowstorm, he is back, does a good job again. And again, through the winter.

Soon he begins to come to the door to ask for a loan for this or that emergency. Some of the time he pays me back. But the emergencies get worse and worse as the weeks and months go by. (I could quote ten pages of notes from my diaries about these "visits.") He is in and out of hospitals—or so he claims, as I pick him up and deliver him to this or that location. He always has documentary evidence or wrist-identification bands. He needs such and such for medicine; he needs so and so to escape a gang threat.

Jewel, our "cleaning lady" and by now our close friend, on one of his visits overhears our conversation and tells me afterward, "That's just jive talk; don't believe him." My wife and daughters keep nagging me to cut it off, partly because to help him I often find myself traveling into "dangerous territory"—driving him to this or that ghetto hospital or friend's apartment seeking help.

But I keep on believing him, as he talks more and more favorably about getting a job, with my help.

Finally, things come to a climax that you've been predicting.

March 17, 1998 [Letter to daughters, who have warned me about being gullible with Joe]
The "Joe" problem goes on and on, never fully resolved. I thought I had him set up for an appointment with counselors and job-helpers, but had not heard from him for about a week, after giving him $40 for medicine.

Saturday night we have friends in for dinner. As we sit down for hors d'oeuvres, the back doorbell rings. When that happens, it's always Joe. I signal to turn him away. He goes on ringing, shouting, "Wayne, Wayne, ahm desperate, ya gotta help me, I'm scared man, I gotta tell ya bout it."[1] Finally I let him in—to explain to him why we've reached the end: I can't go on helping.

"Look, Joe, we have company. I've told you before, no more money until you take a job. . . ." He interrupts.

"Wayne, I gotta tell ya, man, I'm really scared. They after me."

"Who's after you?"

"Them Purto Rickans. They gonna kill me, man."

"Wait a minute, Joe, I can't listen to your story now. We got company in there. . . .

---

1. One reader—and one of my more cautious Selves—warns that I must drop all of the "street dialect" here and have Joe talk just like me. "Isn't it both racist and elitist to have him talk like a character out of *Huck Finn* or *Their Eyes Were Watching God?*" To which MoralB replies, "Just how dishonest are you suggesting I should be, transcribing this letter, after claiming total honesty here?"

Again he interrupts, his eyes rolling, brighter than I've ever seen them. Sweat rolling down. He grabs my arm (several times in the conversation he grabs me, circles me with his arms, and I gently push him to sit back down).

"They grab me like this, and like this. . . . No, I'm telling you man, you gotta listen. I wuz in that house, my fren's house over on 46th where you took me once, and these two guys come in, wid guns, shoutin, 'We looking for dat reefer; where is he?' I din't know nothing about it; they shout at me, grab me (he grabs *me*) take out a gun 'n point it at me. I'm good at handlin' that kinna thing, I grab the gun, dey come at me, I shoot that Purto Rickin inna leg, 'n I run. But they run after me. Gotta git outa town, man. They got a gang wid them teardrop tattoos. . . ."

"Hey, wait a minute, Joe. *You* have one of those on your right eye?"

"Yeah, but I tole ya bout dat, din't I?"—and he babbles out a short, somewhat different version of the story he told last time I asked him about whether the tattoo stood for gangs.

"I gotta git outa here, man, goin back to Mississippi. . . ."

"Look, Joe, this is the last time! You understand? If you come again I'm gonna call the police . . ." (etc.), until, finally, feeling that Laura and Leigh have heard enough in the other room, I give him $120 to get to Mississippi. He leaves, weeping tears of gratitude.

We then have a fairly good time with our friends, one of them saying, "That guy's tone sounds totally phony to me." When Phyllis and I get to bed, we're both a bit apprehensive. I'm saddened, wondering what on earth to do about this lost soul. (I had just that morning read a quotation from the New Testament in which Jesus rescues the down-and-outer by being kind to him! The New Testament doesn't face the problems that are faced by those of us who don't have Jesus's powers.

At 3 AM we're again waked with the back doorbell! Joe rings again and again. We consult and decide not to answer. I feel sick about it; it's cold outside, and he must be desperate again. He rings the front doorbell, and again the back. We don't answer.

At 6:45, the back doorbell rings again. I get up, go to the door, sure that he's been sleeping on the porch—on snow, temperature below freezing, windy. He is visibly shivering. I let him in. He has tears running down his cheeks; his hands feel frozen.

"I hate doing this, Wayne, but I'm scared to death. I been cryin', cause I can't get outta town."

I'm furious.

"Joe, I gave you money last night for transportation. What happened to it?"

"When I was headed for da train, da cops come up behin' me, and since I'd shot that guy inna leg I had to run, right? I run, they caught up with me, one from the front, and arrested me for resistin' arrest. Took me to jail. A thousand bucks bond, so I hadda pay 'em the hundred bucks as ten percent bond."

He pulls out a sheet describing all that, but under another name.

"I give 'em not my name but one a the others I use. I was lucky, man, cause I had left my wallet 'n all identification hidden in a bag, so they couldn't check my name, but now, Wayne . . . " He weeps a bit, still shivering. Phyllis comes downstairs, shouts angrily at him—and then prepares him a cup of coffee, which he accepts, and some toast, which he rejects.

The story could go on and on. We must have talked for thirty minutes, Phyll and I leaving several times to discuss things privately. At one point she bursts out at him in extreme anger—she rightly feels that I have been suckered into too much of this, and she's angry at me, without saying so.

To shorten matters, after he begs for enough cash to get to Mississippi, I finally give him enough for bus fare to Hammond, Indiana, where "I gotta friend who might help me git to Miss'ippi." I offer an aggressive message of finality:

"If you come for money again, I'll call the cops. No more phone calls, no more doorbell ringing. This is the last time, Joe. We're sorry about that, but it's definite."

"Can't I even call ya to tell ya that things goin' better?"

"Not any collect calls, Joe."

By this time Phyll has given him one of my sweaters, some warm socks (his feet are really almost frozen—I felt them, as a test of his story about sleeping on that porch), and a scarf, and off he goes, *perhaps* with a sense of having triumphed with clever stories. But I'm feeling fairly sure that part of it has been true—this time.

A day later the phone rings, "Will I take a collect call from Joe Garrett?" I say no and hang up. The phone rings again. I accept it!

"Hi, Wayne, howya doin'?"

"How YOU doin'?"

"I'm great man, I'm in Hammond, and I gotta job already! A friend turned up here and got me a job. Soon as I git paid, I'm gonna start payin ya back. I do wanna thank ya for what you done for me Saddy night and yestady morning. I love ya man. Ya hate me?"

"No, I don't hate ya, Joe, not at all. I just wish that we could get you on your feet."

"I *am* on ma feet, man."

"Good, but remember, no more requests for money."

"No, man, I'm gonna start paying YOU."

Will I call the police if he calls again? I think so; I'm determined to . . . but at the same time I keep on phoning charity services that might take him in, counsel him. The truth is that I find, beneath all the lies and subterfuge, a potentially strong, more-than-salvageable person. My heart goes out to him, as the corny phrase has it. Thinking of the world he lives in brings tears to my eyes.

Next day I get a call from him saying that the man who's hiring him wants a recommendation. Could he have the guy call me? Feeling deeply equivocal, I answer, "Well, I'll be willing to tell him that I've known you a long time and that you can be a good worker."

Later that day I look for our checkbook and can't find it. I have a visual memory that it was sitting on the table near Joe during our last conversation. Phyll and I look everywhere, everywhere; we even search through the garbage. Though it occurs to us to wonder whether Joe stole it, we think it extremely unlikely that he would be both so cruel to those who have helped and so stupid as to think he could get away with it.

After a day of searching, we cancel our checking account.

Several days later I come back from campus and have a voice mail from the bank. A man named Joe Garrett has tried to cash a check against my account. Do I know him? "He came with a check signed with your name, made out to him, for $300.00. Because you had closed the account we were suspicious, but while we were checking, he caught on to our suspicion, and though we'd warned security, he got away!"

I feel both saddened by the immensity of his meanness and stupidity—so much more vicious and stupid than I had ever realized—and amused at my own gullibility. But in the middle of the night the amusement disappears and I just feel haunted with the thought of how awful his goof was and how badly I had been betrayed—and by the loss of all hope of "saving" him. I have a rather bad night, thinking about him, even wanting to weep for and about him. For some reason I feel no anger. But next morning I do phone the police. I want him arrested.

To our total surprise, Joe did come one more time and rang the back doorbell. I went to the door, did not open it, and shouted out at him, "Joe, I'm gonna call the police. You stole my checkbook!" And he slunk away.

I've never seen him since. Curiously enough, even now, I have this strong impulse to talk with Joe, to probe how and why he could do such a thing. The man I thought I knew, the man who "loves ya, man, God bless ya man, I'd die for ya, man, if anybody attacked ya"—couldn't have stolen my checkbook. But the bastard did. Yet here's GullibleB years later, still sometimes scanning the streets, hoping to be able to say, "Hi, Joe, howya doin'?"

What's more, I wish I had his narrative gifts. What an effective cheater I could have been.

Should I now load this chapter with more of the kind of speculation about causes and effects you've met in earlier chapters? I resist.

End of Gullible's Travels.

Chapter Twelve

A Wandering Generalist Longs to Be a True Scholar

From his cradle,
He was a scholar, and a ripe and good one;
Exceeding wise, fair-spoken, and persuading:
Lofty and sour to them that lov'd him not;
But, to those men that sought him, sweet as summer.

—Shakespeare, *Henry VIII*

I pass for a great scholar with him, by relating to him some of the Persian Tales.

—Lady Mary Montagu, letter to Alexander Pope

The world's great men have not commonly been great scholars, nor its great scholars great men.

—Oliver Wendell Holmes

The bookful blockhead, ignorantly read,
With loads of learned lumber in his head,
With his own tongue still edifies his ears,
And always list'ning to himself appears.

—Alexander Pope, "Essay in Criticism"

Where there is much desire to learn, there of necessity will be much arguing, much writing, many opinions; for opinion in good men is but knowledge in the making.

—John Milton, *Areopagitica*

Here is a journal entry by the Wandering Generalist, from five years ago.

November 10, 2000
This morning as I try to decide what should be the next chapters of the *LIFE*, I am a bit harried—surprise!—by diverse obligations pulling in contrasting directions. Here are some of those that dramatize what may be the subject of the next chapter: my inability ever to pin myself down as a true scholar, a genuine *specialist*. I must, right this minute

- phone a local Episcopalian minister to chat about my upcoming talk at his church, on the relation of scientific and religious rhetoric;
- respond to an editor's highly critical suggestions about revision of an already accepted essay on that subject;
- revise my essay for that (what's-its-name?) encyclopedia, comparing my version of philosophical pluralism with cultural relativism;
- answer a graduate student's request for me to serve on his dissertation committee—he's writing on how scientific prose becomes, when written by the best minds, a kind of prose-poem (and what do I know about that?);
- answer a lifetime acquaintance, now an editor, about why I've never completed the oft-contemplated book about Mormonism;
- work on my talk for MLA, on the movie *American Beauty*;
- respond to the invitation, by Professor X, to do a joint article on the rhetoric of evolutionary psychologists—I'll probably say "no";
- respond to my colleague's nagging me to do a selective anthology of my most "important essays," published and unpublished;
- address the two-foot high pile of manuscripts by friends, former students, and strangers (most of which I actually—and sometimes foolishly—agreed in advance to read).

And it's not just such external demands but also a flood of impulses:

- I must figure out whether to respond to a rejection of an essay, the first rejection I've had in a long time. Do I attack the editor? Throw the draft away? Do another draft?

- I still want to finish one or both of my two totally fumbled novels, *Cass* and *Farrago*.
- As I follow, superficially, our political/commercial scene, I long to work on the half-started book, which was to be called *Fee Speech or Free Speech*, an attempt to rescue the First Amendment from those who think it covers speakers, like tobacco advertisers, who lie deliberately and harmfully for the sake of cash.
- I simply must complete the book, already much too long, on *How Many Gods Are Left After God Dies:* the God of "Goodness," of personal and social improvement (Communism/Marxism as key example); the God of Beauty (Art for Art's Sake; my *For the Love of It*); and the God of Truth (science, secular humanism, rationalism).
- Shouldn't I drop the *LIFE* and work instead on that half-baked book about hypocrisy-upward and how to distinguish it from harmful hypocrisy?[1]

As my young self frequently asked of his journal: what's the point of all that, sounding too much like a laundry list?[2] Well, let's push to one side VainB's boasting about his breadth of interests. My real claim is that by dramatizing the absurdly scattered temptations, I can demonstrate the split, with both self-contempt and some pride, between the would-be genuine scholar and the actual meanderer—the guy I sometimes think of as not just a superficial wandering generalist but a Contemptibly Unfocused Naïve Twister.

Scholars are those who dig deep in one single cavern—and go on digging until they come to layers no one else has even suspected. Nobel-winning scientists win because they have pursued some one quark or boson to its depths (or death). Genuine literary scholars pursue single authors or topics for decades—even for a lifetime.

---

1. At almost 84, I decided to return to it, with the possible title "The Curse of 'Sincerity.'" Total sincerity would destroy us day by day.
2. Actually it could go on for pages, especially if I listed the "books to be read" in a stack beside my desk. I'm amused that my daughter Alison, a feminist literary critic and scholar of Victorian literature—among other things—writes the following in the margin of a draft: "This doesn't seem really *scattered*, just active. Wouldn't *most* good 'scholars' in the humanities have a similar diverse set of projects? You dramatize as a distinctive conflict what's really a feature of academia today." Perhaps my whole account understates the extent to which even the most serious scholars worry about "wandering" too much. Reading Louis Menand's new account of nineteenth-century American thinkers, *The Metaphysical Club* (New York: Farrar, Straus & Giroux, 2001), I'm surprised at how many of my intellectual heroes stumbled from field to field at least as loosely as I have: William James, Charles Peirce, John Dewey, et al. Maybe I should blame them for seducing me into "generalism." Or perhaps I should just erase this whole chapter.

Though I'm sure that most of those "specialists" could construct trouble-some lists of demands that get in the way of their central project, some, un-like me, do stick to their center—provoking my envy. They join societies that concentrate on Henry James, or Shakespeare, or Cervantes—or, at the broadest, "Medieval Literature" or "Victorian Feminism." Unlike me, they work up this or that classical language and stick to it through life. They spend years creating a single new edition of one of Shakespeare's plays.

Very little of my work has pursued the decisive conclusions or *proofs* that are pursued by specialists. Most of it has been, as judged by its critics, merely "speculative," "evaluative," "judgmental," "moralistic," even "dogmatic" and "preachy"—what I prefer to call "rhetorical." But VainB has always longed not just to *be* less superficial but to *appear* to be a true scholar.

I find it amusing, though not surprising, that the split between focused scholarship and my actual interests plagued me long before any career choices really emerged. When facing my second college year, I already exaggerated what many sophomores feel as they choose a major:

> *Sept. 9, 1938*
> Reading *The Horse and Buggy Doctor* arouses a faint desire I have always had—to study and become a research physician. I am still planning to ma-jor in Chemistry, but there are so many of the sciences I am interested in, Chem., Physics, Bacteriology (have never studied it) that it worries me for fear I will choose the wrong one. (I would like to obtain my Dr. of Philoso-phy degree before I terminate my formal education.) I believe the best way to be successful (I don't want to be rich) is to choose one line & stick to it, and not philander from one idea to another. I'm going to have to discipline myself to refrain from doing just that.

As everybody who is anybody knows, genuine scholars in English, es-pecially those specializing in rhetorical studies, are highly trained in other languages, especially Latin and maybe Greek—or at least that was true in my generation. My strongest internal evidence of lifetime failure as a scholar (especially as one pretending to be a specialist in rhetoric) is thus my igno-rance of Latin and Greek. My high school offered no language courses in *any* foreign language. (Spanish was offered one fall, but the teacher married and left after the first term.) In college I had only a bit of German and a smaller bit of Spanish. One summer I did try to work up a bit of Latin on my own. In the army, I "got up" some French and conversational German. But I entered graduate school, unlike a majority of my colleagues, with only a hint of Latin, with not even a longing for Greek, and with only the ungrammatical French and German I'd picked up in the army.

Once I decided to become an eighteenth-century *scholar*, I knew that I had to be able to at least pretend to read the many Latin quotations the texts revealed, so I spent quite a few hours again working it up on my own and learning how to find useful ponies.[3] But I never learned to read Latin, really.

Six years after graduation, in England on a Guggenheim fellowship, I decided that my scandalous ignorance should be wiped out. I was a fake scholar and must become genuine. I learned that the London County Council offered free courses, including Latin, and I phoned to inquire.

> "Oh, I'm sorry, sir, but the course has already been going for one week, and we do not accept late registrants."
>
> "I understand that, madam, but I'm not just a plain beginner. I've done a Ph.D. on eighteenth-century British literature, and I've worked up quite a lot of Latin on my own."
>
> Short pause. Then a haughty dismissive tone:
>
> "Sir, one does not work up Latin on one's own." Click!

So the temptation to become a "genuine" scholar—at least in visibly testable terms like Latin—was crushed. Only occasionally through the remaining decades have I felt tempted to settle in on Latin, or Greek, or—at one point—Russian. The wanderer always triumphed.

I do feel a bit comforted when I happen upon complaints by true scholars about their lack of depth or their ignorance of this or that "other field" or their failure to keep a sufficiently clear single focus. For all I know, every scholar feels some sense of shallowness or inadequacy.

Recently, as I read George Steiner's memoir *Errata*, I was not surprised to find piles of evidence about the superiority of his education over mine. But I was shocked, after pages and pages that illustrated that superiority, to find him lamenting his ignorance as compared with genuine scholars. Steiner regrets not having learned Russian or Hebrew. He echoes my lament here by blaming himself for having been a polymath, knowing about too many things but never going deeply enough into any one of them to suit the specialists. If someone as learned as Steiner has such regrets, why should I complain about my shallower education?

For whatever reason, I still do. One voice has constantly nagged, "You're not sufficiently prepared for *that* project." Then I would be tempted to fix things by narrowing down in some one scholarly territory, what might be called the "Twenty-Year-Perseverance-Bug." I did feel like a concentrated

---

3. Chatting with three college students recently, I learned that none of them knew the word "pony": secret translation used to deceive language teachers.

true scholar for a while when working painstakingly on my dissertation on *Tristram Shandy*. For many months I reread that amazingly complex novel, hoping to discover its "unity"—unity that we were taught should be the center of genuine critical inquiry. After I submitted a first draft *proving* that the book was, at least in Sterne's view, completed, if not unified, Ronald Crane, who had inspired the unity quest, shocked me by saying that it would not do because it wasn't scholarly enough, only critical.

"Your dissertation has got to have some genuine solid historical inquiry in it; your critical ideas will be dead and forgotten within ten or twenty years, so you must include some chapters that yield survivable historical *truth!*" So I then worked ten hours a day for four more months tracing Sterne's predecessors and influences, probing territory that nobody else had ever probed so deeply; that seemed then and seems now to be true scholarship.

But when my mentors said that the results were good enough to be published after some revision, I decided against it. The thinker in me was nagging about "higher things," more controversial or challenging issues: how fiction works; why novels, including *Tristram Shandy*, grab us; why public education doesn't improve; how freshman composition could be better taught; and on and on. Meanwhile another Self nagged daily, "You must become a novelist" (see chapter 13). I was so little interested in the factual side of things that when an author later published a book plagiarizing heavily from the facts in my unpublished dissertation, I didn't utter a word of complaint.

Here's how my roiling mind reported itself at age thirty. It was that first year at Haverford College when I was suffering both competitive anxieties and a bit of postpartum depression. "Now that the dissertation is completed, where is my center?"

> I've waited to write this [journal] entry until the other side of my present "manic-depressive" state turned up. Tonight I am manic. To feel thirty is to feel fifteen instead of sixty. Vast energies, disorganized as adolescence, seem mine. Projects unnumbered and unnumberable chase one another in my head—all demanding to be begun at once. What this will end in I know in advance: another depression, because none of the projects will have been accomplished. What to do about it—how to become thirty rather than 12 or 65—I don't know.
>
> My activities of the evening, with the "projects" stimulated by them, should give a fair idea of the state I'm in (Phyllis is ill from pregnancy, I bathe Kathie and put her to bed).

And then he lists, for the hundredth time in his life, a baker's dozen of absolutely irresistible "projects," most of them stimulated by reading a recent issue of the *New Statesman and Nation*; every article seems to have drawn him in. He's trying to write his report with ironic amusement, but the projects, for a man who has never yet published a critical or scholarly article (only a few spoofs in *Furioso*), are in one sense real. The entry ends:

> I idled the whole time (Saturday to Tuesday), and the result is the above insanity, which, as I said, is in the main honestly reported. . . . I didn't mention my sincere desire to cover the history of philosophy, or to write a couple of articles for scholarly journals, but they occurred to me several times during the evening.

For about six years I wandered among the scores of tempting projects, publishing little except those regular brief satires in the journal *Furioso* (later changed to the *Carleton Miscellany*). Few of the projects would deserve the term "scholarly" in *anybody's* definition. My careful note taking during the year I spent "reading ethical philosophy on my own," financed by the Ford Foundation, could not be called real scholarship; it was a quest for philosophical wisdom, something I have no name for (certainly "generalist" doesn't quite fit). I wanted to learn about *everything* but especially the genuine philosophical grounds for ethical judgments—now that God was dead.

Sometimes I did feel, during that philosophical year, somewhat focused for several hours each day, especially as the philosophers' Gods made more and more sense to me, challenging my "atheism." I'm pretty sure that at least sometimes, as I struggled to understand Aquinas or Kant, I thought of myself as a scholar, discovering truth.

It took me some years to realize that my meandering impulses sprang from, or perhaps were even identical to, my rhetorical (my *rhetorological*) effort to understand—and promote—human understanding in every conceivable domain. My two years of hypocritical missionary work, when I was preaching passionately to get believers and doubters like me to talk together productively, had implanted the conviction that the furtherance of understanding was the best of all human vocations.

The trouble with such a pedagogical passion is that it provides no clear limit on the direction of study—no single focus for the "scholar." As Aristotle said, rhetoric has no subject matter; it's universal.

As I worked more and more on the history of rhetoric (never in a fully scholarly way), I soon saw that a serious rhetorician aspires (always hopelessly) to understand everything and everybody and to teach everybody to embrace the same aspiration. WandererB was thus doomed (or liberated, or blessed) to pursue a lifetime of superficial, sometimes openly moralistic, speculative inquiry. Such inquiry could never reach a decisive, empirical platform of proof. It was moralistic in the sense that explicitly or implicitly its motive was always, like my motive for teaching, Work to Improve the World. Can you pin that man down on any standard chart of life goals—especially scholarly goals? I can't.

I find scores of half-playful journal entries like this one, written a year after two of my books came out and four years before the next one would emerge.

> *July 27, 1975 [on vacation in Utah canyon country]*
> Awake at 5:30 . . . couldn't get back—mind full now, no longer threatening total sleep: projects, worries, plans of how and what to teach 15 mos. from now.—No, by God, it's only 14 mos!—my year's leave is almost over and I've not written a single book yet!
> Say what book, what book.

Then, after reporting ideas he'd run into while again reading the *Times Literary Supplement,*

> So, now, a bit too much aroused by . . . thoughts about a bit of everything at once, I seek, for the hundredth time this year, for the steady project that will be mine. I want an intellectual project that would focus my life as clearly, and w/as much excitement *and* chance for *daily plodding movement* as I imagine an entomologist (enty? enta?) finds in settling on spiders—becoming a "spider man"—or an astronomer settling, these days, on X-ray photography. I am spread so thin that when, as during these 4 days of vacation, I am not at my desk, I don't know "what I am about."

Then after listing various books he had brought along,

> I find nothing anywhere suited to help me "answer the next question." I don't know what my next question is. . . .
> Last week, working on M. H. Abrams, I thought: Why not extend my book about diverse prophets [book never realized] into the 19th c., take one in Romantic (Wordsworth), one in high Victorian (George Eliot), one in fin de siecle (G. B. Shaw), one in 20–30 (Bertrand Russell), etc. But this wld leave me . . . spread thinner than . . .
> In any case, I need to do no more than pick any *one* author I love and find difficult—

Thus the tempted-in-every-direction guy almost never managed to work for long on any one author, or period, or genre, or archeological dig. The "loving" pursuit of understanding of this or that presumed truth was to him usually more important than any one bit of hard, solid, but private bit of truth. The moral center was the claim that intellectual understanding is one of the best versions of the Golden Rule: Listen to others as you would have others listen to you. Precise demonstration of truth is important but not as important as the communal pursuit of it. Put in terms of Kant's categorical imperative, When addressing someone else's ideas, your obligation is to treat them as you believe all human beings *ought* to treat one another's ideas. (This did lead me to *try* to understand those authors I discussed—Kenneth Burke, Bertrand Russell, Bakhtin—but it never led me to any moment of the kind enjoyed by one of my students, Robert Denham. After doing a dissertation on Northrop Frye, Frye told him something like "You are the first and only reader who has ever fully understood what I'm trying to say"—and appointed him a lifetime editor of his papers.)

My first book, *The Rhetoric of Fiction*, which at the time I never would have described in moral terms,[4] was an attempt to answer the question, How do novelists win us into understanding and embracing their worlds? Then for thirteen years, while attempting to get students to pursue mutual understanding, I worked on three books pursuing different versions of "understanding"—what I did not yet call "rhetorology."

Now Don't Try to Reason with Me: Essays and Ironies for a Credulous Age was a collection of essays about the difficulties we face when reasoning together.[5] *A Rhetoric of Irony* was a guide about how to avoid misunderstanding irony and achieve the deep human alliance that *understanding* irony can yield. *Modern Dogma and the Rhetoric of Assent* was an effort to undermine standard "modernist" skeptical, hyperrationalist norms for deciding when to change one's mind.

We need, I argued through all of this, not a rhetoric of skeptical doubt but a rhetoric of *assent*, learning how to find beneath our differences some common ground, usually unprovable, from which our arguments spring.

---

4. I did add, very late in the day, a chapter on the morality of narration—too hastily done but an unmistakable prediction of my later works on the ethics of narration.
5. When I came down with a serious illness as the book was about to appear, my journal reads like this: "Still continuing, on and off, the egotistical—narcissistic?—masturbative—pleasure of re-reading *Reason*. . . . I keep looking for flaws—and keep finding them. Chief one: it doesn't ever come to grips with what "reason" can teach about what the world needs *now*—except the need for reason. It avoids the . . . need for a revolutionary way of organizing men's lives together. The defense of reason is sound and even moving, . . . but it is not made by a man who could guide the world out of its many messes. Indeed, the author does not seem to care very much about any but spiritual and moral messes. . . . A strange man, really, whose book could not possibly interest any but a small and narrow-minded [or "moralizing"?] audience. Etc."

Then I moved on into ever deeper waters, an effort to put it all together into a general theory of human understanding—*Critical Understanding: The Powers and Limits of Pluralism.* Some parts of that ambitious book aspired to be scholarly, and some parts seem to me now about the best work I've done. But it has never hooked as many readers as much of my other work. In it I grappled with diverse previous efforts to organize *all* knowledge, with how various "pluralists" had dealt with the diversity, and with how I was to deal with the plurality of pluralisms. Sometimes I find myself thinking, "Could anything be less 'scholarly,' more hopelessly 'general,' than that?" Yet it was certainly the work that came closest to scholarly aspiration.

Retreating to a slightly less vast territory, I continued the moral quest in *The Company We Keep: An Ethics of Fiction,* an effort to deal with every conceivable moral or ethical question that can be raised when we think of narratives as a joining of authors and readers. And, of course, the wandering generalist is still pursuing, even here, the central moral questions: what's good for us and what isn't, and how can we come to any kind of agreement about such questions? (A reader who has read most of my work objects strongly to my refusal to call this one scholarly; but in my view he's also a meandering generalist—though a touch more scholarly than I've been.)

VainB does take some comfort in all this wandering. If hooking many diverse readers were the only goal of critical writing, my choice of the generalist route might come out—to my surprise—looking pretty good. Because of my wandering, I now have responses from current readers in far more diverse areas than would have turned up if I'd stuck with some one author or topic or period.[6] VainB is delighted to encounter large "pockets" of readers who know this or that corner in my tiny pyramid but who haven't even heard of the other corners.[7]

But that's enough Self-touting. The important fact here is that despite the size of his biblio,[8] he is not a genuine scholar and often longs to have been one. Many colleagues who see themselves as "genuine" have suggested that he's just the shallow, fake kind. Usually the suggestion is only tacit, as when a concentratedly scholarly historian friend said recently, "I just feel awful about how much *knowledge* the world will lose when I die, all that's in

---

6. I feel proud to report that one careful reader has complained that I have so little here about my publication life—the meaning, to me, of my various projects as I look back on them. I won't surrender, but I feel comforted by his answer to those who think I've offered too much of such stuff.

7. I'm tempted to report here the diverse responses—but I resist.

8. VainB jumps in to say, "You gotta mention your more than two hundred published articles." How wise of me to clamp him down into this footnote.

my head that I haven't published." As a generalist, I can't think of any package of knowledge that the world will lose. All they'll lose will be a large collection of exhortations—almost all of which duplicate what other exhorters will go on saying.

Sometimes the judgments against my undeserved successes have turned into open attack. Here's the most revealing event, one that feels a bit scarier in memory than it felt at the time.

A colleague, whom I'll call Jack, asked if I'd like to have lunch. The day before we were scheduled, he phoned to ask if I could come to his house instead of the restaurant. I rode my bike to his house and was welcomed in. He seated me in his dining room.

"I'll be with you in a minute; I'll just go and finish preparing the soup."

Jack brings the soup and a couple of sandwiches and sits down opposite me, looking troubled, face flushed.

"You know why I've invited you here, don't you?"

"No, Jack. Why do you ask?"

"It's to tell you how much I hate you!"

Long pause, as I look at him and he looks down at the soup.

"Why are you bothering to tell me about it?"

Short pause.

"Because my therapist told me I should get it out of my system. But it's not getting out of my system. I simply hate you and always will."

Long, long pause. I consider leaving but instead start sipping the soup, wondering about what could be a good way to handle this shocker.

Finally: "Why do you hate me, Jack?"

"Because of your stupid public success, the way your shallow books and articles get all the attention with your silly superficial arguments, while mine, which exhibit genuine thought and deep research, just get ignored. All you have is a grabby style, one that engages readers into *thinking* that you're thinking. I just can't live with the unfairness of it, my powerful mind ignored while your superficial meanderings . . ."

I've found no journal entry to confirm my memories of his diatribe. What I'm sure of is that he went on and on; and when I found that no real conversation was possible, I simply bit my tongue and left, deeply distressed but saying something like "Well, maybe we can talk about it sometime."

Later in the day when I told Phyllis about it she said, no doubt ironically, "It was foolish of you to eat that soup." It hadn't occurred to me that his hatred was deep enough to be dangerous—and I think I was right. If he'd been an Iago, wanting to destroy me, he wouldn't have invited me to his house for lunch.[9]

Everybody talks these days about how self-destructive competitiveness among overspecialized academics is getting worse. (One reader chimes in, "They just don't know how bad it was in the past.") Some accounts make it sound as if nobody ever thinks about anything except winning over others, whether in fame or money or power. I know, from my half century of working with colleagues who love teaching—both specialists and generalists—that that's a terrible exaggeration. But as I read accounts of what the profession feels like, with academic presses increasingly reluctant to publish even the most excellent works if they won't guarantee high sales, I have to admit a bit mournfully that our cultural drives have moved strongly during my lifetime in the direction of "get ahead, at all costs," ignoring both serious prolonged scholarship and the kind of ethical and formal probing I've engaged in.

Maybe some genuine scholars would agree with Jack that my effort to achieve an accessible writing style was simply a selling out to those drives ("Get an audience, at all costs"). All I can say in reply is the old point made by rhetoricians from at least Aristotle on: if you write something without thinking of *some* audience, why bother?

So where does that leave me today, working from chapter to chapter with this *Life*? Well, I confess in total honesty that I fantasize almost daily about settling down and becoming a *real* Shakespeare scholar. But that would get in the way of my desire to go seriously into film studies; the response was so favorable to my MLA talk on the movie *American Beauty* and how my criticism of fiction might relate to it that it's obvious I should now take up a new career as a cinematologist. On the third hand, shouldn't I pursue that project I started a few weeks ago—an in-depth, scholarly study of *musical* harmony—as I worked on my superficial program notes for the Cedille CD of Dvorak's opus 97 and opus 105? Or how about that book on medical ethics and literature that X has proposed? But then I wouldn't have time to do the book on the sadly neglected novels of George Meredith. And it would interfere with my pursuit of other harmonies here.

And besides, after reading yesterday about how many children are dying of starvation at this very moment, surely I should be spending all my time on trying to save some corner of the world.

But what corner?

---

9. Incidentally, Jack's alcoholism worsened and he died not long after, leaving me wondering whether I should feel guilty about how my "fame" had tortured him.

Chapter Thirteen

A Would-be Novelist Mourns behind the Would-be Lover and Would-be Scholar

A systematic, fifteen-year probing of ALL possible sources has revealed, surprisingly, that there are absolutely no quotations about creative writing worthy of insertion as epigraphs for this chapter. Apparently no novelist or poet has ever uttered a quotable opinion about what it means to be creative.

—W. Clayson Booth, director, Humanities Research Institute

I know you're being ironic, but what about Kafka's "I have nothing to say— ever"?

—Brandon Hopkins, graduate editorial assistant

January 15, 2005

This morning, half awake, thinking about turning eighty-four next month, I was suddenly jolted with the thought: I really should call up my novel *Cass* from the old floppy disks, revise it, and *get it published!* Only two or three minutes later, *fully* awake, did I hear a voice shouting, "That would be absurd. You should spend your time showing how that hopeless longing relates to the conflict between the would-be scholar and lover."[1] The non-novelist surrenders, and here we are.

Once I'd become hooked into reading famous novels and poems in my midteens, I inevitably had dreams of becoming a novelist or poet. I had always enjoyed making up stories, some of them the outright self-serving lies that I've reported here, some of them jokey stories intended only to entertain. But the dream of turning that minor gift into true authoring usually felt hopeless. For one thing, I knew that all of the successful writers lived in New York or Chicago or London or Paris. We lived in the sticks, in the boonies, in what we called the "tules," pronounced toolies; obviously I was simply off the chart.

But the dream persisted. In the ninth grade I managed to win the school prize for the best short story, an adventure story that was pretty much stolen in its basic plot from *Tom Sawyer*. In my junior year, induced by my English teacher Gean Clark to read a good deal of the best current fiction (including the "sexy novels" by Aldous Huxley that my sexy contemporary Zola Grant had also introduced me to), I finally wrote a "powerful" short story about falling in love with an English teacher. Miss Clark judged it a rather poor job—I assume rightly—and gave it only a B+.

She couldn't have known that the seemingly confident kid she met in class was constantly quarreling with another Wayne C., who was absurdly vulnerable to even the slightest negative criticism. She probably intended her B+ to mean "Not a bad start, but as the best student in the class, you can

---

1. I hope, dear readers, that when I report these "voices," you don't assume they are "real," like those of *Beautiful Mind* schizophrenics.

surely make it a lot better." But the hypersensitive boy, trained by a widowed mother to respond with abject despair to any criticism while always trying to get ahead, took the B+ as saying something like "You'll never be able to write good fiction. Give it up." Which I did—for a while. I can't remember attempting another story for about nine years—except in my head.

Anyone whose writing ambitions could be that easily crushed should have recognized that he simply had no real drive to become an "author." A genuine budding creator would have gone on writing, like Sylvia Plath or Flannery O'Connor or Saul Bellow, producing poems or stories daily no matter what anyone said about them in the rejection slips. The inner drive in such creators turns out to be uncrushable, even when they accumulate piles of rejections. But Wayne C. was always crushable.

I did go on dreaming of writing *something*. Occasionally I would write a poem for my diary—never submitting it anywhere for publication. Out of respect for you, patient reader, I quote only one more example of the crummy stuff. (See the even worse one in chapter 7.)

(1941)
The moon, heartless wanton,
Glides, still veiled, onto her balcony.
She slides back her veil a little, and a
     little more
Until, seeing that her purpose is accomplished,
Seductively she disappears into her room,
The cloud-thick sky.

The scarcity of such feeble examples demonstrates the absurdity of my occasional dream of becoming a poet or novelist. I more often thought of becoming a journalist. I did get hired for a while as a "stringer," sending American Fork news to the *Salt Lake Tribune*. I later wrote a weekly column for the college paper at Brigham Young University, calling it "From This Booth" because the editor, my cousin and lifetime friend "TY," was also named Booth. The column was full of satire and irony and comic poems—some by me and some falsely claimed as mine.

Sometimes the creative impulse got deflected into political polemic. World War II was heating up, and the nation was failing to see its duty to join up with England. I published several columns and did one radio interview arguing passionately against the "America Firsters." But, of course, such efforts were totally off the creative writing track.

I actually produced no manuscript pages that I thought publishable until I returned from the war in 1946, married Phyllis, and started graduate school.

I did have fantasies throughout those years, even during the war, about becoming a novelist. Here's how I played with the idea in a letter to Phyllis.

> *19 April 45*
> I think of you constantly. What, constantly? Well, almost constantly, ce qui est a peu pres la meme chose. . . . I suppose I shall have to write a novel, a very fine novel, putting in convincing terms your wonder and loveliness, our love at however many thousands of miles away it is; the hedonists, the skeptics, the moderns who have ceased to believe in love like ours, *must* be told of it some way, and a novel is the only way. "But," you say, "Wayne, you never finish anything you start writing. A while ago you told me you were writing for some French journals, and I've never heard anything more about it. And now you talk glibly of a novel. What makes you think you have the talent for writing a novel?" Now is that any way to support me and be my helpmeet? . . . Why not write a novel, in which I could show the thousands of various currents of thought running around me here in France, and inside me away from you? No specific statement about France, or about the soldiers, or about myself, is true, in itself. It would be true only in the context of a large novel.
>
> Undoubtedly I shall always be a writer who never writes anything; but I insist that it is better than being a non-writer who writes carloads.

He then launches in to his decision to become a teacher.

I later joined a "creative writing club" on the Chicago campus, attended regularly, and finally took my turn to read aloud a short story—the manuscript of which I still long to find in my stack of "remains." It was based on a real experience in Paris in early 1945. What follows here is today's crude summary of the story I saw as quite vivid and clever.

> At the Red Cross center a handsome man in his thirties spoke to me in French: "We French people feel very grateful to you Americans for what you have done. Would you like to have dinner with my mother and me to let us express our gratitude?" I eagerly accepted; what a relief from the boredom of my daily eight-hour typing in the G2 (Intelligence) office.
>
> He and I spent the afternoon strolling along the Seine, probing bookstalls on the left bank, discussing literature, mainly Proust and Gide. . . . We then went to have dinner with his mother, a quite good dinner considering the rationing at the time, and then he invited me to go with him to his apartment. I went—and of course the point of the story, as in my actual experience, was that the young Mormon/American hadn't taken in a single hint of the gay host's intentions.

When the seducer finally made his approach clear, I was shocked, scared, stupefied. I fled his apartment, with him following, pleading, accusing me of having misled him. "How could you have not understood what I had in mind? How could you not know that, when I brought up Gide and Proust, I meant to lead to love. Did you just ignore those photos of nude boys that fill my apartment walls . . . ?" And so on. He followed me to the Metro station, pleading all the way, and he was still pleading as the train door shut and I escaped, feeling about as stupid as I have ever felt, before or since.

The response to my reading of the story draft was apathetic—not to say pathetic. The faculty member who directed the Club lambasted it, saying something like "All that homosexual stuff just won't go." None of the other aspiring writers said, "That was terrific," or, "You should publish that." So I simply put it aside and forgot about becoming a "writer," concentrating instead on succeeding as a "scholar."

As I think back on my story of the cheated gay, I believe it could have been turned into something not just publishable but a step toward the forefront of gay studies—perhaps as a hated target, perhaps not. I would have had to do a lot of restructuring, including more work on making plausible the naïveté of the narrator. As the Frenchman had insisted, it was simply incredible that any intelligent young soldier would not have understood the host's intent after the first twenty minutes standing on the Pont looking down the Seine and discussing whether we thought that Gide "went too far" in his open acknowledgments of homosexuality. But how could that experienced French lover, receiving sign after sign that seemed favorable, have suspected that he was dealing with a Mormon boy from Utah, son of 1,000 percent "straight" pioneers (as far as the boy knew), who had never in his life been seriously solicited by a male and who had, in college and as a missionary, "slept with"—that is, shared beds with—dozens of males without the slightest hint of sexual interest?

Anyway, instead of polishing that rescuable story after it was criticized, I put it aside and quit the club. The creative impulse was crushed. I was convinced once again that I did not possess the gifts of a genuine imaginative writer. Was I right? I think so. That is, one Self thinks so; another Self reproaches me almost daily for having been oversensitive to the critique.

The impulse to write did go on rising and falling over the next few years. In 1953 I lament in my journal, "To have fifteen or twenty unfinished stories, novels, books and articles lying around is a very disorganizing experience." In 1954, late at night, I wrote, "I haven't, at this sleepy moment, the slightest doubt about being able to write a passable novel; no, really, I haven't. But it would be only passable, by which I mean good but not great, and so why not go to bed?"

The most serious effort was based on my dissertation experience. *Tristram Shandy* and *Tom Jones* had turned me on to the joys of complex narrative trickery—playful "meta-narration," a form of intrusive, meandering "telling" rather than simply "showing." It was a style that my earlier passion for Dostoevsky and Tolstoy and Dickens had largely overlooked. My probing into millennia of "self-conscious narration" had placed narrative irony at the center of my thinking about all literature, and after publishing a few ironic spoofs— such as a demonstration that Sterne's book had in fact influenced every author back through the past, including Homer—I decided that the time had come for a narratological breakthrough (of course, that fancy term didn't exist yet).

My novel, to be called something like *"Farrago: The Last Derivative Novel,* by Polygamy M. Smith, Ph.D.,"* was designed partly to mock the creative writing program at the University of Iowa. After an epigraph quoted from *Finnegans Wake*—"Bringem young, Bringem young, Bringem young"—it began with the following fake acknowledgment.

> This novel was originally written as a dissertation in partial fulfillment of the requirements for the degree of Doctor of Philosophy and submitted to the faculty of the Division of the Humanities, Department of English Language and Creative Writing, at Epicoene University (Co-Educational), Epicoene, Wisconsin. The degree was awarded with highest honors.

The hero/narrator, Polygamy Smith, was the son of polygamous Mormons, grappling with how to tell his complex story. He dedicates it to "Venia and Zephania, whose failure to marry my father made this book possible." This is not the place to quote it at length, but as I now read over the manuscript, my Failed Creative Self curses me for not having pursued it further. It was, for that time, an avant-garde work; if polished and pushed, it might have placed as forerunner of John Barth's *Giles Goat-Boy* and the flood of Philip Roth's trickeries.

Of course, by now it would strike any up-to-date reader as old hat—and by no means as good as the works of Roth and Barth. Like me, many readers are a bit tired of the excessive Tristram-Shandyism of works like Salman Rushdie's otherwise brilliant *Midnight's Children.* But at that time my novel would have been absolutely "before its time."

So why did I drop it, after months and months of serious labor? Again it was the lack of praise. I was receiving rejection slips right and left (not only for the book drafts), usually accompanied with little encouraging notes about revision but never with "please resubmit."

August 15, 1951
Funny thing about my many rejection slips. As soon as I get one more, my total summer's output will have been rejected. I should have got a job in a factory somewhere.

Another discouragement was that Phyllis was deeply skeptical about the budding novel. In May of 1950, when I had told her I was thinking of maybe shifting the center from polygamy to polyandry, "She was critical and immediately my enthusiasm turned to gloom. Surely it wasn't worth bothering about." Then the final rejection slip of the summer arrived. I had submitted fifty or so pages to the fiction contest run by *Furioso* magazine and didn't win.

VainB reacted exactly as he had when Gean Clark gave him only a B+ and when the Writing Club Director rejected the short story. "If it doesn't win, I should give it up." So I just filed it away, consoling myself sometimes with the thought "Someday I'll polish it." (Like all my accounts, this one no doubt oversimplifies matters. After all, throughout my writing of that novel, I was apprehensive about its effects on my devout Mormon relatives and friends. For all I can know for sure, fear of hurting others and being hurt in response was an even stronger motive for dropping it than was my sense of inferiority.)

In August I wrote,

> I was tempted for a while today to say to myself, "Forget the effort to do anything creative and stick to scholarship, where you can be sure to publish everything you write." But I didn't maintain that idea for long. I have too many ideas left undeveloped to drop them easily or lightly. . . . I cannot hope to be anything more than a small writer of small things, I suppose; I have begun too late—I spent too long in idle-dreaming. But I can do those small things well.

So I rejected all temptation to do anything "large"—any other novel—until about 1975, just after publishing two "uncreative" books in 1974. But in 1975 I got turned on by another idea for a satirical novel. I was then, as I am now, a bit fed up with the almost universal habit, even in first-class writers, of dwelling on despair about the world, about life: *everything* is shit, there's nothing in life but awfulness, there's nothing to do but curse (cleverly).

So I decided to do—well, not quite what one could call a novel; the whole point was to be a satire "passing" as a novel—a mocking of the despairers. I was pursuing the opposite of Voltaire's *Candide*; instead of mocking those who are too optimistic, I would mock those who are too pessimistic. The plot would revolve around a beautiful, cheerful college student named Cass Andor (spoofing "Cassandra," the truth-telling, despair-touter in the *Iliad* and the *Aeneid*); she comes to a secular college as a Mormon, full of optimism, and she is slowly immersed in, mentally seduced by, the clever despairers.

As Cass's actual life proceeds in utter good cheer, her ways of talking about life grow nastier and nastier, imitating her philosophical idols, especially young Professor Gemmisant (French for "moaning, wailing, creaking"). She does a chapter of sour-witty aphorisms about life. She has just made one entry consisting of what she has decided not to call *profundities* but *neatlies*— efforts to imitate the wit of the despairers. Here's one of them.

"Love is as tough and inflexible as Hell itself."

By this point in the draft, I portrayed her as excited about a new project that has occurred to her while reading in the crazy collection of banalities that Flaubert uses as the appendix in *Bouvard et Pécuchet*. She has just been sitting there, when suddenly she thinks of a project that would be a lot better than Flaubert's, one that would open up the abyss, open it up right before your eyes. She hasn't been planning it; the neatlies just flowed in, the first one like this:

"One way in which I'm weak is that I never seem to compare myself negatively with other people the admirable way you do."

It wasn't *very* neat, but if you thought about it for a minute, a hole opened right up in the floor and swallowed you. Didn't it?

Now she was trying some others:

"One good mutatis mutandis deserves another."

"I don't think very clearly when I get muddled."

"I can take people's emotionalism; but after it's gone on for a while, I just blow up."

"Who are *you* to claim the right not to be presumptuous?"

"What I want most in life is to be known as the woman who of all women is least concerned about what other people think of her."

"In general one can expect a surprising amount of trouble."

"True confessions of a hypocrite."

"He was forging a history of forgeries."

"Let self-sacrifice be its own reward."

She found that she could make these circular jokes easily enough, though most of them weren't quite as good as Peter De Vries's "Nostalgia isn't what it used to be."[2] Or Oscar Wilde's paradoxes throughout *The*

---

2. Simone Signoret used the quip as the title for her *Life*. Who gets the credit, De Vries or Signoret?

Picture of Dorian Gray. But it was really too easy unless you put in the requirement that they must *wipe out the base.* For example, she had written, when a bit tired, what felt like a clever "Report by the Dean on the Status of Departments":

> Biology is quite lively, but Economics is not valued highly by the students. There seems to be some truth to the claim that Philosophy is in need of analytical self-study. History is forging ahead, while Political Science seems to have lost its power base. Art is in beautiful form, Psychology is developing abnormally, Geometry is tightening its lines, and Algebra is functioning well. Sociology is pulling together, Law seems well regulated, but Medicine is ailing, and the Atomic Physics program is clearly decaying rapidly. Finally, our Geography Department seems to be in good shape; though Geophysics is soaring, and we have mapped out a good program in Cartography. . . ."

But all that was just silliness, she could see now, and she threw it all away.

She had read somewhere about the difference between autological words and heterological words—the first include themselves in their own range of reference, as "English" is an English word and "polysyllabic" is polysyllabic; the second exclude themselves, as "water" is not wet and "German" is not a German word. Polysyllabic is autological; monosyllabic is heterological. She wondered whether the concept couldn't yield some "Nihilistic Circularities."

Is "autological" an autological word? Clearly. But is heterological? She had to think awhile about that, and she thought she felt, indeed she truly felt, the Abyss opening beneath her. Vertiginous depths—a fine full phrase for the emptiness—clearly heterological. Void—that seems empty indeed: autologous.

Does "empty" mean something? If so, the word is not empty: heterologous.

Does "nothingness" mean something?

She knew that she did not know.

She found herself writing:

If nothing is nothing, Autology reigns;
But *if* nothing just *is*,
Heterology gains.

Trivial games, she thought with self-contempt. I try to write something serious about the depths and I end up with stuff like that. She crossed it all out and wrote,

"I set out to express the void, but nothing came to me."

"He found that without ribbon in his typewriter his book defending silence went much faster."

"Which is worse, a full cesspool or a permanently empty one?"

"In this sewer, the empty world, we only think we smell shit."

"Ask your friend what she really thinks of you, then flush hard."

She was troubled with these last two: they didn't seem quite to qualify as circularities—just as neatlies. "I gotta do some sorting," she thought, "and I still gotta long way to go. But if I can keep up at this rate, by golly, someday I'll have earned my membership in the company of those who have exposed this great slaughterhouse, the world."

Reading today over my heroine's effort at invention, I go back and forth—sometimes wondering why the three-hundred-page draft (in several versions) is still sitting here in 2005, unrevised, unfinished, unfinishable, and sometimes concluding that it just doesn't work. I don't see it in its present form as publishable, even as I enjoy some parts. But, a voice whines at me, what kept you from polishing and submitting?

Well, I did send it to one agent, whose only comment in the letter of rejection was that I had failed to include enough "physical details" about the beautiful heroine. I did show it to a brilliant friend, who responded negatively, "Well, I think there may be a novel in here, but it sure needs a lot of work." Which I knew already.

So again, I gave it up; my muse—if she existed—was killed by two negative critiques, one from an agent who soon after died of alcoholism, the other from an admired friend. And now I go on imagining, *sometimes*, that if I had persisted, I could have become an "author."

Meanwhile, of course, AmbitionB was always responding to the more positive receptions of my "uncreative" work. Like Lionel Trilling, I was seduced away from the imaginative world into the conceptual world—but without more than a pale shadow of Trilling's miserable self-reproach about it.[3] Literary and rhetorical criticism, the very concept of which hadn't entered my head until far into graduate study, had begun to rival as a goal my zealous hope to become a good teacher. If a critical essay or book draft could earn praise while my creative efforts earned contempt, what should I do? And besides, ideas about criticism began to exert a genuine appeal of their own.

---

3. For a moving account of how Trilling lived with his disappointments as a "creator," see Cynthia Ozick, "Lionel Trilling's Self-Criticism," *New Yorker* (October 2, 2000), 116–27.

Do I now think that if I had persisted I could have become a top-class novelist? Absolutely not. A pretty good satirist? Maybe. But anyone who studies the lives of the great writers learns that they are obsessed, as I was not, by the imaginative process: they are possessed from childhood on, hour by hour, day by day, with story possibilities, with metaphorical riches, with dreams about fictional worlds. Somehow I lacked that, only meeting it occasionally in my literal dreams at night. Real novelists wake in the morning with ideas about the next dramatic episode or moving metaphor; I have almost always waked with some notion of how to reorganize a messy critical chapter. Only my nighttime dreams have revealed a fully rich imagination.

I suspect that my keeping an almost daily journal account of those dreams, decade by decade, came from my sense that I had, buried in there, a genuinely rich creative imagination. Reading some of the entries now, I often think I may have been right. Please note the admirable humility that explains my resisting VainB's temptation to quote more than one of those journal reports here.

> Last night read a bit more about the *ars moriendi*—the art of dying—in Christian authors of the 17th c. All about how the dying are surrounded by demons competing for their souls, against the efforts of the priest who is administering the sacrament. Then I dreamed, not that I was dying, but that I was trying to write an autobiography, and there were about a dozen demons hovering about my head, trying to get their hands on my fingerboard to erase all of the affirmative sections. I scratch at them; they fight back, flashing electrical shocks at my fingers.

Such moments certainly do not make the stuff of first-class fiction, though some of them still seem to me wonderfully imaginative. Nor do they belong in *this* kind of *LIFE*.

THE CONFLICTING STYLES

A closely related conflict of Selves, one that I'd never even thought about until April Fool's Day this year, ThinkerB might describe like this.

> You've spent much of your life, both as teacher and as publishing critic, touting *understanding*. You have hectored students about how to achieve "total clarity," about addressing broad audiences intelligibly. You have attacked authors who distance themselves from audiences with hoity-toity polysyllabic inhibitory ideologicalism like this. Yet your own writing, sometimes even as would-be scholar and almost always as satirist and would-be novelist,

has often been aggressively elitist—unintelligible except to the narrowest of audiences. Your ironies are often clear only to a precious few, while you nag students to "make it clear: write with a specific audience in mind, and cut the obfuscations!"[4]

As I think of that contrast, it seems to me sharp, dramatic, mysterious—and a bit hypocritical, with no "upward" qualification. It's *this* pose vs. *that* pose: Accessible-Booth vs. Booth-as-Smartass. Did the apostle of clarity never nag the fake novelist about his obscurities? Paradoxically, the conflict and obfuscation can't be explained without either too much complexity or too much clarity. For most of my life, or at least since I read my first Jonathan Swift and Aldous Huxley in high school, one of my Selves has been preoccupied with writing subtle satire addressed to some kind of elite audience. The impulse to attack the ignoramuses, whether fat cats or not, can be found throughout the journals and in spoofy piece after piece, including some unpublished bits written (or at least fantasized about) right up to this morning.[5]

As I reread those elitist satires, what strikes me now is how close they often come to being unintelligible except to an implied audience of "learned" intellectuals. They assume not just close reading but informed, deep reading, sometimes loaded with allusions that even well-read readers will catch only if by accident they have read this or that work I've happened to read.

If you looked at the opening paragraphs of that abandoned novel about Polygamy Smith, you'd be totally baffled. Having just completed a dissertation on *Tristram Shandy* and having read, or "read at," Joyce's *Finnegans Wake* several times, I began the first chapter with parodies of Joyce's obscurities, concluding with an allusion to the final sentence of *Ulysses:* "i can only answer in the affirmative in the affirmative in the affirmative."[6]

One result of the split between that obscure satirist and the prophet of clarity was predictable: my "cleverest," most complex satires were largely ignored, while my best efforts at clear, polished, acceptable prose on critical topics were widely read.[7] VainB nags me to quote a bit from works nobody has ever discussed, like my somewhat bawdy "Lady Chatterley's Lover and the Tachistoscope," hoping that at least one reader might know what a tachistoscope is.

---

4. I probably don't have to point out that this whole section could well be inserted into chapter 12, regarding my egalitarian vs. bourgeois drives.

5. It was a satire attacking defenders of the "free market" as the "fee market."

6. Oh, dear; you don't remember that final line? OK, I'll be kind: "his heart was going like mad and yes I said yes I will Yes."

7. One early reader has suggested that I include something like "Your academic style is wonderfully accessible, as compared with the usual." I refuse to.

The split I'm addressing echoes a cultural split that hundreds have discussed, sometimes attacking the elite, sometimes attacking the vulgar. Already in 1938, Somerset Maugham in *The Summing Up* was lamenting how the popular taste of audiences he had to appeal to had degraded the aesthetic quality of his dramas. As audiences have become less well educated, he claims, they have been harder and harder to please without downgrading one's own interests:

> In thus yielding to the fashion [of slangy, colloquial speech] it seems to me that dramatists have gravely handicapped themselves. For this slangy, clipped, broken speech they reproduce is only the speech of a class, the speech of the young, ill-educated well-to-do, who are described in the papers as the smart set. They are the persons who figure in the gossip columns and in the pages of illustrated weeklies. (99)

I never escaped the split, pursuing conflicting goals without even noticing the conflict. While hounding students and colleagues about their failures to make everything perfectly clear, I was simultaneously teaching literature courses where they met a Proust whose sentences, in French or translation, often baffled me. While writing as if to please Strunk and White one day, I would next day turn out stuff so dense that I can't understand it when I reread it now.

I'm sure that you've noticed and perhaps even been bored by my relatively "plainspoken" style throughout this book, mostly purged of beautiful metaphors. Would you enjoy all of this *LIFE* more if it had as many metaphors and similes as the opening of Eudora Welty's *Losing Battles*?

> When the rooster crowed, the moon had still not left the world but was going down on flushed cheek, one day short of the full. A long thin cloud crossed it slowly, drawing itself out like a name being called. The air changed, as if a mile or so away a wooden door had swung open, and a warm smell, more of warmth than wet, from a river at low stage, moved upward into the clay hills that stood in darkness.
>
> Then a house appeared on its ridge, like an old man's silver watch pulled once more out of its pocket. A dog leaped up from where he'd lain like a stone and began barking for today as if he meant never to stop.

So there we have in every sentence at least one metaphor or a "like" or an "as if." Should I succumb to the temptation to go back through this whole book, changing the first sentence of the preface, for example, from

Every autobiographer faces problems that no novelist faces: as I write, my actual story still runs on.

to

Every autobiographer faces soul-destroying problems that no novelist faces: as I write, my actual story still runs on, like some elderly tail-dragging crocodile that has lost its way home.

Though Welty too often goes over the brink, actually tempting me to threaten her with my revision machete, she reminds me of a memory of how Norman Maclean hyped up *A River Runs Through It*. A former student of his, by then a top cat at Yale, responded to Maclean's trembling request for advice about a stinky draft with, "It's gotta have more metaphors." So Norman went back through the draft, sneaking in metaphors *as if* he were *brightening the river scene* by *planting flowers along the bank*.

Actually, unlike this monochromatic stuff of mine, he turned it into a *coup de théâtre*. Shouldn't I just crawl along humbly in his path, like a dachshund feeling crushed by his master's curse, and . . .

Suddenly a chorus of voices chant at me:

"Drop that clumsy stuff! You are not, dammit, a novelist. You're a would-be LIFER."

So I obey.

Chapter Fourteen

The Committed Father and Husband, as Lover, Shouts "For Shame!" at All the Other Selves

Suppose I were to dare to believe that one could be a professor and a man! and a writer!

—Lionel Trilling

All unhappy families resemble each other; each happy family is happy in its own way.

—Tolstoy, as he turns in his grave

Parentage is a very important profession; but no test for fitness for it is ever imposed in the interest of the children.
—George Bernard Shaw, *Everybody's Political What's What*

To be honest, to be kind—to earn a little and to spend a little less, to make upon the whole a family happier for his presence, to renounce when that shall be necessary and not be embittered . . . here is a task for all that a man has of fortitude and delicacy.
—Robert Louis Stevenson, "A Christmas Sermon"

. . . poor Brutus, with himself at war,
Forgets the shows of love to other men.
—Shakespeare, *Julius Caesar*

A national poll of scholars' children, age twenty-two to fifty-five, reveals the shocking fact that 83 percent of them remember their fathers as having "prioritized" research over family.
—Booth Foundation Research Center

Long before Phyllis and I were married, I had developed "indubitable" convictions about what marriage should be—of course, with the male in charge. Many of those views had been changed by the time I found the girl of my dreams. I was sure that she and I could come as close to a perfect, *fully equal* marriage with a perfect family as anyone ever had. And being a good husband and father was even more important than anything else. Sometimes the thought turned into "I must be at least as loving a parent as Mama was, or as Daddy was for six years—and would have been had he lived."

I was determined, and Phyllis agreed, that the right parental path was to have six children.[1] We both loved children so much that we thought the more the better—up to a point. I had reveled in playing with my aunts' and uncles' infants, and I even sometimes nagged the parents about the proper, *loving* way to respond to kids who misbehaved. ("Aunt Zina, you shouldn't bother Grant so much about not wiping his running nose; he has a bad cold!")

I was envious of friends who already had children. Whenever I saw Phyllis playing with kids at her nursery school, I felt envious of her techniques and could see that she would be the ideal mother.

However, when we moved into graduate work shortly after marrying, we both soon felt a bit overwhelmed by the demands of the academic world—so much more threatening than we had experienced at BYU. VainB felt surrounded by hundreds of fellow students who were threateningly more learned than he could ever become. And it was clear that even with the GI Bill and Phyllis's tiny nursery school pay, we did not have enough income to support a child.

Because our main income was the $82.50 per month provided by the GI Bill, I worked for a year serving lunches at Phyllis's nursery school, my "salary" simply the noon meal itself. We both remember my expressing anxiety for fear the kids would eat all the food before I got my share; in effect I was

---

1. I'm surprised to find how many relatives reveal in their memoirs and lives that they set their child-goal at six. One of Phyllis's sisters has six; four of our nephews and nieces have six. Where did that weird target come from? I once had a Jewish colleague at Chicago who, when congratulated on his sixth child, explained that he and his wife had agreed that they must have six children, one for each of the million who had been killed in the Holocaust. That point wouldn't arise in Utah, but it's astonishing these days out there to see how many families are of that size.

Phyllis and I on the Midway, University of Chicago, circa 1947

Utah, 1952, *left to right,* Richie, Phyllis, Mother, Kathie, Lucille, Bruce, Merrill

echoing the seven-year-old boy who, at Grampa Clayson's, for the first time in his life experienced competition at the trough.

So we postponed pregnancy for almost two years—still planning finally to have six children, Phyllis with no clear career plans other than teaching nursery school.

Katherine's birth in December of 1948 was an awakening in two senses. I remember LOVER saying often, "The birth of your first child is the greatest of all educational experiences; for the first time in life you realize that you are not Number One. You have been taught the essential lesson of life: some 'other' is more important than you are." (Oh, yes, marrying a genuinely loved one *almost* rivals this Self-measurement; you see your spouse as equal to you in importance. But worth even more? I've worked at that.)

Most of my Selves still embrace joyfully that anti-VainB lesson from life. To have children, and then grandchildren, is a pleasure unrivaled and at the same time an admonition to reject the notion that you are the narcissistic "center." I am certain that if I came to a crisis where I had to risk losing my life to save the life of either daughter or any one of our three grandkids, there

Richie

My three children in Richmond, Indiana

Kathie

Alison

would be not a moment of internal debate. They are more important, not just to me, than I am. I learned that judgment on December 16, 1948, Kathie's birthday, as I first held her in my arms.

The second awakening was considerably less pleasant. Caring for children can be—as I actually put it then sometimes—a pain in the ass. Phyllis would not have expressed our surprising new burdens in that language; she had not been in the army. But after four months of our tending Katherine, in a moment when Katherine was crying inconsolably, what Phyllis said was "Now at last I know why a parent might throw a child out the window."

Neither of us ever got close to such violent rejection, but I did say, one day when I was diaper-changing or bottle-feeding and felt desperate to be working on my students' papers, "Phyllis, we're just not the kind of people who should *have* children." To which she replied (and we've joked about it again and again over the years), "Well, if *we're* not, who *is?*"

With all the mixtures of loving bliss and exasperating midnight howling and breast infections, to us one thing was clear: to have six kids would be absurd. To have even one howler and shitter already felt sometimes like more than enough. We ended up finally with three, but Phyllis remembers that after Richard was two, she wanted one more and I opposed it; *two* were enough. I wanted some free time to perform adequately as a totally devoted teacher, and VainB wanted some time for getting ahead.[2]

I don't now feel the least bit reproachful about not abiding by the implicit six-pack goal. I know too many mothers who have been miserably overwhelmed by having to take on an unfair share of domestic chores with too many children. One Mormon father, whom I've already mentioned, claims to feel guilty about fathering nine; he learned only quite late in life to think about the planet's overpopulation.

What now disgusts me—mildly but genuinely—is that I let my career intrude unfairly on Phyllis's life and on my share of the duties with the kids. Before we were married, I solemnly swore to her that we were to be totally equal. EgalitarianB was proud to proclaim women equal to men in all respects. I had passionately rejected the Mormon male chauvinism, embracing what *felt* like a full version of feminism. Women were (as they are for me now) at least the full equals of men, and men should take on *at least* half of the responsibilities of marriage, realizing women's *at least* equal freedoms. I openly declared that I would be responsible for *at least* 50 percent of the

---

2. Darling Alison: when you read this, do not take it as the same dreadful message that two mothers we know have shamefully inflicted on their kids, in effect contributing to miserable lives: "I never wanted you." For one thing, Phyllis wanted you; for another, from the moment of your birth, I wanted *you.*

Publicity photo when I became dean

household chores. She didn't demand that; I volunteered it. (Only later did I learn, as she joked about it, that her definition of 100 percent was far different from mine.)

"Converted" may be the right term for what had happened to me, because it entailed a huge transformation from some of my earlier chauvinist views. I'm shocked to find the following journal entry. In July of 1940, after reading some Schopenhauer, the nineteen-year-old wrote this in his diary.

> Schopenhauer's opinions of women are what I have been thinking secretly, for some time, though of course my thoughts have been non-integrated. Women *are* inferior to men in things 'of the mind,' and 'things of the heart' too, I almost believe. In instinct only (mother love, desire for mate, etc) are they possibly superior. Of course, I shall find one superior to all other women, and consequently superior to most men, and shall marry her.

When Phyllis reads a passage like that now, she is contemptuous of the arrogant bastard, and I agree with her. I'm sure it was his Mormon upbringing that had prepared him to accept Schopenhauer's abominable arguments naïvely. (She and I disagree about whether the boy was attempting clever irony in the final sentence.) If I had been reared in these later decades by Wayne and Phyllis Booth, I never could have considered, even for a moment, accepting Schopenhauer's views. I'm afraid that some Mormon youths are even at this moment being corrupted in that direction.

So after writing like that, how did I fall into a bland version of "premature feminism"? I think it came from having lived with a fabulous mama, a woman obviously superior to most of the men I met and obviously too often mistreated by the male-dominated world. She had actually taught me that when we needed house repair, I should get Uncle Eli to phone the company because when dealing with a woman customer, they always cheat.

What happened, then, to would-be LOVER's promise of 50 percent dutifulness? The answer is too easily predictable: as academic pressures mounted, my domestic contribution lapsed from 50 percent on down and down until, at some points, it came too close to nothing more than doing the dishes. By the time I committed the male chauvinist atrocity that I reported in chapter 5, not even consulting Phyllis as I chose to move us from Haverford College to Earlham College, she was performing probably about three quarters of the domestic work.

A Bit of Peripheral Self-Exculpation

As I've talked with Kathie and Alison about all that, it's been wonderful to hear them deny that I was as neglectful as memory says I was. They remind me that I did most of the dishes, teaching them how to have fun doing it. I did most of the grocery shopping. And, they reassuringly claim, I did a lot of game playing. At bedtime I sang songs and read to them and made up fairy stories. Kathie reports this episode that I've totally forgotten, where I went a bit too far in the game playing:

> We had for some reason a lot of trash to be burnt and you decided to play some games with the flame, maybe to teach us a bit about how oxygen works. So you took a heavy blanket, covered the burning trash, then flipped the blanket up, sending sparks into the sky like a mild explosion. You did it again and again—until suddenly a neighbor woman appeared, furious. "Don't you see that you're landing black soot on my laundry over there!"

But at least I was trying to entertain the kids. As you might guess, I could make a long list of delightful times with them. So I wasn't a son of a bitch after all, right? I even at one point, considerably later, signed on for a while as a volunteer play therapist in Phyllis's new "Theraplay" program, working with troubled inner-city kids. This can hardly count as "parenting," but doesn't it demonstrate my effort to be "on her side"?

BACK TO THE MAIN STORY

Though I could contrive a favorable version of the loving father, the truth is that for most of each day through most every year, I was teaching or writing. Phyllis remembers—though I can't remember her talking much about it at the time—that *her* life was often in abeyance: her hope for a career had simply been shoved aside by her half-successful husband and her duties with the children. Her friends were mainly my academic associates and their mates. Though she managed to work half-time in the Earlham nursery school, even there she was simultaneously tending our children; and though she came to love many of our common friends—especially those who played chamber music with us—her life often felt *subordinate.*

The results were not tragic, as they too often are when men engage in such unfair treatment of their families. The kids flourished, becoming splendid teachers, masters of storytelling, music lovers, generously effective parents. (As I write in 2005, Kathie, mother of one teenager, has recently been Education Officer at the Ashmolean Museum of Art and Archaeology in Oxford. Richard had hoped to become an actor but knew enough about acting as a profession to prepare for English teaching as a fallback. Alison, with two teenage children, is a full professor of English at the University of Virginia.)

Phyllis's career has also been flourishing—I'm almost tempted to say incredibly. Her ideas about child psychology grew, and she took up a career that in my view is now "doing more good in the world" than I have done, as she conducts workshops in South Korea, Finland, England, and so on. And I can honestly and proudly say that VainB does not intrude to express envy that these days she is receiving more lecture requests, more telephone calls, more emails than I am. (But as Phyllis says about all my ironies, that thought did in fact occur to me.)

Could I perhaps console the neglectful father with the thought that her work in Theraplay (she's even doing some autobiographical essays about it) was *improved* by having the duties of parenting shoved upon her? Hardly. What is clear is that I was often blinded by my ambitions, ignoring what my fulfilling this or that professional "assignment"—a three-day lecture trip, say—was doing to her and the kids "back home."

It's not at all hard to find sad evidence of moments when the children were treated as less important than my professional success. Of course, I'll never know for sure which choices actually harmed them, and I don't know whether they would now say they were harmed by the following choice. But to both Phyllis and me it now seems that we were a bit careless on this one.

1963

I was invited to go to South Africa for four months as part of a "United States–South Africa Leadership Exchange Program" initiated by The American Friends Service Committee; they were hoping to help "cure," or at least abate, some of the atrocities of apartheid. My assignment was to visit schools and colleges lecturing "on the teaching of English."

After a lot of discussion and internal debate about what it meant to our kids to be "farmed out" for four months, I accepted. How could budding scholar VainB refuse—unless he thought a bit harder about what the kids needed during those four months?

Kathie was almost fifteen, and neighbors with children about her age agreed to take her in for the late summer. We shipped Richard, age twelve, and Alison, age nine, off to stay with Phyllis's parents in Long Beach, California. All three then spent the second two months of the four back with my mother, newly married to her second husband, in Pocatello, Idaho.

We had a challenging, interesting, sometimes harrowing, sometimes thrilling time in South Africa, with its beauty and visible misery and almost universal anxiety. Most of those we talked with about apartheid were discouraged liberals; they were all predicting ultimate open warfare, though "we keep hoping it won't occur until after our grandchildren have left." My lectures went well, were printed—adding to the totals in my growing bibliography (terribly important for VainB, right?). We wrote the kids regularly but did not phone them even once, so far as I can remember.

Do my letters reveal any of my anxiety or guilt about having orphaned them for four months? Only obliquely. Too many are irony laden like this one, written to the two in California.

We leave here at 3:00 for the airport, and it's almost beginning to look as if we'll make it. We've just kept steadily at preparations ever since we left you last night. And Tippie [our young dog] looks very happy over there. I think he'll be a good dog from now on, *with no bad behavior ever.* [Only after our return did we learn that the chaos of living in a house that was being remodeled during our absence had worsened the effects of his early months in an animal shelter. Within a few years, after he had bit a neighbor the third time, he had to be "put down," to the children's great distress.] The house looks very empty with you two going away and leaving us like that.

What did we ever do to deserve such treatment? . . . We do miss you—and we promise to feel very very bad all day long every day, more or less, except perhaps Sundays through Saturdays. . . .

You see, I'm raving. . . .

Dad

Those attempted ironies clearly reveal that the guilty thought about "who's to blame" had occurred to me. By transferring it to a joke about *their* guilt—irony that I'm sure they had long since been trained to decipher—the proud father is trying to get himself off the hook.[3] Or what about this disguised confession in a letter to Alison?

It's interesting to read of your attempts to resist weeping. In spite of the weeping, you sound basically quite happy. Are you? We surely hope so. It's quite an adventure to go away from home so long at your age, and we wouldn't want you to weep too (I mean too) many times. A few times is (are?) natural, though.

Actually the three kids seemed to do really well during that four-month gap, thanks largely to the generosity of their grandparents. Though Alison was often sad, Kathie responded with a good deal of caring for her. The only real problem from everyone's point of view was that the grandparents discovered more evidence than they'd ever had before about our "misbehavior" as lapsing Mormons. And then they baptized the kids as Mormons, after consulting us for permission.

December 23, 2000, Charlottesville, Virginia
This morning thinking about this memory, I asked Alison, now forty-six, whether she remembers feeling anger or resentment about our abandoning her for four months. She first said she felt and feels no resentment about it at all. But then after a brief pause, she added, "But I just can't imagine myself doing any such thing with Aaron and Emily!" Do I dare now to raise the same question with Katherine? I very much doubt it. Would she have "abandoned" Robin when she was only nine in order to spend four months in South Africa? Surely not.[4]

---

3. This is just one of thousands of ironic strokes in my correspondence that seem a bit risky. But all the evidence is that the three had all learned quickly how to detect irony. David Izakowitz, Alison's husband, claims that one of her strongest initial appeals for him was that she knew how to respond to his "Jewish irony."
4. Editing the manuscript, Kathie writes: "No, I wouldn't have done it. When she was eleven I did put her in boarding school for three months, but I saw her every three weeks."

Such signs of regrettable neglect, rarely criticized at the time, are found throughout the years. But sometimes my correspondence does offer implicit signs of my uneasiness. When Alison was about to turn twelve, she went to a summer camp, and I typed her a two-page, single-spaced letter full of attempts at humor, self-reproach, and invitations into the kind of literary-speculative life that she later joined. (The letter fascinates me now, partly because it seems a bit misguided, indeed confusing, as it might be viewed by a twelve-year-old. Unless you feel very mature and attuned to ironies, just skip this entry.)

Early Summer, 1965

Well, now, look what you got yourself into. There you are, no doubt gaily going about your camply activities, bustling, bouncing along with not a serious thought in your pretty lil head, and here I come along on a hot, convalescent Sunday afternoon, feeling all philosophical and loving and pensive, intruding (with what gaiety and bounce I can muster) into your carefree, bug-ridden life. Though of course by the time you get this letter, you'll no doubt be tired and sweaty and impatient with life, sitting in the cabin, trying to read this in the midst of unlimited racket, in a dim light—will the effect, I wonder, be to make you feel ready for, up to, capable of reading such a marvelous letter-to-a-beloved daughter as this one is undoubtedly going to turn out to be? . . .

[Then, after brief description of the home scene, with brother Richard acting up a bit] Phyllis is looking glum. Makes it hard for father to maintain tone of gaiety and philosophical profundity with which he intended to flood this letter. She goes about scowling a bit, looking like Ophelia going off to drown herself.

[Then after quoting some Robert Graves, dramatizing how he feels after a minor operation and urging her to write a poem] After trying to coax poems out of my Talented Elevener, what do I do now? Why, now I philosophize. I should wax eloquent about Life. But what am I to say about life to Alison, who knows in her bones all that she needs to know to live is right where she is? Could I say that she knows better how to make the right use of the Life she has when she goes to camp than I do when I lie here in the house and stew about not "accomplishing" something? . . . I should be—but see how it comes out, in the wrong form—"accomplishing something"—I should be writing another book, . . . I should be getting some essays written on this, on that, on the other; how am I to make sure that you children—and then I draw myself back and remember that *that's* not the way to do it. The way to do it is the way *you* do it (by it, I mean the whole business of living) when you're not anxious but just wholly With It. . . . Do I ramble?

And I do ramble on and on, playing more such games with her. Some of it would perhaps be redeemable if better written; there is some sane advice. But too much of it sounds like some cheap self-help book. Tacitly throughout is my worry that she'll get caught up in the wrong "American" passions.

What I do like is my emphasis on the advice that I still have to give myself almost daily—a kind of summary of the main theme of *For the Love of It:*

> Play games—but only if you play them with people you love because it's fun to be playing games with those people, not when you play them to kill time. Last night Richard and I played some chess and some poker, and both things were Real, not because chess and poker are anything much, but because he's so much fun to be *with.*

And so on—the "devoted father" trying his best to make up with a somewhat self-involved letter for the lack of attention he feels he's been showing to his daughter when she's at home.

I could offer many more examples of how my deep desire to be the best father and husband in history crashed under other ambitions. At this very moment, should I not be writing a loving letter to Katherine and Alison? Is my sense of guilt about neglecting them not justified? Reading a *LIFE* of Thomas Jefferson recently, I was impressed by how much more *written* attention he gave his daughters than I've given mine—though emailing has to some degree revived the intimacy. (We'll never know whether he outclassed me in the amount of eye-to-eye contact.) Should I feel guilty about the fact that Phyllis does almost all of the cooking these days, while I only do the dishes and dispose the garbage?[5] Or should I simply, honestly, sincerely, express my gratitude for how Phyllis has triumphed over my early dominance?

Recently Phyllis and I exchanged readings of our current work; I read a chapter of hers, she a chapter of mine. The point? Her career has flourished, though belatedly, postponed by my sinful careerism. She has "saved" us both, and she manages quite well these days to keep this arrogant husband/father down to earth.

---

5. The fact is that a great deal of the household labor is done by a wonderful woman we've hired for nearly thirty years: Jewel Spencer now feels more like a friend, she says, than an employee. EqualityB is a bit embarrassed by that: surely there's something wrong in a world in which anybody is paid a low wage—even if it's higher than the average—to clean somebody else's house. That's hardly how one treats a genuinely close friend. But BourgeoisB triumphs again.

Kathie Booth Stevens and her family—Robert, Robin, and Heather the dog—in the garden of Pembroke College, Oxford

Alison Booth and her family, David, Emily, and Aaron Izakowitz

Postscript (based on Kathie's editing, October 2001)

Feeling a bit overwhelmed as I work on revision for the umpteenth time, I open Kathie's envelope containing her editing of this chapter—and I'm almost in tears, tears of joy!

> It's a bit disingenuous to flagellate yourself about neglect of us or abuse of Mom. You have probably done much better on both counts than other men of your generation. You should talk more about your family involvement. What did you enjoy/invest in? Fun of camping, telling stories, playing games, chatting, singing. . . .

I'm not going to take her advice, but it thrills me and floods me with memories of moments when we did revel in being together (expanding on my earlier boasting). Her note strongly tempts me to add in accounts of a few of those wonderful episodes, but to do so would belie the main point of this chapter: even if Kathie is justified in her praise, it remains absolutely true, as her phrase "in your generation" reveals, that I should have done more of the good things she remembers. Nobody but VainB would have suffered from the slight diminishment in my total publication record.

Chapter Fifteen

The Man of Peace Tries to Tame the Slugger

We are as ugly as animals in our fashion, and unless we deal with the ugliness in ourselves, unless we deal with the violence in ourselves, the brutality in ourselves, and find some way to sublimate it, . . . we're never going to get anywhere with anything.

—Norman Mailer

Beware the fury of a patient man.

—John Dryden

Anger is a short madness.

—Horace, *Epistles* I.ii.62

Twist ye, twine ye! Even so
Mingle shades of joy and woe,
Hope and fear, and peace and strife,
In the thread of human life.

—Sir Walter Scott, *Guy Mannering*

I was angry with my friend;
I told my wrath, my wrath did end.
I was angry with my foe:
I told it not, my wrath did grow.

—William Blake, "A Poison Tree"

2000

As I was revising a speech for a "Christianity and Literature" conference, my computer suddenly went blank, losing about ninety minutes of the most satisfactory revising I'd done in a long time. I tried every conceivable recovery stroke, and the text would not return. Time rushed on. I had lost.

Feeling more and more frustrated, I was interrupted by Phyllis, who needed the machine for emailing; her computer had crashed. Not so much angry at her—what would be the point of that?—but furious at how life, or circumstance, was treating my work plans, I jumped up, grabbed the book closest to hand, and flung it violently to the floor.

After Phyllis had comforted me a bit—I was almost weeping from embarrassment about my outburst—I picked up the valued reference book and found that I had badly damaged the spine. Was I angry at Slugger-Booth for that discovery? No. Just disgusted that he is a part of me.

Most people who know me would be surprised, I think, if they saw a tape of that outburst. They think of me as an unusually peaceful, nonviolent man—a "dialogist" or "rhetorologist," always working to achieve peaceful reconciliation between disputants through the pursuit of understanding. Many have accused me of being too much on the side of hypocritical tongue biting, cooperating when any *sincere* man would fight back. Yet what they would see in that flare-up is, I insist, a real Self in me.

The fact is that when that Self tries to take over in public, even suffering fantasies of committing real violence, I am quite skillful at transforming into—or pretending to transform into—a friendly, peaceful, cheerful pursuer of joint understanding. One Self forgives offenses honestly, easily, almost habitually, attempting not just to exhibit but to practice understanding. Another Self often defeats the peace lover—or tries to.

As an adult I've never slugged or physically battled with anyone, but I've often felt tempted. As a dean I once pounded a table with my fist, shocking everyone, especially the famous art critic whose ideas had angered me. Once when arguing about religion with colleagues at the faculty club, my fist again got out of hand, as it were. But since adulthood only our children and

Phyllis and one friend have seen me destroy things in anger. (That friend saw me destroy my tennis racket, furious at him for criticizing my playing.)

As a father, I did—far too often—spank or slap the kids, always reproaching myself for it afterward. (I swear that I always did it gently. Would my Kathie and Alison agree?[1])

PROFOUND HISTORY OF PERSONAL VIOLENCE

In a world where the daily papers are full of appalling violence, it may seem absurd for me to report my far less destructive outbursts. May 2001: as I write, the McVeigh bombing and forthcoming execution fills every journal with speculation about where his kind of "evil" comes from. May 2003: as I revise, the world is even fuller of accusations and speculations about who is evil and where evil destructiveness comes from; the Iraq war has escalated angry violence in all directions. January 8, 2005: as I revise again, news accounts are full not just of rising violence in Iraq but of actual genocide in Sudan. So where do my minor offenses fit in all that?

Obviously this chapter would be more gripping if I had ever bombed a federal building or if I'd been accused of murder because someone had seen me loading the pistol. But the structure of the soul division would be the same—as we see in many late confessions by repentant murderers.

ThinkerB and the LOVER have always been on the side of combating violence by turning to rhetorical reconciliations. Sometimes, as I'll describe below, I've even been tempted to proclaim myself a complete pacifist: all violence, and especially all killing, all warfare, is wrong. Only threats like the Nazis under Hitler were enough to cancel my full pacifism.

The adrenalin flow I have often experienced must be to some degree "inherited" by every human being; it's as if most parts of me just close down as some fluid floods in, taking over my whole body. Most skillful novelists portray their protagonists as committing such regretful outbursts, though some, like Dickens, idolize (mistakenly?) some heroines; Florence in *Dombey and Son* is portrayed as totally loving, no matter how badly treated.

The evolutionary inheritance of violence has been grappled with at least from the moment when that brilliant author of *Genesis* decided to tell a story about Cain's angry murder of Abel. Religions have both condemned it and exploited it; some secularists now argue that the vast majority of atrocities are committed not from evolutionary survival drive but out of religious commitment. October 2001: terrorists are claiming their acts are holy, while we

---

1.   Alison: "I don't remember really. I do remember your spanking Richie." Kathie: "Probably not gently—but never inflicting real bodily harm."

antiterrorists defend our violent response as holy. July 2002: Prime Minister Sharon reportedly sees his bombing of innocent children as part of obeying Jehovah's commands. July 2004: President Bush makes it clear that in attacking Iraq he was following the voice of God.

My Mormonism was ambivalent about violence. Having suffered from violent mobs, we were taught part of the time to hope for revenge against those who killed Joseph Smith, and our history was full of angry violence against angry enemies. Yet we worshipped Jesus, the prince of peace. That ambivalence left me with one more division of Selves. After Daddy died, I was paradoxically both "machoed" and "pacified" by Mama. Making every effort to be "the man of our family now" and yet to be the "good boy" Mama could be proud of, I was led to avoid most "boys-will-be-boys" ways. I didn't hang out with "wild" kids. Mama would blame me if I came home showing signs of having been in a fistfight. For her, to hit somebody was just one more kind of naughtiness—except when one's child deserved punishment, as I sometimes did.

Behind Mama's back I did do quite a lot of fighting until my later teens. And I did it usually feeling some pride—so long as my enemy was smaller, as were almost all boys my age. But once I had skipped the third grade and was surrounded by guys a year older, I was doomed. In any fight, I was sure to lose—sure, indeed, to give up before even putting up a good battle. One of my current Selves is still ashamed about how often I would say to those older guys, "I know you can lick me."

For whatever reason, probably my excessive weeping about Daddy, I became the "sissy," the popular butt of jokes. In junior high school one time I was challenged by another guy for a "duel" behind the schoolhouse, to take place later during recess with many classmates watching and laughing. We fought a bit, but I soon retreated, weeping and again muttering something like "I know you can lick me."

Thus from age six to about twelve, I engaged in dozens of physical battles with other boys. I always lost with my classmates, older and tougher, and only sometimes won when fighting my previous classmates my age.

Grade 8

A group of us eighth-graders are walking down Center Street, past Grampa Clayson's orchard joined to a pig lot. Doug Mercer starts kicking out the picket slats in the fence. I tell him to stop. He kicks out another one. I jump him, he comes at me; I keep on flailing, while shouting, "I know you can lick me, I know you can lick me, but you're not going to . . ." Can't remember whether he kicked out any more slats, but I know I did not lick him. I fell to the ground and he stopped, as he and the others laughed at me. Total humiliation—but not a cure for violence.

Does my pacifist-inclined Self feel guilty about having lunged at Doug? Not really—it was Doug who should have felt guilty for kicking the slats. But my lunging does make a strong illustration of my failure to attempt dialogue or diplomacy or "rhetorology." I should have said, "Doug, do you really think it's right to break those pickets, with pigs in there that will come out onto the street? Why are you doing it?"

That's a wild dream, about as hopeless as my many current efforts to reconcile science and religion.

Most early violent encounters were thus inflicted on me by others—or at least by the "circumstance" of my trying not to appear a sissy. But the more challenging ones were those that sprang from the irrepressible Slugger within. Here's a rough selection.

Age Four or Four and a Half

My overworked, always hurrying Mama—she was teaching full-time to support Daddy's college studies—was dressing me up to go to some kind of gathering, probably a Church service. We discovered that there were no stockings in the apartment; they were all hanging outside on the clothesline. She told me to sit quietly while she went outside to get the stockings. I sat for a few moments. She did not return. I felt increasingly distressed, then angry. Finally, after what may have been five minutes but felt like eternity, I lost my temper, grabbed a hammer, and pounded its claws eight or ten times into the linoleum floor cover, creating deep slashes that remained with us for many years as scars, as we hauled that linoleum along with our furniture from apartment to apartment.

The story of that misdeed became a family legend, and it was added to other outbursts when an uncle came to college and boarded with us. I was told years later that as he observed the many angry outbursts of the self-centered, volatile five-year-old, he finally said to Mama, "Lillian, you've got to do something about that child. If he goes on like that, he's going to become a criminal." I don't know what Mama did about it, except for Church advisers, but her own rigorous supervision to control my temper never ceased over the years. And the wild outbursts did not go away.

My most appalling memory has been retold many times, as I've tried to figure out its meaning.

Age Ten or Eleven

At Grampa Clayson's, my daily chores include filling the coal bucket with a mixture of large and small pieces of coal. I have been told many times not to cheat by filling it fast with *large* lumps; I must mix large lumps with the smaller stuff remaining from previous breakings-up of the huge blocks the coalman delivers. CheaterB finds that he can save time by sneaking larger pieces into the coal bucket, filling it quickly, not bothering about the smaller bits. One night Uncle Joe, in effect my boss, comes into the shed, sees what I've done, and chews me out for it. Already furious at him because of his many mistreatments, I raise the ax and aim it at his head, blade foremost. At the last second, some other Self in me turns the blade away, and I hit him with the *blunt* side, knocking him down.

He lies there a moment or two, then rises, sobbing, with some blood on his forehead; he flees, apparently for once scared of me.

Whatever happened next has been totally forgotten. Over the years I have again and again imagined the consequences if I had not turned that blade away. I could have killed him—a tragic turning point in my life. Though I wouldn't have been executed, severe punishment would almost certainly have changed my character radically downward: reform school does that.

Skipping all the other youthful battles of SluggerB, fast forward to London in 1956–57. We now have three children, tended mainly by Phyllis as I work on *The Rhetoric of Fiction*. Living for a year on a "half-year" Guggenheim Fellowship and borrowed cash, we have managed to afford, barely, at least one "cultural event" per week: a play, a concert, an opera.

One night, she and I are enraptured by a wonderful production of Verdi's *Otello*, one that at several points brings me to tears. Suddenly at the end, when Othello strikes and then kills his beloved Desdemona, I am almost sobbing, and I take a silent oath (later that night I report it to Phyllis) that I will never strike or slap our kids again. I proclaim that "We just shouldn't teach 'em violence by practicing it."

I keep that oath—for a week or two. Then one day when we are a bit overanxious about getting all five of us on the road for some scheduled train, seven-year-old Kathie raises some issue that will slow us down—and insists on raising it. I shout at her, she shouts back, and I slap her, rather hard—and I immediately break into miserable sobs. I have violated my own *utterly sincere* oath.

As I am putting Kathie to bed that night, I am almost weeping again. "Kathie, dear, I just don't know what to do when I lose my temper about something you do wrong." And Kathie looks up at me and says, "Well, Daddy, you could always pray." (Unlike some of my remembered quotations, this wonderful one is confirmed by both Kathie and Phyllis!)

I don't know how I would have described that violation then; I can't find anything about it in my journals. But now it's clear: the Slugger overwhelmed all other Selves, and immediately the other Selves labored to crush him. That in no way explains where the Son of a Bitch came from. Or why he goes on committing other minor outbursts about twice a month, like the following.

> *March 2000*
> I am practicing the cello, and Phyllis intrudes with "those last two notes are way out of tune." Already tense, I blow it; the adrenalin flows, I stand up and shout at her, "Shut up!" and then—not with any temptation to hit *her*—the Slugger brandishes the cello bow and shouts, "When you interrupt like that I feel like throwing my bow out the window!" Somehow I manage not to throw it, maybe just because I remember that it's worth thousands of dollars.

THE PACIFIST CONFRONTS NECESSARY WAR

I could go on and on with further episodes of how I've violated my own standards, with my peaceful self each time flooded with embarrassment. Only recently has ThinkerB seen how all that relates to his intellectual conflicts about pacifism and the need for war against violent enemies who threaten one's very existence.

In high school I had been converted for a while to complete pacifism by Earl (Hap) Holmstead, a fine history teacher who had barely survived as an infantryman in World War I and was certain that *all* war is cruel and unjustified. He had somehow persuaded me to read Bertrand Russell's powerful arguments about the stupidity and needless cruelty of that war—indeed of all war. But when news about rising threats from the Nazis arrived, I began to equivocate, like this.

> *August 16, 1937*
> Armis [Ashby, born on *Armis*tice Day] & I have been talking about war and what we would do if war broke out. . . . Japan is invading China, there is a civil war on in Spain, with Italy, Germany & Russia secretly participating. . . . A war is, it seems to me, inevitable. Whether or not the U.S. enters into the war is problematical, but quite probable, although at present, the general sentiment, as well as thought, is against war participation of any kind by the U.S. The only trouble is, most of the people now against war [including himself] would be willing & eager to declare war at the first bit of propaganda such as was dished out in the [first] world war by the newspapers.

After some speculation about how Congress will react,

In two more years I will be in the draft age. [This turned out not to be true.]
Armis said that he would not go to war even if drafted, that he would inten-
tionally disable himself so as to avoid the draft, rather than go to war, kill
off human beings, and run the risk of having his own life cut short. . . . I am
in a quandary. If I were to employ some means to avoid being drafted, I am
afraid I would feel that I was not doing my part, letting other people fight
to protect me. I don't think I would volunteer, but as I feel now I would
accept the draft. After all, I'm not so important that my death through war
. . . should be very much of a calamity.

And I then went on speculating about the meaning of life and death and
war. As a half-baked pacifist, I soon met the realities of the threat by Japan
and Germany (as I saw it) to conquer the world. To stop them, it was increasingly clear that we—I—had to give up any form of pacifism. I later learned
that Bertrand Russell had the same experience about World War II. Having
been a jailed pacifist during WWI, he knew that to fail to fight Hitler, as the
America Firsters were urging, would be sheer wickedness.

But the path to full rejection of the America Firsters was inevitably troubling. Here's how the nearly seventeen-year-old continued to equivocate
about it in 1938, as he read the national journals, mostly left-wing.

Jan. 26, 1938, Wednesday
In the last few months Japan has been invading China, quite successfully.
The U.S. has had one gunboat, the *Panay*, sunk.

The last year or two, more even than the last 20, there has been a lot
of Pacifistic doctrine spread, with hardly any persons sticking up for war, or
heavy armament. With the so-called *Panay* incident, and other war scares
in other parts of the world, a marked, to me at least, change in the attitude
of U.S. citizens has occured. Many people have advocated an aggressive
attitude and the congress has appropriated more for armaments, navy &
army, than ever before in peace times. There are still many who cry "peace,
isolation, etc." Almost everybody is still for peace, but the thing is, they are
beginning to think that we can obtain peace by displaying "a big stick." I
am in favor of being prepared for invasion, but I would be willing to bet
that if the American sentiment keeps shifting as it is now, we will be in a
war with somebody, probably one or all of the Fascist nations, within four
years.[2] I hope to goodness we are not, but I can see the same shift occuring
that came between 1914 & 1917 and I am worried. Oh, well. (Since 1918

---

2. Should I take stupid pride in that adolescent's accurate prescience about the coming
war? Well, I shouldn't, but I do.

an alarming number of dictatorships have sprung up. Russia, in the name of Communism, has established probably the worst, with Italy (Mussolini) and Germany (Hitler) running close.)

By 1940, the equivocation ended: I was actively campaigning on Roosevelt's side, producing several local articles and radio interviews claiming that if we did not support "England's cause," we ourselves were doomed. I often sounded about the way Prime Minister Blair sounded in early October 2001, as he tried to persuade his citizens to join America in the "war" against terrorism. Yet editing this chapter in May 2003, I was even more angry about how many, especially in America, joined President Bush's totally unjustified preemptive strike. Editing in January 2004, I joined those who opposed an immediate withdrawal; the mess we have created must be addressed by those who created it. And by *now*, making final edits in March 2005, I don't know what the hell I would do if I were president.

In other conflicts, such as the Gulf War ("Desert Storm") and especially in the Vietnam scandal, I openly though blandly protested against war—still not a theoretical pacifist but appalled by . . . well, enough of that. As I emailed the President and Congress after 9/11, urging them to think harder about the consequences if they engaged in massive violence, I still blame myself for doing it all so mildly. (March 15, 2003: will I join the peace march downtown today, lambasting the U.S. militancy? No, I don't want to be identified with extremists, some of whom are more ignorant than even the warmongers. Yet I blame that Self for instead sitting here quietly, addressing some future audience about how the U.S. is now raising the likelihood of future disaster.)[3]

Such fence straddling has not been confined to wars. I could fill this book with examples of splits between what I believe and how the Slugger actually behaved.

I am, for example, strongly opposed to all capital punishment; I give some money annually to movements against it. Among my many reasons, the strongest is my conviction that when the state kills people, it teaches the world that killing "in a good cause" is a virtuous act—the very principle that motivates suicide terrorists. Yet I cannot deny that if a hood were threatening to kill or rape my grandchild, or indeed any child, I would not hesitate to kill him—in the unlikely event that I had a weapon handy. And I would do it even if it were clear that the act might harm some innocent bystander, "collateral damage"—the euphemism invented in the Gulf War and now used to defend our attacks on innocent civilians in Afghanistan, in Iraq, and who can predict where else?

---

3.   As the move to war exploded, I did actually do some protest marching.

That degree of self-division about violence may be defensible: it drama-tizes the need for the "casuistry" or "phronesis" or "balance of evils" that I discuss elsewhere. But the deeper division, always expressed in less spectacular ways, is harder to defend—a Self who would destroy a highly valued book by flinging it to the floor or destroy a tennis racket in blind rage against a beloved friend or slap his child in anger. I both laugh and cringe at such memories of physical outbursts, even as I feel guilty for having lied to save myself from the Battle of the Bulge. (There I go again, repeating a shameful confession that HypocriteB insists should be censored.)

Facing those conflicts, I'm a bit comforted by the fact that nobody seems able to reconcile our biological history of survival-by-killing and our various religious versions of the commandment, Thou shalt not kill.[4] How do the devout believers in "love thy enemies" deal with the blatant conflict exhibited when they believe that God orders them to kill 'em all? And how does God Himself reconcile His commandment with His decision to kill off the whole of creation—saving only Noah's clan? Thou shalt turn the other cheek instead of fighting back, and thou shalt forgive thine enemies rather than attacking them. Right? But how many professed Christians are conscientious objectors, as I could never quite talk myself into being?

So, taking some comfort from the universality of hypocrisy about vio-lence, with all human beings openly or secretly my siblings in this matter, it still troubles me when I often find myself unable to turn the other cheek, even when the offence has been minor.

I must now end with a matter that may seem to many readers anticlimactic: the conflict between a defender of animal rights and the hypocrite who eats meat regularly. Am I a vegetarian? Obviously not. Do I think vegetarians are justified in their nonviolent criticism of us who feed on violence against animals? Yes, in theory; Pacifist-Booth would prefer a world with no violence of any kind. Do I ever wear clothing made from animal fur? Well, yes, but not often. And when I do, I always remember, painfully, the most violent job I was ever paid for.

American Fork, 1937

Armis's father has hired me to work on his fox farm, caring for the foxes, forcing medical pills down their throats, learning how to avoid being bitten by the victims (I still have visible scars). I write in my journal: "we are cut-ting the tendons that lead to the toes in their front feet so they cannot dig." Some violence so far but not a lot.

---

4.   Some recent defenders of the Bible have insisted that the commandment is "Thou shalt not *murder*," with other forms of killing, in good causes, justified.

I soon learn how the foxes have been killed: put them into a little airtight wagon behind the car, and asphyxiate them with gas fumes. But then the boss decides that for some reason that process diminishes the quality of the fur, so he develops another form of killing: we are ordered to grab the fox by the neck, pulling the head back so it can't bite, force it to the ground, place our heel over the heart, and stand on the fox for the few seconds or minute required before it dies.

As I obey the order, I quickly feel nausea, revulsion, inner pain. But I go on obeying, not even mentioning the revulsion in my diary. I just do what I'm told, fox after fox, for some months. Killing, killing, killing, of the most painful kind, for my "salary" of thirty cents an hour.

What appalls me now is remembering a rapid diminishment of my horror. The habit of killing killed the nausea, and of course I never protested, since protest would have been pointless. Right?

Is it any wonder that I now *wonder* whether those who kill the beef sources I eat ever *wonder* guiltily about their repeated killings? Obviously I cannot argue that what they are doing is wrong, unless I become a vegetarian. Yet the very thought of their job horrifies me. And all I can do is give a little support to those animal rights groups that try to make the killings as painless as possible.[5]

As I may have mentioned just once or twice before, Booth is himself a divided creature, aware that deep down there is a potential killer in him and that life itself, both a blessing and a curse, will finally kill him.

---

5.   For a first-class bit of grappling with animal rights issues, see J. M. Coetzee's recent novel, *Elizabeth Costello* (2003).

Two of my many selves

Interlude

A Potpourri of Chapters I Refuse to Write (Let Alone Include)

My Most Famous Hoax: One That Would-Be-Witty Wayne Thought Clever and That Only *Some* of His Friends Laughed At

Decades Ago

My colleague James Chandler has been working for some time on a book to be called *England in 1819*. He and I have been discussing hoaxes of various kinds, so I decide to test him. After obtaining some stationery from a friend at Stony Brook, I write a subtly fake letter and have the friend mail it from New York.

> Dear Professor Chandler:
> Since I am soon to publish a book entitled *England in 1818–1820*, I have been shocked to learn of your project on the year 1819. My lawyers have advised me that the best route for me is to sue, if you persist in your project.

And so on, for a full page, with several subtle clues that the letter could not be genuine. It names a few alternatives to legal battle. I sign it "Asst. Prof. Harley Simperson" and wait for Jim's response.

For some weeks, whenever we meet, he gives no hint of having seen the letter. Then one day at my office the secretary says, "Someone called saying that your keynote address, scheduled for Mandel Hall at three today, has been shifted to Brendel Hall. If you have any questions, you can call him at 2-7856." In absolute panic—I have totally forgotten about the lecture—GullibleB calls the number. The answerer has a strong French accent. It takes me quite a while to figure out that it is Jim.

He later confesses that he had taken my hoax seriously for several minutes, actually discussing it with colleagues who, in all seriousness, advised

263

him to sue back. Only when he thought, shortly after, about that signature, "Simperson," did he catch on.

Both his and my hoaxing, I would now argue, especially after hearing him tell an audience about it last week, built a friendship considerably closer than ever would have occurred if we hadn't hoaxed.

25,729 JOKES I'VE HEARD AND RETOLD AND SOMETIMES RESISTED RETELLING

(All deleted, because you've already heard them all.)

INNUMERABLE PORNOGRAPHIC STORIES THAT TURNED LUSTERB ON AND SHOCKED PURITANB

_____
_____
_____
_____
_____

502 ANGRY LETTERS, FACE-TO-FACE ATTACKS, AND REJECTION SLIPS THAT VAINB RECEIVED FROM STUDENTS, TEACHERS, READERS, RELATIVES, AND EDITORS: COMPLAINTS ABOUT SOME OFFENSE OR STUPIDITY, IMAGINED OR REAL (One Only)

Letter from Cambridge University Press (from memory)
There are some admirable moments in this MS *[The Rhetoric of Fiction]* but we feel it will find very few readers, partly because they will be put off by the word "rhetoric."

THE BUNGLER, LOUT, OAF, CLOD, YOKEL, HICK, COMMITS 748 STUPIDITIES-GOOFS-GAFFS-BOOBOOS-BLUNDERS-BONERS-BLOOMERS-HOWLERS-BOTCHES-FAUX PASES (Such as That Misspelling) AND PREMATURE SENIOR MOMENTS (One Only)

Long-Distance Phone Call to University of Nebraska (from memory)
WB: I hate to bother you, Sam, but I'm a bit puzzled about not having received from you yet a full schedule of our conference. This is the first time

I can remember when a chairman has failed to post a conference schedule this late—only two weeks before we start.

Sam: Well, Wayne, I understand your anxiety, but have you forgotten that the conference is not for April 10 *this* year but for April 10 *a year from now?*

MULTIPLE COPIES OF MORE THAN FIFTY "CHRISTMAS LETTERS" SENT TO "EVERYBODY," ATTEMPTING TO AVOID THE BOREDOM THAT SUCH LETTERS TOO OFTEN YIELD (Two Only)

Example #1

To all Beloveds, The Shortest Christmas Letter in History

"End of muddy crushmess.". . . Joyce, *Finnegans Wake*

Example #2

Anti-Christmas (Delayed Chanukah?) Letter, Dec. 25, 1998

Dearly Beloved, Intimate, Never-Neglected Friends:

The major event of this entire year has been my struggle over whether to write a Christmas/Chanukah letter. [Then, two single-spaced pages describing the internal debate.]

375,423 DUTIES THAT THE LOYAL HUSBAND PERFORMED WHEN REQUESTED BY PHYLLIS (Two Only)

Example #1, occurring right at this moment as I write, a pleasant one: "Could you please rub some of this lotion on my back?"

Example #2: "Please, please, always shut the closet door after you've put your coat in it."

THE ONLY THREE ORDERS THAT THE LOYAL HUSBAND EVER REFUSED TO OBEY (One Only—the Others Are Too Embarrassing)

I have dressed up for a dinner party—actually put on a necktie and jacket for the first time in weeks. Phyllis looks at me, says that it's the wrong necktie with that jacket and those pants. I'm suddenly angry, shout back at her, and refuse to change—thus going to the party dressed worse than if I had obeyed.

4,011 OCCASIONS WHEN MORALB, NOBLY HONEST AT LEAST THREE
TIMES A WEEK, HAS BLURTED OUT "TRUTHS" (SOME LATER
DISCOVERED TO BE FALSE) THAT EITHER PHYLLIS OR FRIENDS HAVE
CURSED HIM FOR DISCLOSING

How could I give even one example without offending Phyllis or a friend?

FIVE ABANDONED PROJECTS THAT, IF PURSUED, WOULD HAVE
TRANSFORMED THE WORLD (One Only)

The American Academy of Arts and Sciences agreed to my proposal for a
collection of essays by prominent thinkers on the subject "How We Americans Educate—And *Mis*educate—Our Children, *OUTSIDE* of the School-
room." Many top-rankers responded favorably to my invitation. And then,
for reasons I cannot reconstruct, I dropped it. Or can I blame the AAAS?

SEVENTY-SIX UNINTENTIONAL, ARROGANT CRUELTIES AGAINST
OTHERS (One Only)

When Phyllis and I are "courting," back in 1944, she decides to show me
some poems she's written. Other readers have praised them, and she hopes
for my favorable opinion. Most of my comments are, instead, critical suggestions for improvement. She sees the suggestions as so negative that—as
she remembers it now—the episode permanently killed her impulse to
write poetry.

ABOUT 9,000 DREAMS RECORDED IN LIFER'S JOURNAL, EVERY ONE
OF WHICH WOULD ILLUSTRATE AT LEAST ONE OF HIS SELF-SPLITS
(One Only)

Feb. 21, 1954

I wake from an afternoon nap, having fallen asleep after a somewhat hurried
and harried love bout (some students were directly below us, and the bed
squeaked quite 'orribly; we were afraid Richard [age 2 ½] would wake any
minute; and there was a strong chance that Kathie [age 5+] would come into
the room any time, even though we had moved the dresser in front of the
door: we must get a key). Phyllis woke first. When I woke I started talking:

Now what on earth could make me dream this dream? I am wielding a
blow-torch. The flame dies, indicating that I'm out of fuel. I carefully turn

off the valve, carefully remove the lid, even more carefully remove the lid of the supply can, pour meticulously a new supply into the torch, restore the lid to the supply can, restore the lid to the torch, and then pump up the air pressure and relight the torch. Now what on earth is there about that dream that is in any way significant?

Pause. Phyllis laughs, and then, casually, as she leaves the room, "Except perhaps that you pumped something up that had petered out?"

EIGHT DISASTROUS PERFORMANCES AS AN AMATEUR ACTOR (Two Only)

Second Year in College

As a college sophomore, I am to perform the priest in Yeats's *The Land of Heart's Desire*. The director is appalled at my pronunciation of "daughter" as "dodder," or—at best—dotter, when the priest is to shout about the missing crucifix. I work at it manfully: doughtah, dowtah, dewtah, and finally the boss accepts at dress rehearsal my "rough translation into British." Then, in the actual performance, the whole cast gets confused several lines before my scheduled command, and to pull things together I point at the blank wall and shout, ignoring all training, "Dodder!"

University of Chicago, about 1955

I have agreed, stupidly, to play Duncan in a campus performance of *Macbeth*. Director, even stupider than I am, insists that character Macbeth must be performed as totally blind from the beginning, yielding impossible problems for everyone, not just Duncan. Rehearsals get worse and worse. At the single performance, within three minutes the audience is laughing at almost every line, including most of mine. Humiliation for all.

UNCOUNTABLE GAMES I'VE LOVED TO PLAY BECAUSE THEY RULED ASIDE ALL SPLITS—EXCEPT WHEN EGO OR AMBITION INTRUDED (Hundreds)

No. 1

"If you're really clever you can do things backwards. My name is En-yaw Nos-yalc H-toob. What's yours?"

Maxine, after a half-minute's thought: "It's En-ix-am Rol-yat."

Why have I never played that adolescent game with Phyllis—the lovely Sillyhp?

Nos. 2–2,000

Jacks, rook, *Monopoly*, softball, touch football, backyard basketball, mumblety-peg (boy, was I good at it!), singing songs backwards, singing songs in two-part harmony, parodying songs' texts, making up crazy rhymes, playing Hinky Pinky, chatting in Igpay Atinlay (Pig Latin) or Alfalfa Language (Calfan ouflay tawlfawk alflang lalfangwidge). Inventing private household language (for example, "Aiuto," the Italian for "Help!" which in our family means, "Help! I'm on the toilet and we're out of paper!").

HUNDREDS OF WICKED TEMPTATIONS THAT WERE JUST BARELY DEFEATED BY THE MORALIST

In the Fifties at Earlham College, I learned from a friend that his wife's parents were cheating drastically on their income tax, just keeping hard cash in their safe. I knew that the IRS was paying citizens a fraction of the take for reporting such fraud—the moral thing to do, right? I also knew in my heart that to betray a friend's confidence was absolutely wrong. We were desperate for cash, so after some painful inner casuistry, I decided to turn my friend's parents in to the IRS, secretly.

I sneaked to a public phone, to ensure that my call could not be traced. I dialed the IRS, and as the phone rang, I suddenly slammed down the phone and slunk away, ashamed of myself. I still am—though I still think that all tax cheaters should be caught.

10,537 FANTASTICALLY GENEROUS GESTURES FROM INNUMERABLE FRIENDS AND RELATIVES, NONE OF WHOM HAVE BEEN ADEQUATELY CREDITED HERE (THEY'VE OFTEN RESCUED THIS OR THAT "SELF" FROM GLOOM)

Examples censored. One friend said this week, "If your book doesn't report our fun together, I'll be furious." I couldn't get him to see that to feature him would injure the egos of those unmentioned.

INCREDIBLE, UNCOUNTABLE STACK OF GENEROUS GESTURES OF *MINE* TO FRIENDS AND RELATIVES, DESPITE IMMENSE COST OR HARM TO MYSELF

Just give me a minute or two—I'll surely be able to remember one.

Part Three

Aging, Religion, and—Surprise!—the Quest for a Plausible Harmony

As you would predict, the following two chapters have been the most challenging. How is one to complete a book like this without dealing with every major question that theologians and philosophers have faced since somebody, somewhere, first asked, "What is the meaning of life?"

In an early draft, written just after I turned eighty, I had a long, tedious chapter entitled "JOURNAL ENTRIES, FROM WHAT MAY WELL BE MY FINAL YEAR." Though now, turned eighty-four, that seems a bit silly, I still do wonder whether this one will prove to be the final one. But of course the question should not be Is my life over? The question still is, as it has been throughout, Can I make any sense of it all—especially of all the conflicts among my Selves?

So my advice is this: if speculation about aging bores you, and if expanding such speculation into metaphorical explorations of religious questions feels pointless, stop reading right now. Perhaps it would be less annoying for you to go read the tedious novel by the famous Joseph Heller, *Portrait of an Artist, as an Old Man*, written as Heller faced death at age seventy-six, or some of May Sarton's later works; in 1970 she began to introduce readers to "the foreign country of old age," publishing her journals as *At Seventy* (1984), *After the Stroke* (1988), and *Endgame* (1992). Can I now allow VainB to intrude and tell you that none of the scores of oldsters' works I've read has dealt as fully and honestly with Soul-Splits (and their occasional harmonies) as I have done here? Can I allow ThinkerB to join, finally, VainB and claim that only a lamentably few thinkers have ever joined me in the pseudoreligious speculation of the kind you will find in chapter 17?

Will at least one reader catch the subtle similarities between my wild religious speculation and Mormon doctrine? Perhaps I can escape excommunication after all.

269

Chapter Sixteen

The Old Fart Debates with a Bunch of Young Booths, While Posing as Younger Than 84

Crabbèd age and youth cannot live together:
Youth is full of pleasance, age is full of care.

—Shakespeare, "The Passionate Pilgrim"

How blessed is he, who leads a country life,
Unvex'd with anxious cares, and void of strife!
Who studying peace, and shunning civil rage,
Enjoy'd his youth, and now enjoys his age.

—John Dryden, "To John Driden of Chesterton"

In my fortieth year, I was as clear and decided on some subjects as at present.
And, in many respects, superior to my present self; yet, now, in my eightieth,
I possess advantages which I would not exchange for these.

—Goethe

We are happier in many ways when we are old than when we were young. The
young sow wild oats. The old grow sage.

—Winston Churchill

Age is the bilge
we cannot shake from the mop.

—Robert Lowell

The better you express the losses, the less you've lost. To hold back the losses,
to capture the beauty that was, is to turn the loss into something else: a triumph
of the imagination.

—W. Booth, *The Art of Growing Older*

All of this mess will look better in retrospect, if we ever get back to retrospect.

—Entry in my journal, 1940

August 22, 2000

Yesterday decided to begin a chapter on Youth and Timeflow (really on Aging). Did a bit [which became a first draft of this chapter]. Phyllis interrupted to ask if I'd be interested in reading a journal entry of hers. First time ever, I think. And reading it, I discovered, lo and behold, that *she* is troubled by thoughts of aging—at 74. She never talks about it much. But in the journal she laments seeing herself in the mirror looking old, and feeling depressed about never getting things done at the proper level of excellence. . . . It was striking—and in some ways even reassuring—to see how much overlap there is between our feelings at this moment: anxiety about achievement, about aging, about how to keep our loving marriage as alive as it once was.

Then we had a fine chat about it all, about how we might work to improve the (already amazingly good) lovematch. . . . We agreed that we can't expect the same *kind* of love that earlier decades yielded: old folks can't pretend that they're still really young—especially as, in my case, impotence threatens. Anyway, the chat made me feel that the "harmony" theme of the book ain't an entire hoax; any couple who could be as close as we are after 54 years, while having as many signs of aging on both sides, has had amazingly good fortune—and of course Vain-Booth must add: deserves an amazing amount of credit for the achievement.

December 10, 2000 [Chicago]

A big snowstorm today, the kind of storm that would have thrilled me almost uncontrollably from childhood until—well, let's say until about fifteen years ago. I loved walking in snow, shoveling snow, throwing snowballs, holding my face up to falling snow. Writing to Phyllis from Paris, early in 1945, I reported the sheer bliss that snow can yield:

> When it snows in Paris, I love you. Even when the snow turns to slush, I love you. But when, as today, it remains beautiful, when it remains snow, I love you immeasurably. . . . This storm has been something special. Starting yesterday afternoon with a quick burst of

Relaxing at Villa Serbelloni, 1976

snow of the kind that we used to say "makes good packers," it settled down by night into a slow, beautiful, dry snow. The streets were made wonderfully slippery, and I had the uniquely undignified pleasure of ignoring the Parisians on the Champs-Elysees to the extent of using the sidewalks as a slippery-slide. The exhilaration extended almost to the point of intoxication.

Don't get me wrong, though. It takes a very special kind of snow-storm to arouse my sympathy. . . . Right now I would be willing to romp in the mud if I could be near you while doing it.

But this morning here in Chicago, not fifty years but fifty-five years later, the old man whom he [back then] predicted emerges. As I go out to shovel the snow, I do at first suddenly feel a pale version of the old thrill: it is so beautiful! But then, as I start shoveling and go on to sweeping, with my back in pain, my left knee throbbing, my breath a bit short, I catch myself muttering, aloud, "This is awful; I hate winter." Then of course I think again about that initial thirty-second thrill, and I remember the many times, like the Paris moment, when I felt sheer exhilaration.

I stop shoveling, breathe calmly a bit, looking about at the beautiful patterns of snow on the trees and roofs, and the thrill—a pale version of it—returns. But I do not, could not even pretend, to go get the skis from our basement and do some cross-country skiing on it. And I suddenly remember the crazy risks I took when young, as I reveled in snowfall in the mountains.

In episodes like that one, diverse young Booths and the reluctant old man live together daily, sometimes quarreling. The old man judges the young man or boy as foolish, often even stupid; the young man, confined to a weaker voice because of having to rely on memory, pleads with the old guy to go with the flow: think young even when old. Only rarely do they join, as they do right now, looking out at the heavy snowstorm, and both find it thrilling.

Almost everyone who has written about old age has noted how emotions shift about; youthful desires and achievements fade—most obviously the lustful ones. But writers too rarely note how diverse pleasures rise and fall and rise again, depending more on accident than choice. The oldster whose hearing has been lost suddenly rediscovers visual art; the newly blinded one rediscovers music and audio tapes. The old fart who has not cuddled an infant for decades is suddenly overwhelmed with the discovery that—as a friend put it to me—cuddling a "new grandchild is the deepest pleasure I can ever remember."

Losses and Gains

Some of the changes, as I'm ambushed by age, are almost too trivial to mention. Should I confess here that even though I'm still pretty good at aiming a bit of spit at a sidewalk crack, I am not quite as accurate as I was when my young friends and I competed in that game in American Fork? (Obviously I shouldn't report it, since nobody with any gentlemanly decency ever spits on a sidewalk!) Need I confess that I'm predictably a bit more wobbly on my bike than I used to be? Should I bother you with the decline in all five of my senses, hearing worst of all?[1] Should I repeat my dubious claim that my cello playing is "getting better all the time," as I go on taking lessons but feel my fingers stiffer and stiffer? Should I report my outlandish senior moment of

---

1. Fortunately the new hearing aids cure that one, partially, and my listening to music is not badly impaired.

yesterday when my careless cash recordings convinced me that our bank balance was nine thousand dollars higher than it actually was? Should I include journal entries like the following?

March 15, 2002 (Phyllis's birthday)
Both of us feeling gloomy this morning, in spite of a fairly good session last night playing Brahms sextets. . . . The fact is that my mind just doesn't work as efficiently as it once did. . . . It takes me longer . . . to work out an essay outline: far more rambling, far more temptations into the irrelevant. . . . My mind, not just my typing, substitutes an irrelevant word for the word I intend to say . . . "waifer" for "waiter" . . .

April 17, 2002
Why am I, in addition to feeling despair about the world, feeling so disorganized, muddleheaded? . . . Maybe some secret virus has hit—but I don't feel physically ill: just mentally distraught. Stupidly anxious about . . .

As I run through the scores of other entries I'm astonished at how the gloomy ones outnumber the blissful reports. That's always been somewhat the case, but obviously it's increasing. Why am I more tempted to sit down and record feeling "logey"—my youthful term for melancholia—than to record feeling blissful? Isn't the answer obvious? When you're experiencing a genuine "high," why bother to interrupt it with writing about it? And when you're feeling "down in the dumps," "grumpy," "lost in the woods," you will often find that writing about it helps wipe it out.

To me the most mysterious sharp loss of ecstasies is in my response to visual art. I didn't fall in love with art as early as music. Until I was in my late teens, painting and sculpture were never on our landscape.[2] Our schools taught a great deal of music, no painting or art history. Music was our only artistic center. We had no good museums in Utah, and I can't remember being taken to visit even poor ones, if indeed there were any. Then, sometime in my freshman year at BYU, I chanced on a book reproducing, as its title offered, "One Hundred World-Famous Paintings" and felt my life transformed.

August 2, 1940 [a few months after living with the book]
Yesterday I bought two picture frames (dull silver, a little too gaudy but the best in town within my price range) and put "The Avenue," Hobemma, or is it Hobbema?, and "Man in Armor," Rembrandt,[3] in them and hung

---

2. Phyllis as editor: "Pun intended?" Author: "Isn't it obvious, dear?"
3. The attribution to Rembrandt was questioned many decades later.

them up. It is one of the most important things that have happened to me for—well, in all my life. I had in my hands "100 World's famous Paintings," and I was crazy about them. I picked out the above two pictures as among my favorites, and decided to hang them up. I didn't realize that a picture is doubled, tripled, in value when hung in plain sight in a good frame, over what it is worth in a collection to be glanced at cursorily now and then. Every time I come into my room I get a thrill. . . . I believe that after having looked at them both 500 times, I will like them even better than I do now. Then I shall carefully pack these two and frame two more, until I get about 25 of the ones I like best. Then I'll start over. . . . I feel like a boy with a new bicycle; a husband with a new, no, not wife, child; a child with a new doll. I keep having to look at them to be sure they are still there.

Reading that today I'm startled—and envious. Nothing like that could happen to me now. Oh, yes, we do go occasionally to art museums, and once in a while I'll get some real pleasure from paintings, as I did at the recent "Gauguin–Van Gogh" and "Manet and the Sea" exhibits at Chicago's Art Institute. Visiting the Ashmolean in Oxford with Phyllis and daughter Katherine "educating" me about how to look at some paintings by totally unknown Renaissance artists, I found it all—well, I can't say exciting, but it was rewarding. But the passionate commitment to seeing, the embrace of the visual, the longing to visit art museums—these have somehow diminished. And as I think about it, I suddenly long for the green age that could yield that kind of passion. Whatever happened to it?

September 4, 2001

I'm delighted to report a slight revival in visual interest. I was invited to give a talk at our Art Institute, on how artists (poets and painters) deal with aging. Preparing the talk, I had to run superficially through my art book collection, and through the galleries of the Institute, and my former fascination with art was quickly revived. We've been going to the gallery more often since then.

Longing for lost passion for art doesn't usually extend to a longing to go back to those youthful years. I'm pretty sure that the boy who loved those extremely inadequate reproductions had far more miserable moments per day or week than I do now. In fact, whenever I "wish I were younger," the wish takes me back to the middle years, not to adolescence. At the same time I envy the vigorous excitement of that young man. Even my current love of music, still strong and rewarding, doesn't lead me as often now to sit down and listen as steadily as I did then—often in tears. Only our chamber playing rivals those early years of ravishing discovery. Musical bliss has not just remained with me but in some ways increased and deepened as our chamber playing has taken over.

What about literature? Well, I have to confess—feeling ashamed—that "great literature" grabs me somewhat less than it did when I was twenty. Partly because of my writing life, I spend far fewer hours per day reading than I did when young. Many a novel that thrilled me then I find unreadable now. *The Magic Mountain*, which had been a page-turner when I was nineteen, was sometimes almost a chore as I reread it recently; it took me perhaps two weeks, as other books kept intruding, some of them equally slow going. While it's true that some of the novels I had found boring when young excite me now, such as *Great Expectations* and *The Wings of the Dove*, the general temperature has gone down.

The same is almost as true about works by thinkers I've admired or even tried to emulate. As I write this paragraph in winter 2005, I should be reading some more of Aristotle's *Ethics* in preparation for a class tomorrow. I was startled earlier today by how impatient I sometimes felt as I read my "assignment"; passages that bored me today had thrilled me in my twenties and thirties.

Longing for Maturity vs. Longing for Youth

What interests me even more than such declines is that these days I don't experience nearly as many moments longing for youth as I did back then longing to be older—or at least to *appear* older. I wanted to appear more mature, more masterful. In my generation, unlike today, "mastery" was possessed only by the older ones.[4] But can't we count as a gain the fact that one spends less time now *longing* to be different?

More seriously, I find my grandchildren and my college students much of the time *rightly* exerting their mastery over me—mastery not just of computer techniques but also of a vast range of cultural matters that "everybody who is anybody" ought to master. They hear music on the radio and recognize the singer; they read *New Yorker* cartoons that depend on jargon I've never heard, and then have to teach me what's funny. The truth is that today, for the first time in human history, to be old is to be lacking in what is widely seen as essential education in the "wisdom" of your particular culture. It's not surprising that so many of us old farts spend a great deal of time and energy and money putting on youthful masks.

---

4. Today the elderly are on the whole viewed not just as economic but comic burdens. If you don't believe me, just tot up the comic butts on TV and figure out the proportions.

As a kid, the masks were all flashed in the other direction. I was always sure that if I could just appear older, everything would be better for me.

The silliest masking occurred when I was about seventeen. It was obvious to me that people who wore eyeglasses were more mature than those who did not. Since I was failing, always, in my effort to get on sports teams with my contemporaries, I had few resources for *appearing* older, so I decided—I'm sure without thinking about it quite as directly as I am doing now—to get eyeglasses.

The doctor said my eyes were OK. I told him about all the pain I experienced when reading. He finally gave in and prescribed a pair, which I went on wearing much of the time each day throughout college, posing not just as "older" but as "more scholarly" than almost everybody else. (At the same time, the hypochondriac in me, the man who knew that he could never live longer than his father had lived, feared that his eyesight was indeed failing. And after a while I became genuinely myopic.)

The books I actually read are full of penned comments in the margins. In *The Magic Mountain*, I find page after page of attempted dialogue with Mann. He concludes the book with "Out of this universal feast of death, out of this extremity of fever, kindling the rain-washed evening sky to a fiery glow, may it be that Love one day shall mount?"—and I find on that final page this judgment on Mann—and on me.

> *7/31/40:* [Mann's statement is] up to now, a futile wish, or surmise. worth re-reading many times. The conversations of Naptha and Settembrini are priceless anaesthetics—if I may coin a word:[5] the constant attack at formerly taken for granted viewpoints, first by S. & then by N., is stimulating, to say the least, and to say it poorly.
>
> It is a magic book, more magic than the mountain.
>
> A Classic.

Who is the young man's implied audience there? Is it intended for me, reading it more than sixty years later? I think that though the enthusiasm is genuine, the motive for *writing* about it is a bit silly: show your maturity. Someone will read this someday and be impressed. In fact as I reread the book now it's clear that much of it must have been unintelligible to me then—classical allusions, long passages in French and some Latin, neither of which I had studied.

I could go on through the years tracing the "maturity urge" into the effort to appear as a fully learned scholar. Surely growing my first beard at

---

5. Phyllis and I have trouble figuring out what the kid means with his coinage. Is it just playing with "anti-aesthetic"?

thirty-five had some of that in it; in England for a year, I wanted to look more scholarly.

But then, somewhere along the line, my posing began to work in the opposite direction. No longer "I'd like to be older" but "I'd like to be—and appear—younger."

When did that reversal occur? Hard to say. It doesn't appear in the journals for decades. Rather, one finds "philosophical" speculation about time and how it flows, as in this one.

> *Sept. 9, 1940*
> About the end of every summer I get a sudden feeling of the fleeting quality of time—summers go so rapidly.

Of course, he is unconsciously aware, having lost so many loved ones, of how life itself goes rapidly. But he never mentions the effect those deaths have had on his thinking.

> *Summer 1942*
> It is this farewell to summer, that has gone so fast, that gives such a beautifully sad quality to Autumn. When I think back on certain fall days, I get a tightening feeling in my stomach that is poignantly pleasant. . . . I can't, for some inexplicable reason, become nostalgic thinking of past summer or winter days, although they seem to be pleasantest in my memory (at least strongest), but almost any fall or spring day I have ever noticed . . . causes the above mentioned nostalgic tightening. What is it?

Then, after tracing some memories of "highs" in nature,

> Back to the fleeting quality of summers. . . . A whole summer . . . takes less time to go through than, say, a day of dusty windiness. . . . Now the mountains are coloring autumnally, and I become aware that in addition to my own method of marking time [the journal entries] . . . there is the old intruder, Time, with a very large capital T, marking time with loud taps of his foot, very very impatient, very very uncompromising.
>
> School, that generally dry, occasionally fine and spicy, imprisoner of mentality, is about to begin. And the Freshmen, with their almost fetal look underneath their almost octegenarian pretenses, will be cluttering up the campus and my Time. I am old before my time, young after my time.

The desire to appear more mature did not wipe out all anxiety about growing old.

Feb. 21, 1941, 10:30 PM
Tomorrow, in a couple of hours, I will be twenty years old, which will be something entirely new, as near as I can tell, in my life. I don't feel comfortable about it; in fact, I feel rather sad and ill at ease over the fact, which is, nevertheless, incontrovertible and inevitable. I feel old, and a little tragic—I feel that what I have planned and am planning as a successful, happy life is going to be tragically unsuccessful and unhappy.

But of course, such an attitude is unnecessarily theatrical, juvinilly (sp?) so.

My mood of frustration (sexual (?)) will pass, and I will be happy in my life—I will be. But my very determination to be happy is likely to defeat me, just as my determination to get only the best girl for a wife is preventing me from getting any girl at all. By the time a man, happy or unhappy, is twenty, he should have accomplished a certain amount of fetal preparation, at least. (Mendelssohn had written Midsummer Night's dream Suite by 17). I should, then, take stock of my "accomplishments," file them, and gird up my loins for continued assault at the abandon-all-hope gate of success.

I don't feel like taking stock—I feel like crying—I have felt like crying a lot lately for the first time since my emotional reversion at about 12 years. I laugh and joke, but melodramatically enough, I don't feel all that I show.

(It feels good, here in 2005, to see that young guy anticipating chapter 3 on how the griever masked his grief.) Then,

I am young, and I shouldn't be hunting furiously for a wife—I should be playing unconcernedly rather than worrying senilely (to coin a word). I really cut rather a ridiculous figure, hopping about the feminine landscape, peeping under bushes, up trees (family), chasing diffidently, hopelessly, but always chasing doe after doe, nearly catching one, becoming frightened or disappointed and changing my already erratic course to follow another, a little more diffidently, a little more hopelessly, on into my thirties, forties, and finally visiting my friends and their daughters & sons—I say, returning to a lost original subject for this sentence, that I cut a ridiculous figure, but I don't believe, really, that I do. I am not ridiculous—I am Wayne Booth, the best catch any girl will ever get. The line forms to the left—don't crowd: but no line forms, there is no crowding. I am not recognized as a catch, but I don't laugh at me. Ha!
. . . Birthdays do give one to think.

The first serious, far less jokey worrying about aging occurred when I was turning thirty. Four months after my twenty-ninth birthday, I received the Ph.D., and we moved to Haverford College. I suddenly found myself often feeling—well, just plain old. Phyllis was pregnant with Richard, and we were having no lovemaking. I had no real project to replace the passionate drive of the dissertation. Suddenly life seemed to have no point. The journals surprise me even now with the roller-coaster ups and downs.

> *November 27, 1950 [Haverford]*
> So I'll talk about my own miserable mood these days. It is miserable, in general. No zest for life, no interest in my daily chores, no great feeling of anticipation for the future. . . . And the old subjects no longer excite me. Discussion gets nowhere, activity gets nowhere, unless it can be joyful, which mine no longer is. I never really needed a God, or a reasonable substitute for a God, until now, and I was never in less of a position to be willing to accept one. About the only thing that could save me would be a love affair, and yet really, I love Phyllis as much as I could possibly love anyone. The general feeling is: you have your academic goals, you have your personal goals, you have your intellectual goals, all attained, or if not attained, at least carefully and hopelessly defined. What you are to be is quite clearly settled, once and for all. You are nearly thirty, and you might as well be sixty.
>
> What can tear me out of all this I don't know. Perhaps some big success with the writing I'm doing—but the writing I'm doing will never, barring unjust accidents, produce any stir. It's just not worth that much, even the novel *[Farrago]*.
>
> Yet, with all this, I am plagued with . . . annoyance that I'm not "getting anything done." If I were consistent, the above mood should make me at least indifferent to "success," and yet I lust after success and esteem more than ever before. My detestation for my new boss, for example, goes far beyond what he deserves.

I don't remember how often through that year I felt that way, only that there were decisive moments of crisis when I repeated, "What on earth can I do with this life, now that I am no longer young?"

The "If Only" Drive

Reading now my many accounts of feeling both childish and "in my later years," I'm struck by this frequent message, sometimes explicit: "If only I could turn back the clock"; "If only I could start over and get a genuine education." The overt message is often cheerful and futuristic, with no mention of the past—only "I gotta improve beyond what I am now." Sometimes it is almost despairing; my life is over, and it's a mess. Both directions imply a longing to be able to turn the clock back and start over.

Fortunately I don't often suffer these days from the "if only" syndrome. I feel that my life has been so fortunate, so lucky, so blessed with the right choices and chances that I only very rarely find myself wishing, "If only I had done this or that—if only I had kept on writing novels, etc." The most absurd "if only" I can think of is when VainB says, "If only you had worked harder at publicity, hiring an agent, you could be more famous now . . ."

These days, it's mainly If Only I Were Still Younger, or Could Appear to Be!

I can remember no such moments, through my forties, fifties, and sixties, of hypocritically posing as younger. There were a few times, as I turned thirty-five, when I would catch myself in absurd fantasies about life being over; no man should or could live longer than his father had lived.[6] But at forty I had the thrill of enthusiastic response to my first book. Sudden "achievement" made me feel very young and mature at the same time! Through my fifties and sixties I was comfortable with being fifty or sixty.

Since I was feeling totally happy in my marriage, I never allowed myself to "come on" to any of my female students or colleagues, and I had no motive to put on youthful masculinity. A couple of times when an especially attractive student was graduating and leaving, I would say to her something like "I want you to know that if I were not happily married and if I were twenty or thirty years younger, I would have courted you." That was not posing as younger than I was but as actually a bit older than I felt.

So it was only into my seventies somewhere that the hypocritical wish not just to be but to appear younger came on the scene. The pose was aided by having a white beard and white hair that went on looking roughly unchanged over two decades. I didn't look a lot older at eighty-four than I had looked at sixty-five—unless the looker got up really close to see the skin behind the beard and flowing hair. These days far too much effort is spent on hiding the diverse forms of "limping." HypocriteB behaves in conversations as if totally vigorous and cheerful, even when feeling worn or depressed. (Phyllis says that pose often doesn't work for her; she sees the depression.) I pretend to have heard a fellow diner's comment and invent a response that attempts to hide the non sequitur.

As I think of that posing today, comparing it with my youthful efforts to appear older, I think it's maybe a bit more defensible, more useful to the world. Those youthful efforts to look older did nothing for or to the world, except perhaps negatively—making others feel put down. My elderly posing is usually a way to keep "the world" itself more cheerful, less despairing: Hypocrisy-upward, right? What would be the good of letting my grandkids see

---

6. Paul Auster's *The New York Trilogy* deals wonderfully with this problem: how a man is to deal with being older than his father.

my moments of despair? Then suddenly ThinkerB rushes in here—what on earth is the good of letting them, or anyone, read about those moments?

In any case, by now, at eighty-four, it is no longer simply a hypocritical pose. It is (but only part of the time) a genuine longing to be younger than I am—not to go back and live my life over, but to recover what life felt like at, say, forty. I could do things then that I can't do now. I could feel things then that I can't now. The range of possibilities in life usually felt broader and richer then than they often feel to me now. (For example, though I've always felt overwhelmed by the number of unread books on my shelves, books that ought to be read, back then I had some future in which they could be read. Now time is running out; how many books can I expect to read before I die? Even if I were to rival that French woman who lived to 126, could I even re-read all of Dickens, whose *Dombey and Son* recently took me about a month to complete, partly because of my preoccupation with this *LIFE*?[7])

The strongest "if only" drive occurs when I think about unfinished projects. *If only* I had completed that really splendid project "Yielding," about how diverse religious positions might deal with grief. *If only* I had completed "A Modernist Repents," a "brilliant" presaging of the better forms of some postmodernist critiques of modernism. *If only* I had had the guts to ignore the editor's rejection of the proposal for a book on "Fee Speech and Free Speech." *If only* I had finished *Cass*—and so on. What a fine author I could have been!

Suddenly LusterB snarls, "How come you've never mentioned 'If only I could repair my impotence'?" To which ThinkerB cheerfully replies, "Have you forgotten how wonderfully the aged Cephalus answers when Socrates asks how he deals with 'the threshold of old age'?" And then VainB whispers, "Don't forget to cite the passage; it's *Republic*, 329! Remember how impressed you were when you read it in 1946!"

> When Sophocles was asked, "How about your service of Aphrodite, Sopho-cles—is your natural force still unabated?" he answered, Hush, man, most gladly have I escaped this thing you talk of, as if I had run away from a raging and savage beast of a master. I thought it a good answer then and now I think so still more. For in very truth there comes to old age a great tranquility in such matters and a blessed release. When the fierce tensions of

---

7. A recent survey that has had considerable media attention claims that a vast majority of Americans consider themselves brighter, more mature, happier than they were in the past; the subjects also claim that most other people, in contrast, are fading. I suspect that the interviewers carelessly neglected us oldsters; all of us know we are fading. Except, of course, in the moments when we are constructing new and better Selves in our autobiographies.

the passions and desires relax, then is the word of Sophocles approved, and we are rid of many and mad masters. . . . If men are temperate and cheerful even old age is only moderately burdensome. But if the reverse, old age, Socrates, and *youth* [my italics] are hard for such dispositions.

With sex properly dismissed, how about the potentially boring subject of memory loss? Everybody I know over age fifty complains about an increase in memory problems. Whenever I find myself lamenting memory loss, I find comfort in a memory that some oldsters lack: the absent-minded professor can call up strong memories of memory failure from the earliest years on. Am I more forgetful now than I was at age ten, when Gramma Booth told me to invite Mama and sister Lucille to a dinner celebrating my birthday—and I forgot about the invitation? No current senior moment embarrasses me any more than that one did.

Or how about this one as a GI in Paris, March 5, 1945? After writing to Phyllis about a curious band concert, I reported,

I finally got to the library [where I had been headed before getting distracted by the public concert]. Yesterday I had left a pair of pants there, which I had had laundered and was taking to be pressed, forgetting about them until I was back here in town. So last night I phoned, with the officers and GI's laughing the while, and explained to the French woman at the library desk that I had left my pants, "mes pantallons," on a bench. All sorts of obvious wisecracks were made at this end of the line, and the girl on the other end laughed, too, but she did find them and promised to save them for me. Today when I arrived and asked for them, the girl said, "Oh, so you're the famous man who left his pants in the library." "Yes, but fortunately they were an extra pair." "That's what we all wondered about." And, blushing just a little, I took my pants and made an overly graceful exit.

So, back to the second journal entry at the beginning of this chapter: Why should I here today, after shoveling heavy snow for fifteen minutes, curse myself for forgetting to turn off the burglar alarm when I came back in the house? Par for my course? But the comfort doesn't carry very far. I have to admit that when I was thirty, if I'd wanted to name the author of "My Last Duchess," I wouldn't have had to wait for ten minutes before I could suppress the name Matthew Arnold and call up Robert Browning. And what was the name of the guy who wrote *1984*—oh, yes, Lionel Trilling—no, wait a minute. That can't be right. Yesterday in a conversation about politics, I had to pause for about five seconds after I referred to Bush as Gore and couldn't remember the name of our unmemorable "President" Bush.

"Senior moments" thus fill our lives, but it is still a comfort to remember many similar junior moments throughout my life. The truth is that I've always explained them away by claiming, arrogantly, that "My mind is always on higher things"—even when the "thing" was actually "higher" than what my mind was dwelling on. Can one take pride in resembling that ancient Greek philosopher who became comically famous for falling into a cistern because his entire being was concentrated on studying the heavens?

Depression?

What I've said so far understates my many gloomier moments about aging. Though much of the time I feel buoyant, almost "young again" (especially, VainB intrudes, after hearing yesterday that a beautiful young colleague had told another young colleague that she sees me as handsome), I must record a melancholic moment or two.

> *July 18, 1999 [shortly after considering the possibility of a LIFE, to be called "Another Summing Up"—echoing Maugham]*
>
> For a few weeks I've been almost completely free of outside pressures, and as I've battled within myself about just which "free" path to choose, I remember my fantasy in college: my ideal life will come when I can live in a tiny apartment, with a desk and typewriter and some bookshelves, with nothing to do but read and write.
>
> It's not quite true that these days I have *nothing* to do but read and write: I have my life with Phyllis and our music playing [a list of musical events follows]. . . . All of that has filled a few hours with focused, joyful playing. But what feels awful about these weeks, and especially the past three or four days, is a rising number of moments of just plain miserable self-loathing: not just melancholia or ennui or apathy or boredom or doleful dumps or blues but something approaching the current medical meaning of "depression": a really dangerous and perhaps unprecedented low. . . .
>
> Enough for now. I'm tempted to find a therapist, because it would be wrong to go on with these angry outbursts, and this sense of miserable self-loathing. . . .
>
> Well, the truth is that this vile "meditation" has me feeling considerably better than I did a while ago. Often, when I'm surveying possible "cures," I think of joining or rejoining some congregation (actually attended LDS Sunday School last week), or at least daily meditation (Spinozist prayer). . . . Why can't ZenB drive me (note that keyword, drive) to meditate for an hour daily, and exercise for an hour daily, and get rid of this absurd "drive" to accomplish something, every minute.

Along with the occasional self-loathing and despair about losing powers, I have inevitably experienced what almost all oldsters do: a strong sense that the world is going to hell in a handcart. Here's how I put it in summer 2000.

> Though the surface, in America, is perhaps more cheerful than ever,[8] the path we're on is into total doom. . . .
>
> I admit that such Doomcalls are always absurd, even when they turn out to be justified: they're absurd unless the calls themselves have a chance, as none these days has, of averting the doom. Noah was right when he shouted to his kinfolk, Git on that boat, right now! But I have no boat, the world has no boat. As Machiavelli is said to have said, and as I have reported ten times here and there—after he had traced doomcalls over the centuries, "The difference is that this time the call of doom is real." In sum: the path of "capitalism," "consumerism," "militarism" (we still have hundreds of nuclear weapons aimed at Russia, and they have 'em aimed at us, while we go on fiddling with an impossible and absurdly threatening missile defense system)—but there I go, instead of getting down to "work."

Actually it's not hard to think of "youthful" moments when despair about the world made even more sense than now. Here's how I put it on January 1, 2001, when the media were full of apocalyptic predictions.

> Nobody in America can possibly feel as doom-ridden as we all felt in 1963? [1962, that is], as the Cuban crisis came to a head. I was certain that the nuclear bombs were about to fall—and that we could do nothing about it. (My family did not follow the many who built, and even dwelt, in bomb shelters: we knew that would be useless.) When Kathie, then thirteen, asked me, "Daddy, are we going to have war and get bombed?" I hypocritically tried to smile and said, "Oh, certainly not, Kathie; just don't worry about it." While my stomach was churning with fear. She remembers spotting that I was telling a lie.
>
> Almost equal doom-fever hit us and our friends way back in 1948 when news of the Soviet atomic bomb arrived. One couple we knew and admired made a deliberate decision never to have children, because they knew every child would be incinerated by the Soviets. Perhaps even more discouraging was life in the early forties. I was fairly sure that the Nazis

---

8. A bit amusing, that, as I revise over the years and on to winter 2005, with all of the depressing events since 1999: stock losses, corporate crime revelations, hatred of Americans mounting around the world, the scene in Iraq looking more and more like a genuine quagmire. If and when this book comes out, will things look better or worse? Two Selves within answer in total contradiction.

would win the war; the end of life as we loved it was near. I remember looking at our refrigerator and wondering, "Will they deprive us of *that*, because
of our having fought them?"

I must then ask, Shouldn't any doomthinker just get down to work, instead of shouting "the end is nigh" on some street corner? Yes, because he has
known for decades that sooner or later the world *will* be annihilated—by
asteroid, by environmental pollution, by sun decay, by fire or ice—and he
has long since declared that the importance of *now* does not depend on the
importance of *then*. The point (LOVER and ZenB almost snarl at me) is not to
hope for any prolonged future; the point is to live today and leave the fruits
in the hands of a "God" who is "simultaneously" creating other planets, some
of which will discover the good things that we've discovered, and also the bad
things, and then get destroyed while yet others are created. Some creatures on
those other planets will discover, as I have, a sense of gratitude to this eternal
"Range of Possibilities and Powers"—Supreme Being—and then they'll get
destroyed too, while others are "created"; and some clever prophet will get in
touch with "God," invent some "Gold Plates," and become famous publishing a book about how . . . And so on.

Now, then, do I show this to Phyllis or save it for her—or someone—to
read after I die? Should I just scrap the whole chapter? I think so. Anyway, for
now I'll just ask her to give me some therapy time. And the Zen Buddhist in
me will go right now and meditate for a while; then LOVER will practice the
Brahms G major, then exercise, with both of them chanting at the old fart's
allowing himself to be plagued by ambition and pride, "To hell with that
achievement drive. Live the life you've been granted; leave the fruits in the
hands of Spinoza's God, who created it all in the first place. . . ."

Or I might resist all that and just follow what many an aging hypocritical
philosopher has advised: "Pursue only the more affirmative side, as you did in
the last third of *The Art of Growing Older*, tracing more of the blessings than
pains tied to getting old. Act younger and you'll feel younger."

Chapter Seventeen

Harmony at Last?

There are moments, and it is only a matter of a few seconds, when you feel the presence of the eternal harmony. . . . A terrible thing is the frightful clearness with which it manifests itself and the rapture with which it fills you. . . . During these five seconds I live a whole human existence, and for that I would give my whole life and not think that I was paying too dearly.

—Dostoevsky

*It has amazed me that the most incongruous traits should exist in the same person and for all that yield **a plausible harmony**. I have often asked myself how characteristics, seemingly irreconcilable, can exist in the same person. I have known crooks who were capable of self-sacrifice, sneak-thieves who were sweet-natured and harlots for whom it was a point of honour to give good value for money.*

—Somerset Maugham, *The Summing Up*

Other Lifers' efforts to pursue harmony of soul have always at least half failed, as mine must do. Sometimes the Lifers do attempt to present a full harmony throughout, behind the many threats that life presents; careful readers then detect the deception. The more serious Lifers confess openly to frustrating failure. Most of them do celebrate moments of *feeling* fully in harmony: "Ah, at last, *this* is the harmony, the life I've been longing for." But their efforts to move beyond those moments and produce full harmony by *thinking* about the conflicts always fall short.

This chapter begins with a brief summary of the innumerable moments of centering that might be called *temporary* harmonies. In each of them, the rivalry among Booths is briefly silenced, as some total concentration is achieved, blissful or tragic. Part two is an attempt to explain why no one can escape soul splits. At the heart of "things" is a strong conflict among three "absolutes": Supreme Being "orders" us to pursue Truth *but also* to pursue Beauty *and also* to pursue Goodness—the universal welfare of all God's creatures.

Part three is my final quest for the most plausible harmony among these three inescapably conflicting human goals.

If, like one of my more critical readers, you feel you've had enough evidence about the brief moments of concentrated bliss or grief or despair and enough evidence of inherent conflict, just skip now to part three.

PART I: EMOTIONAL CENTERINGS

Everyone's life, like this book, contains many unfuzzy, unified moments, blissful or awful; the sense of suffering splits simply disappears. Whether or not some thinker later intrudes to label them *illusions* of unity, the fact remains that as we experience them we have no conscious thought about conflict. The bliss or pain takes over the whole of life. Only when other ecstasies or pains or telephone calls or household chores intervene do we start thinking about conflict again and perhaps even pursue a plausible harmony.

Throughout this book you have encountered these four radically different temporary harmonies that simply shove aside ThinkerB's *implausible* quest:

290

Hiking with Phyllis

Clowning with Max Dalby and Phyllis, 1989

Serious amateuring

1. *Temporary Blissful Centerings*—the kind that make me long for more of the same. (Most of them do not quite deserve the label "epiphanies," but some of them come close to it.)

- Making love—not just having sex but *loving* my lifelong partner, Phyllis
- Cuddling a newborn child or grandchild
- Playing games—with children, with friends, with anybody who is fully engaged with the game
- Listening to powerful music: classical or jazz or even the Beatles (after my son converted me to them)
- *Playing* music, the supreme bliss I describe in *For the Love of It*
- Receiving a letter from Phyllis, especially when I was desperately lonely in the army
- Reading any novel or poem slowly, deliciously, totally absorbed (In the army, with no time pressures as I waited for the next assignment, many days were rescued by Sterne's *Tristram Shandy*, Fielding's *Tom Jones*, Wharton's *The Age of Innocence*—and some murder mysteries not worth mentioning.)

- Writing a draft of something that feels good or even polishing (here) what was before just a messy paragraph or chapter (When things are going well, the blissful escape from time may last for four or five hours; I look at my watch and am shocked that it is not nine AM but already one PM.)
- Working many hours with marvelously collegial friends, Marshall Gregory, Joe Williams, and Greg Colomb on textbooks, for days and weeks and months (Of course, splits frequently intervene, but the hours of actual work usually feel totally concentrated.)
- Teaching a class when the discussion goes *right,* especially when, in the midst of a passionate discussion, a student intervenes to say, "Mr. Booth, we've already gone past closing time and I have another class now. Could a bunch of us get together later today and talk it over?"
- Looking at a flower, or a shimmering lake, or a magnified photo of an insect, or a rainbow flash from a prism, feeling a flood of gratitude to the God/Nature that created such marvels
- Lighting a well-laid fire, whether in an inside fireplace or an open (safe) "firepit" in the mountains, staring at the flames as they mount
- Chatting with colleagues at lunch, time flowing so fast that we're almost late for class[1]
- Feeling absolutely radiant, blissful harmony as I walk Grand-daughter Robin's dog Heather through Christ Church Meadow; sunshine on rain-flooded fields; Heather amazingly alert to every detail, including other dogs in the distance; the combo of Nature and the history of Christ Church's manipulation of Nature—the sheer power and mystery of the *Creation* of all this—and I am *here,* part of that creation
- Experiencing equal bliss as the "boys' choir" in Christ Church Cathedral sings a Mozart mass (The boys, like the conductor, are really *into* the music. Phyllis and I are sitting within touching distance from them and can observe almost every face. Obviously they—most of them—are equally transformed. In tears, I put my hand on her knee and she puts her hand on mine—always our way of sharing musical thrills.)
- Attending Catholic mass in a tiny chapel in Flavigny, France, singing the hymns, reveling in the deeply probing sermons by the

---

1. If I provided an index and any one of those friends found himself not listed, he'd no doubt feel hurt, justifiably. But the list would take a couple of pages in itself.

On Phyllis's Plateau with Phyllis, August 2003

One of my many pictures of the cabin we built in Wildwood, Utah

priest who has welcomed us even though he knows that we are Mormons

- Meditating silently in Quaker Meeting, surrounded by friends who interrupt only infrequently to report what their spirit dictates
- Attending the bat and bar mitzvahs of grandkids Emily and Aaron—total "spiritual elevation" or "religious ecstasy," even while unable to do any justice to the hymns
- Singing the Mormon hymn "Come, Come, Ye Saints" at my missionary homecoming service

Such moments from my life (and I hope you have had many similar ones in yours) could fill this book, with HypocriteB happily posing as totally, blissfully unified—almost sounding like one of those silly chicken-soup self-help manuals. Often the centerings make me wonder, "What more than *this* need you ask for?" Some of them edge toward the religious harmony we come to in part three: we feel "salvationally unified," raised out of the time-bound world. And many of them produce no sense of internal conflict, even as ThinkerB works on this book asking how to put them all together.

2. *Temporary Comic Centerings*—the kind that now lead me to mildly contemptuous amusement.

- At age thirteen, I manage, after prolonged wrestling, to throw Cornwall Hammond to the ground and sit on him, demanding his apology. Blissful unity: I've won!
- In 1956 I receive a Guggenheim fellowship: total bliss—for VainB.
- In 1960 I receive John Crowe Ransom's strongly favorable reading of the manuscript of *The Rhetoric of Fiction:* I've won!

And so on. Well, these days, looking back on such amusing unified moments, none of my Selves blames the Would-be Winner *heavily* even for such silly egotism. "I" only laugh at "him."

3. *Temporary Regrettable Centerings*—the kind that make my more defensible Selves, especially LOVER, cringe, either with shame or guilt or puzzlement about my behavior, or moan, "*If only* . . . ."

- At age eight, I tease my three-year-old sister and make her cry; I'm the boss.
- SluggerB knocks my uncle down with the ax (chapter 15); I've won.
- The would-be thinker snarls at Mama, "Any man who can read Plato shouldn't have to spend his time varnishing this furniture"; I'm the master intellectual of the family, and that's what a *man* ought to be.

4. *Temporary Miserable Centerings*—moments of totally concentrated misery, the kind that have led many philosophers and some religionists to pronounce them as revelations of the full truth about life: life is awful, deadly, and only fools can deny it. I've again and again mocked such extreme cynicism, especially in that abandoned novel *Cass Andor.* But the very impulse to attack the extreme negation means that it has sometimes occurred to me.

- The soldier longs for home and love, fearing that the Nazis will win.
- The college administrator hates his job and longs for escape.
- A favorite colleague dies young: Sheldon Sacks and Arthur Heiserman and Perrin Lowry, in their (and my) late forties, and Ronald Crane (in his eighties) in the same decade. And on to many more recent ones.
- A loved one dies: my father; my grandmother; my best friend Junior Halliday; my mother; my son; a favorite cousin, Thornton Booth (T. Y.); Max Dalby, just last week. (When I heard about T. Y., and then Max, I was shattered each time—though not really

surprised because each had informed me that it was coming soon, and besides, our life is flooded with such news these days. When T. Y. first told me about the illness, for hours my whole soul was concentrated on that "unified" feeling: the approaching loss of a loved one. When I phoned him about it, he turned the unity into a comforting "split." Since he sounded cheerful, I asked him why. "Well, I've been expecting it all along. And besides, this will protect everybody from my becoming senile.")

- National or international tragedy occurs. (Like many Americans, I was totally "unified" for a while after the 9/11 attack. I felt shattered—my faith in God temporarily disunified—when the recent tsunami struck lower Asia. In the months following our war on Iraq, I have suffered many mornings of total misery about what we have done to "the world.")

Oh, and there is a fifth temporary harmony, which you have *not* seen here.

5. *Faked Blissful Centerings*—the kind that constitute a large share of what is offered in the flood of self-help books. It's hardly surprising that our bookstore shelves are obsessed with offerings of harmony, some tempting, many comically absurd. Just after I wrote the first draft of this book, a stranger mailed me a copy of one of the best-selling books on the market, *Chicken Soup for the Soul: 101 Stories to Open the Heart and Rekindle the Spirit*. VainB already felt a bit arrogantly envious of the fame and mildly contemptuous of the work, glancing through the table of contents, introduction, and concluding notes about the authors' fabulous successes in "saving" people. They've published book after book that promised "Chicken Soup" for this or that soul: Christians, Kids, Mothers, Teenagers, and on and on. My first impulse—just ignore such a book!

But then I caught myself in a bit of conflict. ThinkerB felt that to be honest he should read some of this to see what offerings of harmony are really popular with Americans. VainB moaned, "Why should such stuff have so much success, when my own efforts to improve the world have been so badly neglected and my book, if ever published, will never sell more than a fraction . . . ?" And on with other voices. ThinkerB leapt back in and laughed contemptuously at VainB: "What a fool you are to feel anything but amusement at a book like that." "I" calmed them down by reading the book's epigraph, a Chinese proverb about harmony.

If there is light in the soul,
There will be beauty in the person.
If there is beauty in the person,

There will be harmony in the house.
If there is harmony in the house,
There will be order in the nation.
If there is order in the nation,
There will be peace in the world.

ThinkerB whispered, "Bullshit!" (With one of Phyllis's Theraplay conferences going on in a nearby room, he couldn't shout it.) "That poem, full of wishes, some of which I share, is crazy in the claim that the search for internal light or beauty or peace will yield total peace in the world. And these guys—the Chinese poet and the chicken-soup salesmen quoting him—are ignoring all of the problems I'm grappling with. You guys never mention how much real good is done in the world by people who pretend to be harmoniously cheerful when they're actually torn apart."

PART 2: DIALOGUE AMONG THE SELVES, MOVING TOWARD HARMONY

The word "plausible" in my subtitle carries a lot of weight for me; I can't hope for anything decisive. One dictionary definition of plausible is "giving a deceptive version of truth." But let's take the other one: "apparently valid, likely, or acceptable"—acceptable to both sides after discussion. Any full pursuit of that version of plausible harmony will lead us on to part three.

In chapter 6, I portrayed the missionary experiencing a rising awareness of the inescapable conflict among genuine values and diverse rhetorics, with the resulting need for casuistry and hypocrisy-upward. I was thus won early into a pursuit of diverse forms of dialogue, diplomacy, conciliation, and reconciliation. Sometimes it has been sheer bargaining, sometimes contemptible hedging. But at its best it's what I've dubbed rhetorology: the pursuit of genuine reconciliation.[2]

Whatever we call it, it is the joint pursuit of common ground shared by disputants in the hope that some sort of genuine discussion of the conflict becomes possible.

What happens when this rhetorologist works to achieve real dialogue among a batch of rivaling Selves? He soon discovers that all of the disputes boil down to a simple conflict of three irrefutable, ultimate, universal values, oversimplified with the labels Truth, Goodness, and Beauty. Most serious LIFERS have had to deal, though usually only implicitly, with the inherent conflict among those three values or "absolutes": the pursuit of truth,

---

2.   See my Introduction to *Roads to Reconciliation: Conflict and Dialogue in the Twenty-First Century* (2004).

however defined; the pursuit of "goodness," improvement in one's self or in some part of the world; and the pursuit of beauty or the perfecting of "beautiful" or "sublime" feelings burning with a hard, gemlike flame. Truth should *never* be violated. *But* one should *never* deliberately harm others or fail to attempt to do good in the world. *But* to violate beauty and to further ugliness is *always* wrong.[3] Yet circumstances present us every day, almost every hour, with conflicts among these three absolutes, requiring choices that violate one or the other (which is why many have declared that there is no such thing as an "absolute").[4]

As you've seen, my actual life has moved back and forth as this or that one of the three supreme values temporarily reigns. Most often, both as a fringe Mormon and as a teacher and scholar, MoralB has led me to talk as if for me, in contrast to many others I admire, the supreme value of the three is "goodness" and that the pursuit of goodness dictates negotiation—and that negotiation dictates some forms of hypocrisy—pretending to accept fully what, in your heart, is considerably lower on the list. Unlike St. Augustine, who worshipped truth so passionately that he would refuse to lie even if the lie would save the life of a friend, I would put saving my friend ahead of truth.[5]

I may be sure, for example, that a friend is just plain wrong in her *literal* reading of the Tower of Babel story. I fear, deep down, that she is absurdly dogmatic—that she can never be expected to see how impossible this story is if taken literally and how marvelous the story is if read metaphorically. I must choose between flat, rude expression of my actual contempt for her reading or a smiling, friendly, hypocritical invitation to discussion. She may reject me flat out; my "pose" has failed, and I simply give up. But sometimes a genuine "good" is achieved: reconciliation, progress on both sides. She may manage to get me to see just how much pleasure and devotion a literal reading can yield. I may manage to get her to see that she doesn't have to violate nature and reason to discover the rich truths in the story. Whatever happens, it is my belief that when any two contestants—whether two real persons or two of my Selves—come out of an argument with some degree of agreement, achieving

---

3. Throughout Aristotle's *Ethics*, he often seems to put "beauty" at the very top of the values.

4. For a really penetrating recent exploration of how supreme values conflict, see Michael Ignatieff's *The Lesser Evil* (Princeton, NJ: Princeton Univ. Press, 2004). His center is the conflict between violence that is justified in self-defense, though still evil, and violence that is unjustified.

5. Suddenly I remember a moment of grotesque lying that I forgot to include in chapter 2. A friend whose wife agreed to a divorce had to prove in court, under Illinois law, that one of the two had committed adultery. He talked me into lying under oath that the nonexistent affair occurred. "Goodness"—my friend's happiness—counted for more than truth.

that harmony is more important than the question of whether they have arrived at some absolute truth. (Note how I am increasingly forced to use "I" and "my" in place of the third-person Booths; we're moving toward a plausible harmony.)

As I probe my conflicts more and more deeply, I discover that I am ultimately (though often uncomfortably) more of a "goodnesser" than a "truthist" or "aestheticist." But life has taught me that to be what I am is not to be inherently superior to those who place either of the other two at the top. Is the artist who spends her life devoted to painting while neglecting family and friends any less defensible than someone like Jane Addams who spends her life rescuing the troubled and deprived, neglecting art and—often—neglecting her love of philosophy?

Rhetorology thus lands us in religious questions. In claiming that the three values are real, not merely cultural constructs, I am clearly invading the territory that all believers claim as their own.

Part 3: Joining the Divine Chorus, in Spiritual Harmony

A majority of religious questers have dodged the conflict among ultimate values by simply asserting one grand indubitable Truth, leaving the conflicts in the hands of the one true God. Thus the harmony pursuits that feel most successful, at least to the authors themselves, have most often been an absolute discovery or revelation, a full conversion to some ultimate, single, unified truth. For the individual quester, such conversions can feel like total solutions to all problems. C. S. Lewis, in *Surprised by Joy*, reports a youthful life of conflicted thoughts about religion, the conflicts finally and totally resolved when he arrives at full belief not only in God but in Christ's divinity. Reading his book, one receives no hints of the conflicts that he must have experienced afterward in everyday life.

If I believed most religious tracts, I would simply have to confess that all my Selves are simply versions of two sides: God's will vs. Booth's sinful temptations. Yet implicit always is the notion that somehow God's will includes a command to honor all three values—as if there were no problem of conflict.

The history of such dogmatic quests for more-than-plausible harmony would have to include every religion, every belief in any kind of hierophany, whether a "manifestation of the sacred" or the claims by Communists or Fascists or Free Marketists that they have arrived at the ultimate goal of society. The plot of any *LIFE* written about such manifestations would be simple and clear: I sought it, and I found it.

Any rhetorologist who has ever tried to start a dialogue among these Totalists discovers why the outcome too often is violence rather than conciliation. The search for a common ground is in itself a challenge to the claim that "I have *the* one true truth." And the searcher soon confronts the fact that the search for common ground is not just something that this or that misguided thinker imposes on reality. The search is built into the nature of what reality *is*. My diverse Selves, toward so many of which I've expressed contempt—too much ambition, too much cheating, and so on—have always lived with a plain fact about human values: even the best ones, the totally defensible ones, are often forced into conflict by this or that circumstance, this or that "case" of rival "commands."[6] The conflict emerges not just in my rival goals but also in everybody's day by day lives. To obey any one genuine value or to pursue any one "divine" revelation of the whole truth will almost always require violating another one.

Such unavoidable conflicts have led some naïve disciples of the founding "deconstructionists" in recent decades to misinterpret the case, claiming that there is no such thing as a *genuine* value or moral judgment. They are quite right if they mean "there is no value that cannot, in some circumstance, be overridden by some other value." Casuistry is required, not only when dealing with other people, but when dealing with "God."

It is true that some, like Plato and many theologians and my Religious Self (once or twice a month), have seen the three as inherently somehow harmonizable in some lovely picture of the One. While being trained as a "clerk-rifleman," I was often proudly reading Plato in my spare hours—though also often mystified.[7] One night I had a beautiful dream that I remember recording with some excitement—somewhere.

> The night heavens are alight, with three huge overlapping circles, one red, labeled in huge capitals, BEAUTY, one blue, labeled GOODNESS, and one yellow, labeled TRUTH.
>
> In the center the overlapping primary colors are yielding pure radiant white; its intensity overwhelms the others. And in the background is a wonderful chorus singing Bach's *Credo in Unum Deo.*

Obviously that dreamer is convinced that if he thinks long enough and hard enough about it, he will find the One that will harmonize Truth, Goodness, and Beauty. They rival one another at the fringe, but in the center they join.

---

6. Most major thinkers about ethics have confronted my point here: Aristotle, Machiavelli, modern probers of "situation ethics." Much of Isaiah Berlin's career was spent trying to deal with the essential "incommensurability" of genuine values. Stephen Toulmin has also devoted himself to the problem. I'm surprised by how few have made use of the tradition of "casuistry," the Jesuits' effort to deal with *case conflict.*

7. It might just as well have been Parmenides or Plotinus. But at that time I hadn't even heard of them.

That longing for a vision of the central One, totally harmonizing all the conflicts, is revealed throughout my life. In September of 1952 I dreamt again—after a couple of other dreams about being a convicted murderer and being myself murdered—that "someone is singing Bach's B minor mass, 'Credo, in unum . . . .' Suddenly a booming voice interrupted, chanting 'How many would you expect?'"

That skeptical voice predicts the debates among "supreme" values that we've pursued here.

Too many established religions dodge the inherent conflicts by openly embracing one or another of the three—and then privately using casuistry to deal with the actual conflicts. Too often the conflicts are resolved thoughtlessly, simply ignoring or sacrificing a greater good in the name of a narrow commitment to another one. The most extreme version of this distortion is the act of a terrorist who kills thousands pursuing the supreme good: bliss in heaven. In millions of other cases through history, the believer in this or that supreme value happily sacrifices others, just as we are today killing innocents in Iraq in the pursuit of a "good" that some are calling "holy."

That statement might be taken as a hint that I stay strictly on the absolute-truth side. But I think the history of my hypocrisy-upward in the service of what I have seen as "welfare" or "happiness" or "goodness" illustrates my point here: I believe in pursuing truth, but I'm not a *dogmatic* "truther." The multiple truths are themselves too often in conflict, and when they conflict with this or that "good" that I believe in, then thoughtful casuistry, in the *good* sense of the term, must enter the picture.

My favorite allegory for how we Homo sapiens fell into these conflicts is the story of Adam and Eve, which it's just possible you may have encountered elsewhere in some other form.

> Some millions of years ago God created those two and planted them in a purified garden where there were no conflicts. All was harmonious—except for one problem: they could either eat of the tree of knowledge or obey God's command against it. They ate, down there in Africa someplace (or as Joseph Smith taught us Mormons, in Adam ondi Amman, Missouri). And suddenly they fell (or as I would put it, rose) to become conscious of all the conflicts that the very possession of such consciousness creates. Driven out into the real, the fallen, the shit-laden world, they faced—as even the brightest of the chimpanzees had never done—the incommensurabilities I've been describing.

Having thus confessed that I see no conceivable form of complete, ultimate harmony among the three, each of them partly responsible for the Self-Splits

I've reported, I find it interesting that life produces so many moments that go a bit beyond the blissful unities described in part one of this chapter—moments when, like the young soldier dreaming of the ONE, we do feel illuminated by a sense of achieved harmony. They are not just moments of unified bliss but moments filled with an awareness of and sense of gratitude for the very multiplicity of Selves that produce the conflicts. Supreme-Being-Itself seems in some mysterious way to *harmonize* what we cannot intellectually manage to harmonize. "I have grasped, or glimpsed, or been occupied by, and believe in UNUM DEUM, the divine ONE, without Whose Being Nothing would Be. But He/She/It will never be found *fully* realized within me."

WHY THE HARMONY IS NOT TEMPORARY—INDEED IS EVEN A BIT BETTER THAN PLAUSIBLE

Often when meditating about all this, I feel flooded with gratitude for a "fact" I've so far only hinted at here; it's by no means a hard fact in any demonstrable way, but I believe that it's real.

Though the "I" who will never fully harmonize everything will die, no doubt quite soon now, the truth is that the "I" who on occasion has pursued any one of the three genuine values does not die; that value, whether one of the three or the mysterious, incomprehensible chorus of them, is immortal, eternal. Whatever part of it has been in me was there before my birth and made possible those fragments of it that I have reveled in—and often struggled with. They were *discovered*, not invented, by me and by the thousands of predecessors who passed their discoveries on to me. And they will live after the complex, body-laden, conflicted, circumstance-structured, unique "I" has decayed. My diverse soul splits will die off, while Truth, Goodness, and Beauty, and my small share of them—the best of me—go on living not just in other actual living creatures but in the Whole of Things. It was their actual existence in the total range of possibilities in Supreme Being that enabled any one of us to come along and discover them.

A zany way of putting this would be to say, "Aha, at last I have found the One: the Supreme Dialogist who has tried to teach us Rhetorology, the one supreme, unchallengeable fusion of Good/True/Beautiful"—Booth's "God."

Here I join Plato, as many of you will have recognized, in his claim that whatever redeems human life preexists it. Wordsworth puts it beautifully in his "Ode on Intimations of Immortality," stanza V, which I was required to memorize in high school—and still remember.

Our birth is but a sleep and a forgetting:
The Soul that rises with us, our life's Star,

Hath had elsewhere its setting,
And cometh from afar:
Not in entire forgetfulness,
And not in utter nakedness,
But trailing clouds of glory do we come
From God, who is our home.

I've heard many a secularist scoff at that stanza. Indeed, taken literally—as if you and I preexisted in our particularities, fully "ensouled"—it makes no sense to me.[8] But I've loved it from the beginning, initially because it fit into my Mormon picture of our literal preexistence and now because—well, because it coincides with my conviction that Something Bigger than the Big Bang preceded—and made possible—the Big Bang.

All I'm claiming now is that whatever harmony has been achieved in my life, the chorus of all those divided Selves will not disappear from the universe when I die. My having joined everyone (well, *almost* everyone) in biting into that apple and thus becoming conscious of the difference between good and not-good has joined me not just to fellow human beings but to the very inner nature of all things.

When I die, what happens to all of that? Nothing happens to it; it remains where it always was: everywhere. And it will be rediscovered by other Selves, whether on this planet or on innumerable other ones that exist "out there." Evolution—one of Supreme Being's cleverest creations—will create, on planet after planet, other creatures who bite into that apple. They will discover that there is a real difference between good and bad, and then *some* of them will engage in the quest for the difference and pursue harmony among the diverse goods.

For those who detest such wild speculation or who resist religious language, this dream of a kind of immortality, with "the whole of things" mystically harmonized, may seem absurd. It can never be adequately described, will always be unpersuasive to secularists, and will seem offensively mushy to many who think of themselves as *really* religious. But as I embrace the harmony, as I revel in my too rare moments of peace, I see myself as *joining*, though metaphorically, the vast number of religious believers whose *literal* claims I reject: I join those who believe in Christ's redemption and describe

---

8. The claim that *in some sense* each of us has existed even before conception cannot be denied even by the most rigorous genetic evolutionist. And it's hardly surprising to see how many religious speculators come up with something like Tolstoy's nonorthodox reading, in a diary entry written in his final year: "We speak of the life of the soul after death. But if the soul lives 'after death,' it should have lived also 'before life.' Onesided eternity is an absurdity." *Last Diaries*, ed. Leon Stilman (New York: G. P. Putnam's Sons, 1960), 45.

such moments as the simple discovery of Christ's love; I join my Mormon brothers and sisters as they sing "All is well" at the end of the hymn "Come, Come, Ye Saints"; I join even those who claim to have visions of divine personages—except when those Spirits order massacre or stoning to death of prostitutes. I join (in totally different language and with equal inability to persuade any "outsider") the Buddhists and Taoists and hundreds of other groups who find their beliefs and practices to be somehow an embodiment of, or at least connection to, the Whole.

What happened in evolution is just one of innumerable possible realizations of the glories that my God provides and provided long before the Big Bang.[9] He/She/It did not just set things up, as in the clock-winding metaphor that many Deists employed after Newton's discoveries. He/She/It is the total range of possibilities and impossibilities: the *Is* without which nothing would Be. That Being, once you think of what supremity really means, must include every actual fact about evolution—the requirements and possibilities of locomotion, of flight, of germination, of mental complexities. How to walk on two legs was not invented by "us"; it was *discovered*, as was our passion for Truth, as part of Being. Everything that works was always *THERE*, waiting.[10]

It was that Being that laid down the infinitely complex conditions that created my pioneer ancestors who could "invent" and sing the hymn "Come, Come, Ye Saints" and the T. S. Eliot who could finally write the poem I quoted in chapter 3.

Does this mystically speculating Booth have visions and hear "voices"? Not at all. In fact—perhaps deflected by too much "Enlightenment" rationalism—I have had too many prolonged periods in life when none of the above thoughts

---

9. A group of scientists called neurotheologians are claiming these days that they have found in the brain the physical source of such ecstasies—physiological explanation of why religious quest seems never to be killed by scientific discoveries. Some write as if this neurological discovery shows that religious impulses are simply the result of evolution. My way of putting it would be "evolution *discovered* religion."

10. In my decades of speculation about how to define my God, the influences have been too many to list here—or anywhere. Rudolf Otto's *Idea of the Holy* was deeply influential when I was a missionary. Spinoza, especially with his *Ethics*, and Anselm with his ontological proof were among perhaps a dozen philosophers from Plato and Aristotle on to yesterday who deconverted me from the atheism I described in chapter 5. Various "process theologians," or "panentheists," especially Alfred North Whitehead and Charles Hartshorne, have come closest to full evocation of the God—or Allah, or the Eternal—whom I now worship.

even occurred to me. As I've reported, for a few years I was a sometimes proudly professing and more often surreptitious atheist. Even in my many periods of sincere private meditation, going beyond efforts of Deep Thought to what can honestly be called prayer, I have heard no "voices" proclaiming divine truths, seen no visions of divine personages. All claims to such immediate contact with the divine I still take as at best metaphorical or analogical.

But I did have one "sort-of vision," one that powerfully dramatizes both my picture of "the" truth and the necessity of plurality in any vision of Oneness.

Meditating one day, back in the 1960s, I was probing my Selves for answers about how, as a dean, I could deal with the various student uprisings, especially the conflict between my duty as an administrator and my sympathy with the students. Walking along Lake Michigan, hoping to calm myself down, suddenly I had a vivid image—not of the kind many report, when a voice speaks directly to the visionary, but a picture as vivid as a nighttime dream—but with my eyes wide open. It was simply a transforming image of "the whole world" (a bit like that soldier's dream of Truth, Goodness, and Beauty more than twenty years earlier). I'm tempted to call it an epiphany—something like the "spiritual highs" that James Joyce labels in *Stephen Hero* (the early draft of *A Portrait of the Artist*)—but I don't see it as quite *that* spiritual.

I see, in full detail, twelve mountain peaks in a huge circle, each peak occupied by a white-haired, crouching guru in a flowing white robe (most of them, I'm embarrassed to say, were bearded males). Lightning flashes of truth, seemingly of twelve different "stripes" or "colors," are shooting out of all twelve minds, each mind flashing eleven different but genuine truths to each of the other gurus: truths about truth, truths about goodness, truths about beauty. All twelve are somehow receiving, taking in, never rejecting, the flashes from the other eleven.

So—multiple truths were flowing in all directions, in one sense not fully harmonized and never fully harmonizable, but all fitting into a scene in which everyone was communicating fully with everyone else. Each guru was taking in the flashed truths from all the others—practicing what I only now label rhetorology. That seemed to me then and seems to me now the ultimate ideal of human life. No one of the gurus has "the" truth; each one has only a fragment of it. No human being will ever totally grasp the One. But if we try hard enough, we can share diverse views of Him/Her/It.

Something like that image is what the attempt to write this book has reinforced. But I'm still emotionally gripped by other far less metaphoric moments of full harmony—not just the better hours when writing the book but the moments that probing the journals bring to light. Somehow they extend the merely blissful moments with which this chapter began, taking them into harmony with every thought about life.

> *August 26, 2000, still in Wildwood, with ten more days before returning to Chicago*
> Saturday Phyll completed a demanding essay; I "edited" a next-to-the-last draft and found it so impressive that I was in tears at the end: wotta blessing to be married to a woman who not only does her kind of therapy, rescuing that adopted kid "Luis," and then writing about it so beautifully.
>
> So by yesterday morning, we both felt totally free to "do a morning Sabbath" according to our own definition: hiking in the mountains. Scheduled to meet Max [Dalby] and his second wife Marjorie for lunch in SLC at 1:00, we got up early, appraised what looked like a certainly rainy day, said "what the hell will it matter if we're rained on?" and decided to do our favorite hike, up Timpanogas trail to a point we've always called "Phyllis's Plateau." Drove up toward the summit, still expecting more rain, and suddenly as the car climbed out of the mist we were surrounded with one of the most beautiful scenes ever: Wildwood below was totally covered with the radiant white clouds that had made us predict more rain. But above those clouds, where we were now, was nothing but a more brilliant radiance, every high peak, every leaf, every cove, every cliff dripping with the night's rain and flashing in the rising sun. We did not need a camera to "capture that scene" forever.
>
> As we climbed up the rather muddy trail, above Camp Timponekee (sp?), the bliss continued, both of us feeling that this is what we came for, this is what we *are* for. We hiked up two miles, amazed that our knees and hips and hearts were "taking it" (we carried two canes, mostly for me). Light lunch at the top, looking blissfully out over the still incredible glowing scene (including one moose below). Blissful kissing, spiritual ecstasy.
>
> Viewed from the perspective of the emerging Book, all of that could be called total harmony; my Self-Splits were wiped away. This is what life is for, this is, to repeat, what we came for—to the mountains—to life itself.
>
> Maybe some such moment could make the climax of the chaotic *LIFE*...

And now that epiphany does. Four years later, that still seems not just a *plausible* harmony: it's the real thing.

Not quite yet The End

Phyllis, Kathie, and Wayne at home, March 13, 2005

Alison, Phyllis, and Wayne at home, March 13, 2005

This autobiography, in the works since before the turn of this century, was essentially finished by the beginning of 2005. In March of that year, Wayne was diagnosed with an unknown form of dementia. The course of his decline would make a long story, but it was relentlessly short; over a few months he had to give up one by one the things he had done with pleasure all his life. He died on October 10, 2005.

Index

chap. 10 passim; sit-ins, 191–
95; Hutchins College, 103,
104, 182, 187; WB as teacher
and dean: *see* Booth, Wayne
Clayson, life and struggles
Utah, 5, 87, 94, 236n1, 275. *See
also* American Fork, Utah

Valéry, Paul, 117
values, 32, 86, 151, 298–305; WB's
guru dream, 306. *See also* casuistry; *phronesis*
Van Gogh, Vincent, 276
Van Parijs, Philippe, 173n7
vanity. *See* Selves: Vain-Booth
vegetarianism, 260–61
Verdi, Giuseppe, *Otello*, 256
Vietnam War, 176, 191, 194n11,
259
voices. *See* Selves
Voltaire, 91–92; *Candide*, 227

Wacker, Jeanne, 21
Wallace, Henry, 173–74
Weber, Max, *The Protestant Ethic
and the Spirit of Capitalism*, 86
Webster, John, *The Duchess of Malfi*,
103
weeping, 66, 68–69, 73–74, 81,
146, 280. *See also* grief; Selves:
Griever
Wegener, Charles, 74
we-ism, xii–xiii n3
Wells, H. G., 95, 119; *Outline of
History*, 118

Welsch, Alice, 71
Welty, Eudora, *Losing Battles*,
233–34
West, Ray, 203
Wharton, Edith, *The Age of Inno-
cence*, 292; *Ethan Frome*, 55
Whistler, James, 160
Whitehead, Alfred North, 127,
305n10
Wick, Warner, 192
Wilde, Oscar, 77, 117; *The Picture
of Dorian Gray*, v, 228–29
Williams, Joe, 293
Wings of the Dove, The (James), 277
Wittgenstein, Ludwig, ix
Word of Wisdom: 4n1, 13, 25,
31, 140; alcohol ban, 4, 25,
127–28; hot drinks ban, 4, 14,
20, 21, 46, 128; smoking ban,
7, 23
Wordsworth, William, 216, 303–4
World War I, 257, 258
World War II, 257–58, 287. *See also*
Booth, Wayne Clayson, life
and struggles

Yeats, William Butler, *The Land of
Heart's Desire*, 267
Young, Brigham, 5, 12, 172
Young, Karl (English teacher), 97,
99
Young, Kimball, 23
Young, Kip, x

Zion, 5–6